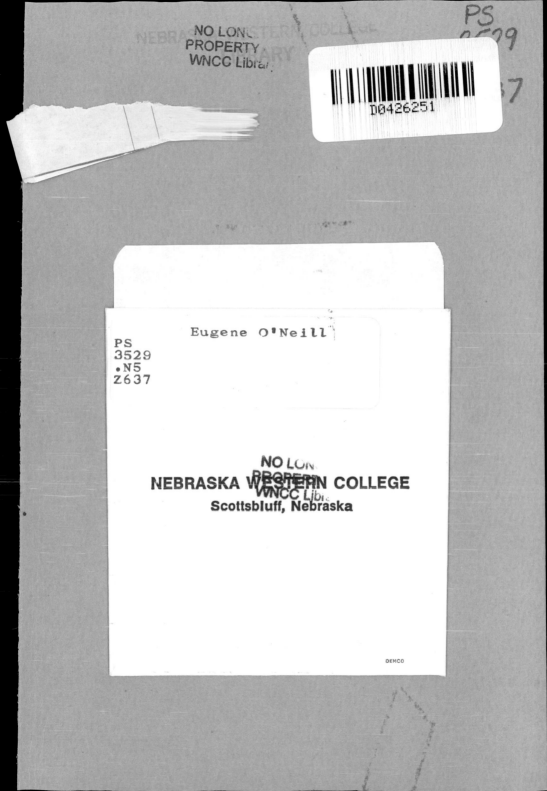

Eugene O'Neill

Eugene O'Neill

A World View

Edited by
Virginia Floyd

FREDERICK UNGAR PUBLISHING CO.

NEW YORK

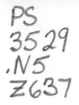
To the memory of
Clifford Leech

*Flights of angels
sing thee to thy rest!*

Copyright © 1979 by Frederick Ungar Publishing Co., Inc.
Printed in the United States of America
Designed by Helen Roberts

Library of Congress Cataloging in Publication Data
Main entry under title:

Eugene O'Neill : a world view.

Bibliography: p.
Includes index.
1. O'Neill, Eugene Gladstone, 1888–1953—
Criticism and interpretation—Addresses, essays,
lectures. 2. O'Neill, Eugene Gladstone, 1888–
1953—Stage history—Addresses, essays, lectures.
I. Floyd, Virginia.
PS3529.N5Z637   812'.5'2   79–4826
ISBN 0-8044-2204-4

ACKNOWLEDGMENTS

I wish to express my gratitude to Donald Gallup, Curator, Collection of American Literature, Beinecke Rare Book and Manuscript Library, Yale University, and to Yale University as legatee of the Eugene O'Neill Collection for their permission to use quotations from the dramatist's unpublished notes and notebooks, his Work Diary—transcribed by Donald Gallup—and all other material in this book designated as part of the Yale O'Neill Collection.

V.F.

CONTENTS

PART 1   A EUROPEAN PERSPECTIVE

Introduction   *Virginia Floyd*   3

O'Neill and the Royal Dramatic
Tom Olsson   34

O'Neill's Significance: A Scandinavian and
European View
Timo Tiusanen   61

O'Neill in England—from *Anna Christie* to
Long Day's Journey into Night: 1923–1958
Clifford Leech   68

Platonic Love in O'Neill's *Welded*
Egil Törnqvist   73

The Lasting Challenge of Eugene O'Neill:
A Czechoslovak View
Josef Jařab   84

O'Neill in Poland
Marta Sienicka   101

The Use of the Short Story in O'Neill's and Chekhov's
One-Act Plays: A Hungarian View of O'Neill
Peter Egri   115

One Hundred Percent American Tragedy:
A Soviet View
Maya Koreneva   145

Eugene O'Neill and Georg Kaiser
Horst Frenz   172

PART 2   AN AMERICAN PERSPECTIVE

Introduction   *Virginia Floyd*   189

The Last Confession: O'Neill and
the Catholic Confessional
John Henry Raleigh   212

The Irish Atavism of *A Moon for the Misbegotten*
John Henry Raleigh   229

The Pressure of Puritanism in O'Neill's
New England Plays
Frederick Wilkins   237

Poetry and Mysticism in O'Neill
Albert Bermel   245

O'Neill the Humanist
Esther M. Jackson   252

Exile without Remedy:
The Late Plays of Eugene O'Neill
J. Dennis Rich   257

PART 3   PERFORMERS ON O'NEILL

Introduction   *Virginia Floyd*   279

Reflections on *Long Day's Journey into Night*
      First Curtain Call for Mary Tyrone
      Florence Eldridge   286

      Staging O'Neill's "Simple Play"
      Arvin Brown   288

Another Neurotic Electra:
A New Look at Mary Tyrone
Geraldine Fitzgerald 290

A Meeting with O'Neill
Ingrid Bergman 293

Contributors 297

Index 303

PART 1

A European Perspective

INTRODUCTION

Virginia Floyd

What will a future age say about the fluctuating evaluation of Eugene O'Neill in America? In appraising their country's greatest dramatist, critics, theatre professionals, and academicians were polarized more often than not. The pendulum swung between periods of praise and rejection; the more vociferous frequently drowned out the voices of reason and reflection.

In contrast, against a broader panorama, O'Neill loomed large on the stage of world drama. His reputation, once established abroad, remained relatively intact; his plays were produced and appreciated from the 1920s to the present. European evaluation of the plays has always been more coherent than American. Far more than their American contemporaries with their vacillating attitudes, Europeans seemed to understand what O'Neill was attempting to say, striving to do. Viewing at first his piecemeal efforts and eventually the totality of his work, they valued the plays for their philosophical as well as their artistic statement. It did not take the dramatic impact of a *Long Day's Journey into Night* to activate their directors, fill their theatres.

In the two decades preceding the American première of this play in 1956, O'Neill's worldwide popularity did little to effect a change of attitude in his own country. The dramatist first won national recognition for the plays of his early period. While they were often criticized for their excesses, experimental devices, and poverty of expression, the plays were, at least, produced. O'Neill was theatrically alive! After *Days Without End* in 1934, however, the last play of the early period, O'Neill became a dramaturgic pariah; for over twenty years, from 1934 to 1956, there were no major productions except the 1946 American première of *The Iceman Cometh* in New York and the ill-fated pre-Broadway tour in 1947 of *A Moon for the Misbegotten*. The year of the great thaw, 1956, marked the return of O'Neill to the American theatre with the acclaimed Broadway première of *Long Day's Journey into Night* and an off-Broadway revival of *The Iceman Cometh*. Other successes followed: *A Moon for the Misbegotten* in 1957 and *A Touch of the Poet* in 1958. After the American premières of *Hughie* in 1964 and *More Stately Mansions* in 1967, there was relative silence again. Americans had seen everything O'Neill had in his "bag of tricks." Granted, there were commercial productions of several of the popular plays and experimental stagings of lesser known works in the 1960s and 1970s; most of the canon, however, has been neglected. O'Neill, in this country, still remains a playwright in search of a theatre and an audience. Yet, in Europe, his popularity has been sustained for decades, even during the years of the so-called "great O'Neill silence."

What explanation can be given for the attentive reception accorded O'Neill's work abroad and the benign neglect his work received at home? The fault lies not "in the stars" but "in ourselves." It is these very "selves" that O'Neill holds up for scrutiny; and it is this reflection, perhaps more than the man, that is rejected. American life, as the dramatist depicts it in the hopelessly confused condition of Billy Brown, is lived behind the mask. Like him, the American character is reluctantly split; it wants the best of both worlds: Brown's mask of success, Dion's poetic mask. In 1927 O'Neill made a notation that he wanted to write a "modern Faust play" which would have depicted the American character, as he perceived it, as having sold its life and soul for material things. *Marco Millions* illustrates such an instance. While

Beyond the Horizon focuses on the plight of Robert Mayo, the doomed dreamer-poet, *Marco Millions* could be considered a continuation of the story of Andrew Mayo, the businessman-farmer who journeys to distant places to make his fortune. He would have become, in time, as deformed spiritually as Marco, given O'Neill's attitude to men who seek material possessions. In *Marco Millions*, the Kaan says of Marco: "He has not even a mortal soul, he has only an acquisitive instinct."[1] In 1946, in an interview with the press preceding the première of *The Iceman Cometh*, O'Neill diagnosed the sickness of America:

> The United States, instead of being the most successful country in the world, is the greatest failure . . . because it was given everything, more than any other country. Through moving as rapidly as it has, it hasn't acquired any real roots. Its main idea is that everlasting game of trying to possess your own soul by the possession of something outside it. This was really said in the Bible much better. We are the greatest example of "For what shall it profit a man if he shall gain the whole world and lose his own soul?" We had so much and could have gone either way.[2]

These words can be interpreted as O'Neill's thesis, for they reveal his attitudes to this country and its people; and they suggest the central focus of his work: that Americans are basically a rootless people, that their search to belong leads them to forfeit the only possession of value, the inner self, for material acquisitions.

The seeds of materialism had been sown with the country's founding. As the first settlers and possessors of the land, the Puritans established the national religion—an idealism that equated spiritual well-being with economic prosperity. Later waves of immigrants had to bend and accept the prevailing Puritan work ethic and codes of morality, or they would perish in the strange, harsh environment. The compromise they made, the sacrifice of their heritage and ethnic identity, left them forever wanderers and misfits in the promised land; exteriorly the body moved to adjust, to become assimilated, and craved material comforts, the nourishment of the elusive American Dream; but interiorly the spirit hungered for what it had bartered, ever remembering the *spiritus mundi* of old lands. Consequently, the American character became forever split, reaching with one hand for material things, groping with the other for a lost, shadowy idealism. The melting pot proved to be a crucible; and tested, a unified cultural identity failed to materialize.

Eugene O'Neill was himself caught up in the American dilemma. As a second generation Irish Catholic, he inherited the idealism of Old World faith, values, traditions; as an American, he inhabited a New England terrain, haunted by a Puritan "hangover." The dichotomy of the self, experienced on a personal level yet reflected in the American character, the search by the self to become integrated, to belong, became a major motif of his plays.

O'Neill can be viewed as our native historian, resident physician, and, despite his own apostasy, high priest. As historiographer, he presents the problems of a new, growing nation and its people, baring the sick American soul, holding it up for the world to see its naked greed, despair, and suffering. But he held a Janus-mirror; being the son of an immigrant, he was cognizant of the tragic effects of rootlessness on the human psyche. Following the adage "Physician, heal thyself" proved to be painful. As the dramatist's dedication for *Long Day's Journey into Night* implies, reliving the events recorded in the play caused him much anguish and sorrow. In depicting characters hopelessly trapped in a tangled web of suffering, O'Neill acts not as a modern Mephistopheles, plunging us irrevocably into a national and personal hell, but, rather, as a New World Dante, leading his fellow countrymen on a search for self.

For O'Neill the quest for the meaning of life, of existence, proves to be religious in nature. His concern is not the relation between man and man but the relation between God and man and between man and his divided soul, seeking, as was the playwright himself, for a faith to make it whole. If he plunges us into that "Bottom of the Sea Rathskeller," it must be remembered that Christ Himself descended into hell to redeem. Without a Good Friday, there would have been no resurrection. The catharsis of suffering must necessarily precede redemption. As a country that was, as O'Neill says, "given everything," America has yet to experience its Gethsemane. The dramatist gives us in his plays a vicarious glimpse of it, yet without the certain vision of an Easter Sunday. The canon bears but a "hopeless hope" in early plays like *The Straw*; by the time the "last harbor" at Harry Hope's is reached, even that has nearly expired. The journey from beginning to end is ever an American quest for faith in a world that has lost its faith—religious, national, and personal.

O'Neill made two different attempts to write a cycle of plays to depict the personal and social dilemma caused by man's loss of faith. He makes two references in his Work Diary to the autobiographical "Grand Opus" of his life: March 8, 1927—"Outline of Sea-Mother's Son"; July 21, 1931—"The Sea-Mother's Son" (notes—Nostalgia). In an entry dated October 16, 1928 in one of his notebooks he discusses the basic concept of this work.[3] In the 1930s O'Neill abandoned his biographical theme to work on a historical family cycle, which would have been his greatest major achievement had he finished it—*A Tale of Possessors, Self-Dispossessed*. The title of this work reveals his revulsion from American materialism and indicates the kind of punishment that is meted out for greed. O'Neill described the cycle as

> a psychological drama of a family against the background of the drive toward material progress and the spiritual degeneration of the American people. . . . America is the greatest failure in history . . . we've squandered our soul by trying to possess something outside it, and we'll end as that game usually does, by losing our soul and that thing outside it, too. Some day this country is going to get it— . . . We've followed the same selfish, greedy path as every other country in the world. . . . We've been able to get a very good price for our souls in this country—the greatest price perhaps that has ever been paid—but you'd think that after all these years, and all that man has been through, we'd have sense enough—all of us—to understand the whole secret of human happiness is summed up in that same sentence (from the Bible) [For what shall it profit a man, if he shall gain the whole world and lose his own soul?][4]

The eleven plays of the cycle would have traced over one hundred and fifty years of American history, but they would have been primarily a saga of the immigrant Irish and their descendants and their conflict with the Yankees, possessors of the land—dating from *The Greed of the Meek* in 1755, the first play of the cycle, to *The Life of Bessie Bowan* in 1932, which O'Neill stated in 1943 was to be the basis for the last play. In February of 1943, he discarded part of Act One of that play, labeling it "no good," but even at that time he was still determined to continue the work, as he writes in his Work Diary, "now with many changes." Unfortunately, he never completed his work, and he burned the unfinished manuscripts. The destruction of the cycle plays is an irreparable loss to modern drama. However, I believe O'Neill's work on these historial Irish-American plays, which have semiautobiographical elements, inspired him to attempt his great autobiographical masterpiece, *Long Day's Journey into Night*. In June 1939, he notes in his Work Diary: "Feel fed up and stale on the Cycle after 4½ years of not thinking of any other work—read over notes on various ideas for single plays—decide to outline two that seem to appeal most and see—the Jimmy the P[riest]—H[ell] H[ole]—Gorden idea—and N[ew] L[ondon] family one." The family, of course, was his own.

Only two of the cycle plays survived: *A Touch of the Poet* and *More Stately Mansions*. It can be argued that O'Neill perhaps unconsciously did achieve his goal, combining elements of both proposed cycles. These two surviving works when combined with *Long Day's Journey into Night* and *A Moon for the Misbegotten* do form what can be termed a "New England Cycle." Comprised of semi- and totally autobiographical plays, they are unified by the theme of the attempt of the Irish immigrant and his descendants to survive in a hostile, alien land—a struggle the dramatist knew well from his heritage, environment, and own tormented soul. One of the recurring themes in these last plays, the struggle for place here in this world, is demonstrated in the conflict between the New England Yankees and the Irish, symbolically for land—whether it be a lowly tenant farmer's shack or the more stately mansions. In a sense, the struggle is futile, for the possessors will ever be self-dispossessed. In a historical sense, both the Puritan descendants and the Irish are foreigners. O'Neill's comment, "There is hardly one thing that our government has done that isn't some treachery —against the Indians, against the people of the Northwest, against the small farmers,"[5] reveals his attitude about who has first claim to the land.

A Touch of the Poet, set in 1828, depicts the rise of the Irish immigrant Melody family; in *More Stately Mansions*, set in 1832, Sara Melody defeats the Yankee New England Harfords. *Long Day's Journey into Night* and *A Moon for the Misbegotten* reveal the moral dissolution of the Irish Tyrones nearly a century later. The two surviving cycle plays are crucial for an understanding of the picture of America that O'Neill was trying to draw, the key to his social statement and coda to the early plays. Con Melody represents every immigrant who tried to take root in a Yankee-Puritan stronghold. Suspended between two worlds, he reflects in his character a dual nature: the idealistic poet-hero of the Old World, the realistic Irish misfit in the new. At the end of the play, when Con kills the mare, he kills forever the former noble dreamer and with him his pride and the illusions that made his life bearable. America had destroyed the best that was in him. Sara Melody symbolizes America coming of age and the price the Irish immigrant paid for a more stately mansion. In her ruthless schemes to prosper, she crushes the last vestiges of the poet in her Yankee husband, Simon Harford, and in herself.

In O'Neill's envisioned cycle, the characters of *More Stately Mansions* evolve from those of earlier plays. In the first play of the cycle, *The Greed of the Meek* (1755–75), an Irishman's lust for the land and the Yankee woman who owns it proves to be stronger than his idealistic desire for freedom of the spirit. The situation is reversed in *More Stately Mansions*; the Yankee Simon Harford's lust for his Irish wife Sara destroys his idealistic tendencies. Like her literary forebear, Sara is drawn to materialistic possessions, mercilessly stifling any noble yearnings within her. If completed, the historical cycle, with its predominant theme of greed, would have been O'Neill's definitive indictment of America, of its society and people. The seeds of greed sown in early cycle plays fructify in the nineteenth-century Sara Melody in *More Stately Mansions* and make *Long Day's Journey into Night* inevitable. The two plays studied in tandem demonstrate the social and personal malady merging and overlapping. As a nation, as individuals, Americans become betrayers, having lost their ideals. The macrocosmic and microcosmic dimensions are manifested externally in the dislocation of the self and internally in the lack of belief in something outside the self to give life a valid meaning.

Like some earlier nineteenth-century writers, O'Neill was convinced, as he states, of "the death of the old God and the failure of science and materialism to give any satisfying new one for the surviving primitive religious instinct to find a meaning of life in, to comfort his fears of death with."[6] Nowhere is this "failure of science and materialism" to provide a meaning for life more evident than in *The Hairy Ape*. Through Yank, O'Neill depicts the plight of modern man who has become dislocated, disillusioned, and destroyed by his highly technological world. Yank's struggle to belong proves to be not only futile but ruinous; rejected by all, he dies in an animal's cage. In contrast, Jim Tyrone, the last of O'Neill's long line of misfits, cannot die without spiritual solace. Hovering on the brink of death yet haunted by guilt, this tormented soul must find forgiveness, some semblance of the confessional of his lost Catholicism, before breaching the abyss.

Yank is a victim of a materialistic, indifferent society; Tyrone, of his heredity and environment. His spirit, like Yank's body, is crushed by inner and outer forces. Tyrone's greater degree of awareness does not lessen his isolation. In the end, strengthened by Josie's "absolution," he walks off into the horizon to meet his "ghosts." Only final dissolution can bring an end to the long migration, the search for place, and resolve the dilemma of the dual nature of existence. Both Yank and Tyrone find themselves suspended between heaven and earth. Having lost the vision and hope of the former and locked into a meaningless existence in the latter, they inhabit a kind of hell. Each is a misfit without purpose or place, a transient in an alien land. O'Neill's resolution in both the early and late plays is the same: man can belong only in death. The tragedy in modern society is not that man suffers Yank's dislocation and Tyrone's despair; the tragedy is that he has even lost the will to engage in a quest for a meaning to life and death. Turning back, like Yank, to live complacently on the animal level or reaching out, like Tyrone, to seek oblivion through liquor and sex can bring only moral death and destruction; turning inward to discover the self can provide a degree of awareness of our humanity.

On the national level, the search for the American character must turn ultimately to an exploration of the country's origin, its roots. To discover their national identity, Americans must examine historical reality: they are the offspring of immigrants with special Old World ties; and they are descendants, perhaps even the inheritors, of the Puritan legacy. The conflicting values of Old and New World cultures produce the American dilemma, the split self. The search, therefore, to integrate the self must be of a twofold nature: an outward examination of the significance of European cultural origins and tendencies, and of the effects of the loss; an inward look at what Americans were and are as a people.

This present collection, with its focus on Eugene O'Neill, world dramatist and native son, has such a dual purpose. The essays in the first section by European O'Neill specialists show the bonds that he established with Europe, his return to the Old World of his ancestors for inspiration, acceptance, and presentation of his plays. To complement this European perspective of the playwright, O'Neill experts in the American section examine four aspects that contributed to his formation: Irish Catholicism, New England Puritanism, mysticism, and humanism. A discussion of these formative aspects precedes the second section. In their totality, these essays present a world view of O'Neill—the American and

European influences that affected his work and the evaluation of this work in this country and abroad. O'Neill could
achieve an integrated self only through recognition of what
he was—the son of an immigrant with an Irish Catholic Old
World heritage—and of what his only family home was—an
outsider's domain in Puritan-dominated New England. As
native son, he carved out the terrain of American drama, yet
he wisely rejected the concept of Emersonian self-reliance
and turned to European playwrights and their work for
models. As world dramatist, he was able to transcend national boundaries and native cultural heritage to depict the
universal plight of modern man doomed by fate and his
tragic flaws, yet redeemed by his indomitable spirit and
innate nobility.

A number of essays by European contributors provide
valuable information about O'Neill productions abroad, and
some raise disturbing questions about the attitudes of Americans to their greatest dramatist, to theatre, and, by implication, to the quality of American life. There are undertones
here, if not of disbelief, of sorrow that the playwright has not
been accepted and adequately produced in this country. Other
essays examine how O'Neill thoroughly merged with the
mainstream of European literary, philosophical, and theatrical currents.

Tom Olsson provides an analysis of O'Neill productions
at the Royal Dramatic Theatre in Stockholm from the 1920s
to the present. He discusses the significant role the Swedish
government plays in bringing culture to the people by sub-
sidizing the arts. Not only was the "O'Neill tradition" established at the Royal Dramatic in the capital city, but smaller
repertory companies frequently staged O'Neill throughout
Sweden. Even when O'Neill was rejected in the United
States during the period that has come to be known as "the
great O'Neill silence," Olsson points out that "in Sweden
that silence was not total," and he lists a number of plays
that were presented in those years.

Olsson also provides an insight into the relationship
established between Carlotta O'Neill and Karl Ragnar
Gierow, who became manager of the Royal Dramatic Theatre

in the early 1950s. Carlotta's letters to Gierow reveal the playwright's attitude to his fellow countrymen in the last period of his life—those years of theatrical ostracism in America: his directive that *Long Day's Journey into Night* was never to be produced in the United States; his fears that American directors would "produce this play as a sensational melodrama"; his bequest to the Royal Dramatic to present the world premières of his last plays—*Long Day's Journey, A Touch of the Poet, Hughie,* and *More Stately Mansions.* This great legacy was given, as Carlotta states, because the Swedish people "kept us going in 1953 when this country wasn't interested in O'Neill." The letters are depressing if they accurately reflect the bleakness of the last years of O'Neill's life when no title of a play of his lit up an American marquee. Surely he must have found some consolation when he received word of the highly praised Swedish productions of *The Iceman Cometh* in 1947 and *A Moon for the Misbegotten* in 1953—no doubt contrasting in his mind the success of the two plays there and their failure in this country.

A statement, which Olsson includes, by Karl Ragnar Gierow provides, in my opinion, the best explanation for O'Neill's refusal to allow a production of *Long Day's Journey into Night* here and for his decision to give it to the Royal Dramatic in Stockholm. Gierow claims that O'Neill was filled with doubt because of the rejection he experienced here—that his late works were "in his own country regarded as barren leaves." The news he received from Sweden about the successful productions there seemed to assure him "that after all he might be right. There did exist a theatre deeply interested in his works and eager to do it all justice." Gierow states what he believes to be the reason for the neglect of the dramatist here and his acceptance in Sweden: "we might be especially trained" by Ibsen and Strindberg "to recognize O'Neill's qualities, maybe a little better than his countrymen do."

In his essay, Olsson traces Gierow's delicate negotiations with Carlotta O'Neill to "break into the treasure house of the posthumous O'Neill." Dag Hammarskjöld, then General

Secretary of the United Nations, tried to help Gierow, for he believed the director could give "Stockholm a new chance to show what O'Neill's countrymen do not dare to produce." The play that interested Gierow most, of course, was *Long Day's Journey into Night,* and Olsson presents an informative account of the events leading up to its world première on February 10, 1956, and the reaction of critics and audiences viewing this play's first production. The Royal Dramatic would present three other world premières in the coming years, but none of these was as successful as *Long Day's Journey.*

There is a "hopeless hope" in Olsson's conclusion, for he compares O'Neill to Strindberg, who was for so long rejected but then finally acclaimed in Sweden. He suggests that perhaps young actors and producers may "open up new roads in the work of O'Neill." Given the state of the American theatre, the attitude of its prime movers, and the choice of entertainment pursued by our countrymen, this seems unlikely. Were it not for the relatively few theatre people here devoted to O'Neill, how often would the plays be staged in the United States? Part of the problem—lack of interest in the theatre—is, as Timo Tiusanen observes, that the United States is "by and large a country without a dramaturgic tradition." He suggests one specific way to establish an O'Neill tradition here: Americans should "classicize" O'Neill by following the long-established traditions European countries have in treating their theatre classics. Very logically Tiusanen refutes American critics who find the dramatist's use of language a stumbling block to their appreciation of him and maintains that it is O'Neill's "grand language of the stage" that makes him modern even today. Tiusanen also makes a point here, which is analyzed at greater length by Clifford Leech, that perhaps explains, in part, American apathy to O'Neill. He asks: "Is there still a Puritan prejudice alive in America against the theater—and another against O'Neill as an analyst of 'low' characters?"

We are light years removed from the days of Cotton Mather who called the theatre "the Synagogue of Satan" and even from that era of censorship when O'Neill's early plays, like *Desire Under the Elms*, were considered an affront to moral decency and were raided by police. Puritan ghosts lurked everywhere. Without doubt, O'Neill is more at home with alcoholics, prostitutes, the outcasts of this world than with the rich. Anyone with money in the plays becomes automatically an object for ridicule or scorn. In a country with a Puritan tradition that equated wealth with virtue and weakness of any kind with depravity, O'Neill characters could be a source of contention.

Clifford Leech observes that while his English countrymen are Puritans still, they love "the delights of the flesh which you [Americans] are still intellectually brought up simply to repudiate." Leech was shocked to discover, when he first came to this country, that Puritanism was very much alive. "We thought, wrongly, that O'Neill was 'placing' puritanism historically in *Desire Under the Elms*; we came to find it endemic." In discussing O'Neill's reception in England in the 1920s and 1930s, Leech states, "We worshipped him." This is a curious remark considering that the "we" were, like Americans, inheritors of the Puritan legacy. If anything, the English should have been even more contaminated by the "disease" than Americans in view of the fact that Puritanism originated in England. Perhaps what saved the English from the disastrous effect of Puritanism lingering on into this century, as it did in this country, was their proximity to the continent and the fact that they never drifted out of the liberating mainstream of European thought.

Egil Törnqvist's analysis of O'Neill's *Welded* demonstrates that the dramatist merged with the European literary and philosophical mainstream. Törnqvist notes that *Welded* has been called a "poor imitation of such Strindberg plays as *The Father*, *The Link*, and *The Dance of Death*" and that O'Neill when finishing the play "referred to *The Dance of Death* as an admirable example of the 'real realism' he wanted to explore." O'Neill acknowledged his debt to Strindberg in his Nobel Prize acceptance speech:

> It was reading his plays . . . that, above all else, first gave me the vision of what modern drama could be, and first in-

spired me with the urge to write for the theater myself. If there is anything of lasting worth in my work, it is due to that original impulse . . . which has continued as my inspiration down all the years since then.[7]

Peter Egri has made an interesting remark in discussing the two playwrights—that two significant events took place in 1912: Strindberg died and O'Neill began to write. It is almost as though the younger dramatist symbolically assumed the mantle of his avowed master.

However, as George Jean Nathan observes, *Welded* is "very third-rate Strindberg." O'Neill probably knew that *Welded* would be a failure even as he was writing it. At one point his hero, Michael Cape, who has just completed his play, exclaims: "It's rotten. I hate the whole play!"[8] In an entry in his Work Diary dated March 5, 1924, O'Neill comments on the pre-Broadway Baltimore production: "Saw Welded—rotten!" The play ran only a few weeks in New York, closing in early April, as he says—a "flat failure."

As a result perhaps of his own disastrous short first marriage, O'Neill's early plays deal with sick marriages and unsatisfactory man-woman relationships: *A Wife for a Life, Recklessness, Bread and Butter, Abortion.* The early ideas for plays that he records in his notebooks reflect his fascination for the man-woman theme. While the marital conflict in *Welded* is reminiscent of the one found in Strindberg's *Dance of Death*, O'Neill's view of idealized love, spiritualized love, in his play differs from Strindberg's unredeemed love. Törnqvist observes that when writing *Welded* the American dramatist was trying to get back to the religious in the theatre and that "the analysis of love in the play is less Strindbergian than Platonic." He discusses three of the theories on the nature of love in *The Symposium* that he finds in *Welded*: that of Pausanias, of Aristophanes, and of Socrates or Diotima. He sees the prostitute in the play as a representative of common love—*Aphrodite pandemos*; the two circles of light that intensify Michael and Eleanor Cape as visualizations of Aristophanes' primordial man and Michael's cell split in two; and the play's stairway, the symbol of ascent to a higher plane derived from Diotima's imagery, as O'Neill's equation that love in its highest manifestation is the desire for "absolute beauty beyond the phenomenal world." Thus he establishes his premise that while *Welded* is suggestive of Strindberg's *Dance of Death*, its analysis of love is in the Platonic tradition.

While the first four essays in this section are the work of Western European O'Neill specialists, those of the latter half reflect the views of Eastern Europeans. If Americans have had little direct contact with the Western European mainstream, they are even more removed from the intellectual flow of Eastern European countries. No reason exists to perpetuate this situation, for scholars in these countries, as their essays demonstrate, are making overtures to establish new international bonds.

There were years of theatrical silence for O'Neill in Eastern European countries—almost total silence from 1947 to 1960—but this period does not reflect a rejection of the American dramatist. The main reasons were the war and its aftermath and an inauspicious political atmosphere. While some Western European countries did experience similar horrors of war, a few—like Sweden—remained neutral. This country experienced only difficult restrictions. There was no ravaged aftermath or political tensions to interfere with the Royal Dramatic's O'Neill Tradition. On the contrary, in 1945 this theatre was in the process of expansion, adding a second stage even in the midst of a nationwide building stoppage.

The situation was vastly different in countries that were devastated by Hitler. Josef Jařab reminds us of the infamous Munich Agreement of September 1938, which ended Czechoslovak independence and led to a suppression of free national culture. There was no room, as he says, for the Nobel Prize-winning dramatist in censored theatre repertories. Such war events did not go unnoticed by the dramatist. He was very aware of the great suffering and loss of freedom experienced by Europeans. His Work Diary reveals that the war in Europe had a tremendous psychological effect on him. On May 10, 1940, he writes: "the Big Invasion starts in Europe— glued to radio—to hell with trying [to] work—it's too insignificant in this madmen's world." He makes frequent references to the war: "am determined to shake this off—is becoming a neurosis—can't even save myself by not working and despairing about the future of individual freedom" (June 25, 1940); "Listen Hitler speech—what could be more squalid than a dictator who is also a fifth rate ham!" (July 19, 1940). It is in this time period that he records his first notes in the Work Diary for *The Last Conquest*: "Work on fascinating new idea I get for duality of Man play—Good-Evil, Christ-Devil—begins Temptation on Mount—through to Crucifixion—Devil a modern power realist—symbolical spiritual conflict today and in all times" (August 30, 1940).

Before World War II, theatre flourished in Czechoslovakia. The O'Neill tradition at the Royal Dramatic in Stockholm has its counterpart in the National Theatre in Prague. There are a number of similarities between these two theatres in the formation and development of this tradition. Two men—both writers and translators—played a comparable role in bringing the American dramatist to the attention of the directors of these theatres. Gustaf Hellström introduced the playwright to Sweden; František Götz took the initiative to bring O'Neill to Czechoslovakia. In 1922, two experimental directors—Per Lindberg of the Royal Dramatic and Karel Hugo Hilar of the National Theatre—made every effort to stage the same expressionist play, *The Emperor Jones*; neither succeeded. These two men and the expressionist work of O'Neill exerted an influence on their more traditional theatre associates: Olof Molander and František Götz. Eventually two directors in particular became the driving force to produce O'Neill in their countries and won great acclaim when they did so: Karl Ragnar Gierow at the Royal Dramatic and Karel Hugo Hilar at the National Theatre. Although these two men worked in different time periods, both had a very personal devotion to O'Neill. The supreme achievement of Hilar's career was his 1934 production of the best play of O'Neill's early period, *Mourning Becomes Electra*. Gierow's great triumph came in 1956 with the world première of the dramatist's masterpiece, *Long Day's Journey into Night*.

The two theatres differed, however, in the type of

O'Neill plays staged. The Royal Dramatic did not present the early expressionist works in the 1920s. As Olsson states, the theatre concentrated on the realistic and psychological dramas. In contrast, the National Theatre, with Hilar at the helm, produced a number of O'Neill's experimental plays. Josef Jařab says Hilar felt a strong affinity for O'Neill and shared his "naturally expressionistic vision of man and man's social existence." There is another bond that links the two men. Jařab claims that because of Hilar's early involvement in 1922 with the expressionist stage and his production of the "masterpiece of the national expressionist drama, *The Insect Play*, by the Čapek brothers," he became interested in *The Emperor Jones* and *The Hairy Ape*. Then Jařab mentions, as an afterthought, that Hilar very nearly became involved in the 1922 New York production of *The Insect Play*. Possibly O'Neill saw this production. He was certainly aware of the play, for in 1925 he recorded the following idea in his notebooks: "A symbolic play . . . taking the spider, the praying mantis, etc.—stories of their deep savage life compulsions as insects working out in human form—i.e. the reverse of the usual process (as per Čapek's 'Insect Comedy') of using insect forms in thinly veiled symbolism of humans. The Spider as the absolute arch-type of most feminine instinct." In May of the following year, O'Neill writes in his Work Diary that he is busy "scheming out work on *Strange Interlude*." Nina Leeds, the play's heroine, is most obviously an example of "naked feminine instinct," a parasite preying on the four men who surround her. Whether O'Neill was actually inspired by *The Insect Play* is uncertain. What is certain is that he repaid any possible debt to the Czechs with his plays.

Hilar seemed to grow with O'Neill, personally and artistically, passing through similar phases. As Jařab notes, even in their experimental period, neither adhered to the principles and practices of the German expressionists. Both men realized their method had its limitations and impeded artistic growth. However, because of his expressionist experiments, Hilar modernized traditional theatrical techniques in Czechoslovakia. He also tried to bridge the gap between the

Greek age and his own time in his last "synthetic period" when he directed *Mourning Becomes Electra*, his artistic and personal testament. Hilar's death in 1934 closed a chapter in O'Neill history in Czechoslovakia. Some plays were staged in the late 1930s and 1940s, but it was not until the early 1960s that the real O'Neill revival started. As he did with the plays of O'Neill's early period, Jařab discusses the late works and their many productions in Czechoslovakia in the last two decades.

In an entry dated August 31, 1939 in his Work Diary, O'Neill writes: "up till 3 a.m. to listen Hitler's war speech against Poland." This statement reveals O'Neill's awareness of the imminent suffering of the Polish people. They, in turn, have been aware of the American playwright for over fifty years although he did not make an impact on their theatre to the same degree that he had in other European countries. It may be, as Marta Sienicka suggests, that O'Neill reached Poland too late and in too traditional a form to exert an influence on the theatre there. The first play to be staged was *Anna Christie* in 1929. According to Sienicka, this play marked the beginning of a strange relationship between the Polish theatre and the American dramatist. Before World War II only a few of O'Neill's plays were produced in Poland, and they had moderate success. This was followed by a period of almost total oblivion caused by—among other things—the war, the reconstruction period, and the political situation. There was a notable O'Neill revival in Poland in the early 1960s, but this burst of enthusiasm has now moderated and settled into an "understanding and lasting co-existence."

The one word that perhaps best characterizes the early O'Neill-Polish relationship, however, is "misunderstanding." Polish theatregoers never had the opportunity to see the early experimental plays. What they were given was monotonously produced "heavy naturalistic traditional drama," and their image of O'Neill was one-sided. There was no director in Poland—like Molander and Gierow in Sweden and Hilar in Czechoslovakia—to provide the impetus to stage O'Neill's work. No repertory theatre "adopted" the American dramatist as had the Royal Dramatic in Stockholm and the National

Theatre in Prague. While producers and actors were blamed for misunderstanding and misinterpreting O'Neill's vision, Sienicka believes translators must assume responsibility for not "bringing the true and authentic O'Neill to Poland." As noted earlier, the two men who played a crucial role in bringing O'Neill to the attention of the Swedish and Czech people and directors—Gustaf Hellström and František Götz —were more than mere translators; the first was a writer, the second a dramaturge.

What the Polish people seem to have gotten in their early exposure was O'Neill's naturalism but not his poetry and symbolism, without which the plays become impoverished. They were shocked by the warped or aborted O'Neill, by the "brutality of the form of his expressions and drastic flouting of all conventions: moral, social or dogmatic." The moral sensibilities of the Poles account perhaps for the real "trouble with O'Neill" in Poland. While Catholicism is the dominant religion in this country, it differs greatly from Irish Catholicism which—because of its exposure to Jansenism and Calvinism—was heavily tainted with a persistent strain of Puritanism. Irish Catholics—like the O'Neill family —who settled in New England encountered a type of Puritanism that reinforced their own. Polish directors, theatregoers, and readers of O'Neill are not aware of the cultural and psychological ramifications of Puritanism, according to Sienicka, who says: "American Catholicism with its specific Puritan coloring seems, for the most part, heretical to an average practicing Catholic in Poland. No wonder, then, that the New England Puritanism, so devastatingly present in many O'Neill plays, has disappeared from their Polish interpretations." Strangely enough, the most popular O'Neill dramas in Poland have New England settings and characters who are either lapsed Catholics (*A Moon for the Misbegotten* and *Long Day's Journey into Night*) or guilt-ridden Puritans (*Mourning Becomes Electra* and *Desire Under the Elms*). Like the Czechs, Poles are able to relate to the major themes in *Desire Under the Elms*—especially the struggle to possess the land, a recurring motif in their own literature. Sienicka concludes by saying that while O'Neill may not ever directly influence Polish drama, his plays will have a permanent place in the theatres of her country. Perhaps if these theatres staged O'Neill's early sea plays, especially those in the *Glencairn* cycle, Polish audiences would discover his affinity with their own great writer, Joseph Conrad. Sienicka notes that O'Neill has often been compared to Conrad because their artistic visons were similarly affected by their sea experiences.

This similarity between O'Neill and Conrad, which once again reveals that the American writer is part of the European mainstream, is also noted by the Hungarian O'Neill specialist, Peter Egri. He maintains that there is a strong relationship— especially in plot—between Conrad's story, "The End of the Tether," and O'Neill's one-act play, *Warnings*, and his short story, "S.O.S." Egri sees an even greater affinity, however, between O'Neill and Chekhov as both use the short story in their plays. In comparing the relationship between the two genres found in O'Neill's work to a similar integration in Chekhov's, he demonstrates the organic manner in which the American dramatist was able to become part of a movement in world literature. He holds that O'Neill's shorter dramas resemble the genre of the short story and that his longer plays verge on novels, remaining, nonetheless, excellent dramas. This, too, is an important international link. If O'Neill is viewed as part of a world dramatic movement, it becomes less difficult to understand his international, indeed, universal appeal.

Egri explains in detail some uses of the short story as manifested in the plays of both dramatists and gives numerous examples from their works to demonstrate the ways in which the two genres are closely related. To illustrate the link, he selects for discussion a Chekhov story, "A Defenseless Creature," and the playlet *The Anniversary* and O'Neill's short story "S.O.S." and one-act play *Warnings*. Egri points out the generic proximity of the short story and the one-acter can also be found in O'Neill's other playlets—both those that are demonstrably related to specific short stories and those that are not. One question is obviously raised: are the features typical of the short story that are incorporated in O'Neill's early plays manifested in his later work? Egri finds the integration of the genetic features of the short story and the short play, coupled with a Chekhovian atmosphere, chiefly in O'Neill's late masterpiece *Hughie*. He provides an analysis of the play and in his conclusion comes full circle, summarizing the similarities between Chekhov and O'Neill: their attempt to synthesize "the lyric and the epic into the dramatic, to integrate the short story and the short play into a revealing and moving dramatic unity."

In addition to the Chekhovian traits in O'Neill's work, there are also Gorkian elements—characters, setting, theme— in the dramatist's late play, *The Iceman Cometh*, which some critics see as an American version of *The Lower Depths*. As noted earlier, when O'Neill borrowed from other European dramatists, Strindberg and Čapek, he repaid any debt to them by enriching the theatres of their respective countries— the Royal Dramatic and the National Theatre—with his plays. Any inspiration O'Neill might have derived from Chekhov and Gorky was counterbalanced by the plays he gave Moscow's Kamerny Theatre. That theatre's acclaimed director, Alexander Taïrov, staged these plays so effectively that even the dramatist was compelled to attend their performances. George Jean Nathan states that only on one occasion did O'Neill admit that he had been in a theatre and that one time was for Taïrov's productions.[9]

When O'Neill was living in France, he made a special trip to Paris where the Kamerny company was appearing. Later he wrote words of praise for the company in his Work Diary: Paris "To see Kamerny Theatre from Moscow do *All God's Chillun Got Wings* and *Desire* at Pigalle Theatre" (May 29, 1930); "We see *Desire Under the Elms* in Russian— much impressed—wonderful acting company" (May 30, 1930); "*All God's Chillun*—supper with Alice Koonen, Taïrov, etc." (May 31, 1930). On June 2, 1930, he wrote a letter to the manager of the Kamerny Theatre stating:

> . . . most profound gratitude! Let me humbly confess I came to the theatre with secret misgivings. I did have an author's fear that in the difficult process of transition and transformation into another language and milieu the inner spirit—that indefinable essential quality so dear to the

creator as being for him the soul of his work!—might be excusably, considering the obstacles, distorted or lost. Hence my amazement and gratitude when I saw your productions, which in every way delighted me because they rang so true to the spirit of my work! They were also productions conceived by your director, Alexander Taïrov, with that rarest of all gifts in a director—creative imagination! . . . To see my plays given by such a theatre has always been my dream! The Kamerny Theatre has realized this dream for me. . . . Most gratifying of all was my feeling that, despite the barrier of language, you all felt the kinship with me as I immediately did with you—that we had known one another a long time and were united in old and tried friendship—comradeship!—by the love of the true theatre.[10]

Resembling those two great directors—Molander in Sweden and Hilar in Czechoslovakia—in their early recognition of O'Neill, Taïrov was the first to bring the American dramatist to the attention of his countrymen. In her essay, Maya Koreneva discusses Taïrov's approach to his productions of O'Neill and states that because of the affinity of their views of reality—both of life and the theatre—the two men seemed to have had a "date with each other from the beginning." Taïrov once remarked that if *Desire Under the Elms* "did not exist it should have been invented so fully is it in accord" with his theatrical principles. Koreneva maintains that what attracted Taïrov to O'Neill in the first place was the dramatist's concentration on the foremost social issues of his day.

O'Neill has often been criticized for not addressing contemporary social problems. This accusation can be refuted by a close examination of his plays—specifically those he wrote in the 1920s—and the ideas for others contemplated in this period, which are found in his Work Diary and notebooks. My investigation reveals he had two major social concerns. The first involved racial discrimination against blacks in America. The second social issue, which became an obsession with O'Neill in the 1920s, was broader than the racial problem. Throughout this period he denounced in his plays the economic system he considered responsible for the dehumanization and exploitation not only of blacks but of all Americans: capitalism. Plays such as *The Hairy Ape, Marco Millions, The Great God Brown,* and *Dynamo* attack, to varying degrees, the American capitalist system. *Desire Under the Elms* and *Mourning Becomes Electra,* both 19th-century historical dramas, present a view of the acquisitive American nature in its early, but still fatally dangerous, developmental stages. In two other plays, *The Emperor Jones* and *All God's Chillun Got Wings,* both social concerns are expressed in a single work.

Taïrov put what he called "the tragedy of the white and black races" at the center of his production of *All God's Chillun.* Even though he altered the ending of the play— Ella dies—his vision of the total concept was so like O'Neill's that the dramatist, who would not allow one word to be changed or omitted in American productions, never objected to the liberty taken by the director. Taïrov describes the conflict of *Desire Under the Elms* in terms of "the possessive instinct," using almost the exact words of the playwright's description of it. Koreneva, in noting the similarity of their views, states that this is important as Taïrov did not know O'Neill's statement and based his interpretation on a close reading of the work itself.

Koreneva seems to emulate Taïrov in her ability to interpret O'Neill. She offers a perceptive analysis of his development and efforts to write modern tragedy in terms of American life and experience, finding his basic premise stated in his response to a critic's assertion that tragedy was incompatible with the American character. O'Neill maintains that if Americans could see with the eyes of a soul the valuation and cost of their materialism in terms of eternal verities what "a colossal, one hundred percent American tragedy that would be. Tragedy not native to our soil? Why, we are tragedy, the most appalling yet written or unwritten!" Koreneva shows the progressive stages of the dramatist's attempt to depict his concept of the American tragedy, defining his recurring theme as the "hostility of bourgeois society imposing dull utilitarianism through the tyranny of the moneybag, to art and artist, to the spiritual aspirations of man in general." Some who saw Taïrov's production of *Desire Under the Elms* spoke of it as having an "anti-capitalist slant"—as though it were something the Russian director had put into the play. Neither Taïrov in his productions nor Koreneva in her essay distorts, or adds to, O'Neill but merely reflects what is already there.

Who could improve on the tirade of Long, O'Neill's socialist spokesman in *The Hairy Ape*, against "the damned capitalist clarss"? On the trip to Fifth Avenue when Yank asks where his rich foes are, Long replies: "In church, blarst 'em! Arskin' Jesus to give 'em more money." When first reading Koreneva's title, "One Hundred Percent American Tragedy," I immediately thought of a line from this play. When the wealthy finally emerge from church, they discuss ways to combat radicals (the workers?) and false doctrines (anti-capitalism?) and decide to "organize a hundred percent American bazaar" with everyone contributing "one one-hundredth percent of their income tax." A careful reading of this passage reveals religious, as well as political, overtones which support Koreneva's definition of O'Neill's theme—that the destructive nature of the hostile rich poses a threat to man's spiritual aspirations. It opens with a reference to the high priest of the new Temple of Moloch for wealthy traders, the sincere "Dear Doctor Caiaphas." The high priest presiding at the council that condemned Christ to death was Caiaphas who declared: "It was better that one man die for all the people" (John 18.14). The three other evangelists note that when Christ died "the curtain hanging in the temple was torn in two from top to bottom." O'Neill's passage ends with the wealthy planning to donate the proceeds of their American bazaar "to rehabilitating the veil of the temple." Certain aspects of Yank's plight—his loneliness, alienation, and betrayal and rejection by the masses—reveal a Christ-figure quality in him. In his discussion of a German production of the play, Horst Frenz notes that Monty Jacobs, in the *Vossische Zeitung*, calls attention to Eugen Klöpfer's interpretation of Yank in the union scene: "With dangling arms and dragging steps, as clumsy and artless as an animal, he opens his heart to these men of the world. When they overpower him and throw him to the ground, his simplicity takes on a savior's traits, the characteristics of a despised cross-bearer." Like Brecht, O'Neill wielded a two-edged sword, often striking with one blow both capitalism and Christianity when it became the handmaiden of the former.

Koreneva describes O'Neill's search for a form suitable for his concept of modern tragedy, one that would be the embodiment of the idea of universal tragedy. While he expresses the universality of tragedy in the early sea plays, he excludes the individual from his picture of reality and treats his characters *en masse* as part of their environment. In the early 1920s when O'Neill moved in the opposite direction, depicting the tragic embodied in the sphere of individual consciousness, the protagonist emerges out of the masses, but his tragedy loses its universal characteristics. Koreneva states that the antagonist, who also appears for the first time, is represented by a group of characters embodying the hostile environment. This type of individual tragedy is likewise characteristic of O'Neill's work in the late 1920s, especially *The Great God Brown*, which he viewed as the tragedy of man. Koreneva maintains that when O'Neill tried to synthesize the two forms, universal and individual tragedy, in *Desire Under the Elms* and *Mourning Becomes Electra*, he discovered that he could do so only when he dealt with historical material. Yet, neither play reached full universal tragic dimensions as the circle of protagonists did not comprise all the characters. Not until the late plays was he able to synthesize the two forms, using contemporary themes, and widen the circle of tragic heroes to embrace all the characters. *Long Day's Journey into Night* and *The Iceman Cometh*, she points out, are examples of a perfect embodiment of the idea of universal tragedy.

Koreneva provides the finest analysis to date of the dramatist's progressive stages as he developed his concept of modern tragedy—100 percent American tragedy—but what also emerges from her essay is her appreciation and awareness of those things O'Neill valued most in life: the beauty of natural human relations; the nobility and innate worth of man; the eternal value of courage, compassion, honesty. At the same time, she acknowledges and discusses the contributions O'Neill made as a craftsman and artist, smashing conventions of the commercial theatre by his bold experiments. These experiments, especially O'Neill's foray into expressionism, are the focus of Horst Frenz's essay.

A two-month stay in Russia in 1907 provided Ernst Barlach, the playwright and sculptor who pioneered expressionism in Germany, with new artistic inspiration and strengthened his mystical tendencies. Like the characters in his plays, Barlach was a God-seeking mystic in his life and work, resembling that other early German expressionist, Paul Korfeld, whose primary concern was the souls of his characters. Like these writers, O'Neill was, as he stated, more interested in the relationship between man and God than the relationship between man and man. In his expressionist vision and portrayal of man, the American dramatist has greater philosophical affinity with Barlach and Korfeld than with the more rationalistic playwrights Georg Kaiser and Ernst Toller, to whom he is frequently compared. Attacked by critics for his turn from the social to the metaphysical or psychological sphere, O'Neill was following the lead of German expressionists who dramatized the need for spiritual, as well as social, reform and faith in God.

In his effort to depict the displacement of modern man in the distortions that followed World War I, O'Neill abandoned the realism of his first plays for expressionism. Although *The Emperor Jones* and *The Hairy Ape* contain realistic elements, both use the technical devices of expressionism. However, when O'Neill was charged with having been influenced by Kaiser's *From Morn to Midnight*, he stated that he had not seen the play until 1922, after he had written his own two, adding: "I had read *From Morn to Midnight* before *Hairy Ape* was written but not before the idea for it was planned. The point is that *The Hairy Ape* is a direct descendant of *Jones*, written before I had ever heard of expressionism." O'Neill had read the plays of Strindberg, and he and Central European expressionists were directly influenced by them, depicting modern man as exploited and forced to cope with social inequities. What distinguishes the American playwright from the more rationalistic German expressionists and aligns him more closely with Strindberg is what John Gassner calls his "metaphysical mode of expressionism," for O'Neill examines not only the nature of man's role in society but also the nature of being.

Horst Frenz notes that one reason for O'Neill's reluctance to acknowledge Kaiser's influence may well have been his admiration for Strindberg, whose "supra-naturalism" he appreciated. Frenz claims that O'Neill "stood so much in the center of the various movements of the European drama and felt so close to his European predecessors that he was unaware of the exact nature of their impact on him." In addition to its resemblance to Conrad's *Heart of Darkness* and Ibsen's *Peer Gynt*, *The Emperor Jones* has parallels with Kaiser's *From Morn to Midnight* beyond the common use of expressionistic techniques, according to Frenz. It is conceivable, he maintains, that O'Neill, prior to writing *The Emperor Jones* in 1920, had access to Kaiser's play, for Ashley Dukes's translation was published in the autumn 1919 issue of a Boston magazine, *Poet Lore*.

Frenz asserts that besides the common expressionistic devices of these two plays—the monologues and soliloquies, the projections of the subconscious—there are a number of similarities between Kaiser's Cashier and O'Neill's Brutus Jones: the depiction of the initial situation of each man, the problem of identity, their spiritual testing grounds, and symbols forecasting their tragic end. Frenz also finds resemblances between later plays of the two dramatists, Kaiser's *The Coral* and O'Neill's *The Hairy Ape*: their setting—the ship of a wealthy capitalist with its contrasting stokehole and luxurious upper deck; their lower and upper class representatives—the grimy stoker and the white-clad industrialist's daughter; their theme—exploitation of the workers and the effects of this exploitation on them.

While the basic situation is the same in these two plays, the focus differs. Frenz asserts Kaiser is primarily a reformer, interested in the "liberation of man from social and political evils," in the problems encountered by the masses living in an industrial society; in contrast, O'Neill is "more the mystic concerned with the liberation of man's soul," with individual human lives as they are affected by an industrial society. Frenz illustrates this difference of emphasis in his discussion of Kaiser's *Gas I*, which depicts all classes of men at the mercy of the machine, and O'Neill's *Dynamo*, in which one individual becomes a victim of his own superstition when he begins to worship the machine as a substitute for the deity of his lost faith. While Kaiser and O'Neill both explore man's relationship and responsibility to his fellow man in an industrial society, using expressionist techniques to depict his exploitation and subsequent alienation and despair, the universe that O'Neill creates is governed by some "behind-life" force. The tragic dislocation and destruction of his heroes are caused not by the machine and/or materialism but by the loss or absence of spiritual certainty.

As Frenz demonstrates, O'Neill was indeed aware of and influenced by German expressionists, but he adapted and refined the techniques of Old World playwrights to dramatize the social problems of the New World. That he was able to give these concerns a universal dimension is but further evidence that his international reputation as a major world dramatist is justified.

There are, obviously, several lessons to be learned from the essays in this European section. Clifford Leech and Timo Tiusanen remind Americans that there are still traces of Puritanism in the national character—that they seem to be living in a closed cultural society and are removed from the mainstream of enlightened European thought. As Tiusanen notes, this lingering Puritanism may possibly account for American resistance to theatre and to O'Neill. One way suggested to keep O'Neill alive in this country would be to "classicize" him by finding ever new relevances for his plays. Peter Egri, Horst Frenz, and Egil Törnqvist demonstrate that O'Neill was very much a part of the European mainstream, turning to the Old World for literary, theatrical, and philosophical inspiration. Tom Olsson, Josef Jařab, Marta Sienicka, and Maya Koreneva provide information about the many productions abroad from the 1920s to the present that indicate the dramatist has found a permanent "home" in the theatres of Western and Eastern European countries.

In their totality, the essays offer Americans a European view of O'Neill as a major world playwright. Peter Egri maintains that the more we see O'Neill as part of an international dramatic movement, the more we will be able to understand his international, indeed, universal appeal—and also his American quality. Perhaps those outside the native tradition can best help Americans understand and appreciate their particular legacy of O'Neill. We Americans are still playing what the dramatist calls "that everlasting game of trying to possess our own souls by the possession of something outside them." It is possible that an awareness of what O'Neill was trying to say in his plays may help us discover our roots, our true personal and national identity, and a solution to the dilemma of the split self, the materialist-businessman/idealist-poet dichotomy. When Americans have truly disposed of the Puritan legacy once and for all and replaced their pursuit for material possessions with a quest for spiritual and moral values, O'Neill's work may very well be totally accepted in this country, and America will then enter the theatrical world mainstream.

The European view provided proves that O'Neill was able to transcend international language barriers with a universal vision of man that can be comprehended by all men of good will. Significantly, what O'Neill found *most* gratifying in his encounter with the Moscow Kamerny company was his discovery that the theatre has a unifying language of its own; "you all felt the kinship with me as I immediately did with you—that we had known one another a long time and were united." In these times of international tensions, when men use weapons rather than words to resolve their differences, there is something to be learned from this remark. For the past half century this dramatist with his plays has enabled peoples of various countries, with totally different cultures but with a mutual love of the true theatre, to unite in "old and tried friendship—comradeship!" O'Neill shows us in his words and works that we belong not only to some "behind-life" force but also to the brotherhood of man. If

America does respond to his universal message, it could be we may experience a new harmony with our fellow man, our world, and ourselves.

NOTES

[1] Eugene O'Neill, *Marco Millions* in *Nine Plays*, edited and introduced by Joseph Wood Krutch (New York, 1941), p. 251.

[2] Croswell Bowen, *The Curse of the Misbegotten* (New York, 1959), p. 313.

[3] Information contained in these notebooks is still unpublished but will soon be made available. For the past twenty-five years much of the material that O'Neill and his wife Carlotta sent to Yale in the years prior to the dramatist's death in 1953 and that the playwright's widow gave the university in subsequent years has remained restricted. Donald Gallup, curator of the American Literature Collection at Yale's Beinecke Rare Book and Manuscript Library, has asked me to research and to edit for publication "Eugene O'Neill's Ideas for Plays," and he has given me access to notebooks dating from 1914 to 1943. Dr. Gallup has kindly allowed me to use material for this introduction from the notebooks in the Yale Collection and from the four volumes of O'Neill's Work Diary that he has transcribed.

[4] Bowen, pp. 313–14.

[5] Ibid., pp. 315–17.

[6] Quoted by Joseph Wood Krutch in his introduction to *Nine Plays*, p. xvii.

[7] Quoted by Louis Sheaffer, *O'Neill: Son and Playwright* (Boston, 1968), p. 252. [A letter to Kenneth Macgowan dated September 23, 1922 reveals O'Neill made a conscious effort in *Welded* to imitate the Swedish dramatist: "Am working on the preliminaries to 'Welded' now. Think it demands evolving into some new form of its own if I am to say what I want to. My conception of it as Strindberg 'Dance of Death' formula seems hard to fit in. But have no inkling yet of the 'belonging' method. Little subconscious mind, say I each night, bring home the bacon!"]

[8] Eugene O'Neill, *Welded* in *Six Short Plays* (New York, 1951), p. 265.

[9] George Jean Nathan, "Portrait of O'Neill," in *O'Neill and*

His Plays, eds. Oscar Cargill, N. Bryllion Fagin, and William J. Fisher (New York, 1961), p. 54.
[10] Eugene O'Neill, "A Letter to the Kamerny Theatre," in Cargill et al., pp. 123–24. Three years earlier O'Neill and Danchenko of the Moscow Art Theatre had become friends. Dudley Nichols in a commentary on his own friendship with O'Neill says that he first met the dramatist in 1927

> ... in the apartment in New York of Nemirovich-Danchenko of the Moscow Art Theatre on the day when Gene delivered to Danchenko the script of his new play *Lazarus Laughed.* Danchenko, whom I knew well, was eager, as was Stanislavski, to give this play, ignored in America, its première in Moscow. I remember Danchenko telling O'Neill with glowing eyes and deep sincerity, "*You* are one of us, *you* are a *Russian,*" which was about the highest praise this old Russian could think of.
> (Eugene O'Neill Collection, Yale)

A letter to Kenneth Macgowan dated December 30, 1940 reveals that O'Neill continued to hold the Kamerny and Moscow Art Theatre in high esteem in later years. Explaining the necessity of the scene at the end of *The Iceman Cometh* in which the characters return to their earlier pipe dreams, O'Neill writes:

> They *must* tell these lies as a first step in taking up life again. Moreover, their going through with this pathetic formula heightens by contrast the tension of Larry's waiting for the sound of Parritt hurtling down to the backyard, and the agony he goes through. If our American acting and directing cannot hold this scene up without skimping it, then to hell with our theatre! You know as well as I that the direction and acting of the old Moscow Art Theatre, or Kamerny, could sustain the horrible contrast and tension of this episode and make it one of the most terrible scenes in the play, as it is to me now.
> (Eugene O'Neill Collection, Yale)

O'NEILL AND
THE ROYAL DRAMATIC

Tom Olsson

Theatre in Sweden

In the late eighteenth century Sweden acquired its first two more permanent theatres in Stockholm—the Royal Opera in 1782 and the Royal Dramatic Theatre in 1788. While the former had its own theatre from the beginning, the latter was not to have a house of its own until 1842. At the end of the eighteenth century and throughout most of the nineteenth century, theatre life in Stockholm, and in Sweden as a whole, was totally under royal supervision and monopoly. Earlier, most of the acting companies were French, and they had been brought to Sweden by the royal families. In the eighteenth century actors of Swedish origin began to perform. In those days, however, theatre was a diversion designed only for the royal family and the court. By the end of the nineteenth century, theatre was becoming more and more popular. Private acting companies began touring throughout Sweden.

In the past the Royal Opera and the Royal Dramatic Theatre were subsidized by the king; today the Swedish government assumes financial responsibility. For two decades, 1888–1907, the Royal Dramatic Theatre was run in a more private way by the actors themselves. In 1908 the new and present building that houses the Royal Dramatic Theatre opened its doors on February 18 with Strindberg's *Master*

34

Olof. Since the early 1930s the government has taken great interest in culture; music, theatre, and art were offered to all people. Because the theatre is highly subsidized, the best seats at the Royal Dramatic Theatre can be had for $5.25. Students and those over sixty-five can purchase tickets at half the original cost. In addition to the two royal theatres, there are municipal theatres in several of the larger cities, a central touring company with its administration in Stockholm, and acting groups in many areas. All theatre activity, as well as programming for music and other performing arts, is under either community or government supervision.

Since 1908 the Royal Dramatic Theatre has been directed by an artistic and economic manager. Today two people jointly share the responsibility, and they are elected by the government. These persons are aided by an elected board whose members represent various fields of society and different political parties. The artistic manager is elected for a period of three years, but he can be re-elected for several periods. According to a new law, the manager and the board must now heed advice from a group representing all sections within the theatre in all matters. This also includes the repertoire. The Royal Dramatic Theatre, like most of the European national and municipal theatres, has been mainly a repertory theatre with many different plays on the repertoire and sometimes for many seasons. One has to keep this information in mind in order to understand the surprisingly small number of representations at times.

Introduction of O'Neill in Sweden

In the spring of 1922 *Dagens Nyheter,* the Stockholm daily newspaper, carried four articles on modern American drama; Eugene O'Neill's name was foremost. Three of these articles were written by the author Gustaf Hellström who, at the time, was working as a journalist. From 1918 to 1922 he was a reporter in the United States. From his own statements we know that, in addition to having seen several of O'Neill's plays in New York, he had been in contact with the playwright personally, although this fact has never been verified. Two men of the American theatre, Kenneth Macgowan and Robert Edmond Jones, visited Stockholm and the Royal Dramatic Theatre in the spring of 1922 as part of their European tour to gather material for their book, *Continental Stagecraft*, which was published in New York later that year. Articles on the two men appeared in the Stockholm press, announcing new productions on the experimental stages of New York's Greenwich Village and praising the young American drama, especially O'Neill's work. A year later Macgowan and Jones joined O'Neill to form within the theatre consortium "The Provincetown," the so-called triumvirate, which made its debut in 1924 with Strindberg's *The Spook Sonata*.

Unknown as O'Neill was at that time in Sweden, the newspaper articles and the American visitors must have created an interest in the dramatist within the Royal Dramatic Theatre, for when Gustaf Hellström offered *The Emperor Jones* to the theatre in the summer that year, the management was obviously interested. When negotiations about producing that play began in the early fall, Tore Svennberg, the artistic manager, and Gustaf Hellström, translator and the playwright's representative, conducted them. Discussions were drawn out, however, and when the fall season of 1923 began, the plans of the theatre had completely changed. The more realistic *Anna Christie* was selected to introduce O'Neill to the Swedish audience at the Royal Dramatic. The première took place on the 25th of October with the great actress Tora Teje in the title-role.

The reason for this change can almost certainly be attributed to the play's Swedish aspects. *Anna Christie* was performed only twelve times at the Royal Dramatic Theatre. A production a month later at the Municipal Theatre of Helsingborg was far more successful. It was five years before there was another O'Neill production at the Royal Dramatic Theatre, and by then the Lorensberg Theatre in Gothenburg, which was so vigorous at that time under the management of Per Lindberg, had staged three one-act plays from the nautical cycle *S.S. Glencairn*. Critics saw a far more original author than had been apparent in *Anna Christie*. But Gustaf Hellström's importance as the man who introduced O'Neill in Sweden must not be underestimated. Twenty years later Hellström became a member of the Royal Swedish Academy, which awards the Nobel Prize for Literature.

Strange Interlude at the Royal Dramatic Theatre and O'Neill's Personal Contact with This Theatre

In 1928 Erik Wettergren became the manager at the Royal Dramatic Theatre. Wettergren was anxious to champion the cause of modern drama, both Swedish and foreign. Per Lindberg, who had established a reputation at the Lorensberg Theatre, came to the Royal Dramatic as director in that same year. One of the plays that interested this experimental director was O'Neill's *Strange Interlude*, which had its world première in New York early in 1928. The play opened at the Royal Dramatic at the end of that year and, in terms of audience statistics, was the fourth most successful O'Neill play ever staged at this theatre—fifty-four performances, most of which were in one run. Even the critics were impressed, although they complained about the length of the work (this was not the last time such a complaint was made). Tora Teje and Lars Hanson appeared in this production.

The staging of *Strange Interlude* was important for the Royal Dramatic Theatre in two other ways. Olof Molander, who had been a director at this theatre since the late 1910s, was most certainly affected by this interpretation and gained a more modern view of dramatic production. Molander had always been more or less a traditionalist in his work, despite his early articles on the progressive Gordon Craig and a few attempts to do contemporary drama. He was most probably forced into a new approach by Lindberg's unintentional competition. Molander later progressed in a quite different way, but this was a beginning.

The other, more tangible, thing that happened was that O'Neill, who was staying in France at that time, heard of the success of his work in Stockholm. He wrote to Wettergren personally and requested that the reviews be translated:

> . . . I would consider it a great personal favor if you could have someone write me in English what the reactions of the critics, and especially of the general public, were to my play *Strange Interlude*. I am deeply interested to know this. Of course, the criticisms from the newspapers were sent to me, but as I don't read Swedish and have no friend who does, they left me no wiser!—May I take this opportunity to thank you and everyone connected with the production for the appreciation of the play which your choice of it implies. I wish I could have seen it but I was in China when you first produced it. It is my hope that I may be in Sweden sometime, if it should be revived. I would have loved to see the 'Nina' of Miss Teje. I know her wonderful acting by reputation. I have also heard the finest things of the work of Mr. Kage and Mr. Hanson.

This letter was written on March 26, 1929, but it was missing until March 1975 when I found it in the Royal Dramatic Theatre's archives, along with another original letter by O'Neill and copies of two other letters. These letters and copies of Wettergren's answers had been forgotten all these years, for they had been incorrectly filed.

Probably out of sheer thoughtlessness, Wettergren failed to respond to this letter from O'Neill, who felt offended and wrote to his agent and friend in New York, Dick Madden, in early June of the same year:

> . . . Here is something, Dick. I wrote to someone I thought was the director of the Royal Theatre in Stockholm asking for some dope on the Swedish reaction to *Interlude*. I've had no reply. Now I can't believe even a director would be as discourteous as that, especially in Europe. Something must have gone wrong. Will you kindly take it up through the agent in Sweden [Folmer Hansen, Copenhagen, for this play]—tell them to find out if the letter was ever received, etc., and to write me! I understand they care to do *Jones* there soon—but they'll do no more of my plays at that theatre if that's the stuff they pull. Will you kindly write the agent rightaway? I want to know about *Interlude* in Sweden, having heard such good things about it."

It was yet another five years before the next O'Neill première at the Royal Dramatic—*Mourning Becomes Electra*. Like *Strange Interlude*, it was a European première—or almost at least, as the play opened in Oslo on the same day. This time it was Olof Molander who was holding the reins— in three ways: as director, as translator, and as stage designer. He had produced the trilogy for radio a few months earlier. Now Tora Teje and Lars Hanson were on stage once more in an O'Neill play, and for the first time Märta Ekström. It was a great artistic triumph, even if audiences did not give it due support—it was performed twenty-seven times, but for Molander it was the beginning of a long period of work with O'Neill as well as with Strindberg.

From now on O'Neill productions came thick and fast at the Royal Dramatic and at other big Swedish theatres too, and the Royal Dramatic was not by any means always first. The third of the Royal Dramatic's great directors who took an interest in O'Neill during this period was Alf Sjöberg. In the same year that *Mourning Becomes Electra* was staged, Sjöberg directed *Desire Under the Elms* with Tora Teje, Lars Hanson and Anders Henrikson in the leading roles. This production was not one of the great ones and only had fourteen performances. Sjöberg's production of *Days Without End* in cooperation with the Swedish National Touring Theatre in 1935 was even less successful, only being played four times on the Royal Dramatic stage. It had, however, a measure of success at Gothenburg's Municipal Theatre, where it was put on some eighteen months before the Royal Dramatic production. A decade was to pass before Alf Sjöberg did his best-known production.

The last O'Neill play at the Royal Dramatic before a long gap was the comedy *Ah, Wilderness!* in the autumn of 1935. The critics were confused, but thought that they could see new openings for a playwright formerly only connected with somber tragedies. Their positive criticism helped to make it a genuine long-runner—the third biggest box office success the Royal Dramatic has had with an O'Neill play. It was on the repertoire until the Spring of 1937—much dependent on O'Neill's Nobel Prize for Literature in 1936—

and was performed sixty times. Rune Carlsten was the director, with Olof Winnerstrand—then in his sixtieth year —as Nat Miller, ably supported by Sture Lagerall, Signe Hasso, Märta Ekström and Carl Barcklind.

The years between 1933 and 1946—the dates of the Broadway world premières of *Days Without End* and *The Iceman Cometh* respectively—have been called "the great O'Neill silence." In Sweden that silence was not total. We have seen how the Royal Dramatic played *Ah, Wilderness!* until 1937. In that year Gothenburg's Municipal Theatre's "Studio" stage had been opened with well-received performances of *The Emperor Jones* and *Ile*. A year earlier Per Lindberg had once more tried his hand at O'Neill's experiments. This time with *The Great God Brown* at the Vasa Theatre in Stockholm. Neither critics nor audience understood it, and it was only put on a few times. *Ile* came to the same end when it was given as part of "An American Rhapsody" at the New Theatre in Stockholm in 1942. Apart from these, about ten plays were broadcasted on Swedish radio during those years, several of them directed by Olof Molander.

When the Royal Dramatic opened its second stage— "The Studio," later known as the Small Stage—O'Neill's *All God's Chillun Got Wings* was chosen for the opening program. This was at the suggestion of Pauline Brunius, who had been the theatre's manager since 1938. Other voices had been raised in favor of Strindberg. There is no doubt that the earlier choice of Gothenburg's "Studio" influenced the decision, as the two theatres were in fierce competition at that time. The unofficial opening took place on the 10th of April before royalty, with the manager, Mrs. Brunius, reading a prologue written by Karl Ragnar Gierow. The play was directed by Alf Sjöberg, with Inga Tidblad and Holger Löwenadler in the major roles. (It dealt with problems which had been horribly accentuated by the world war which had just ended—those of racial strife. But the work is not based on this alone—according to O'Neill it is not even the driving force in the drama—but, according to the author, on the opposition between male and female, just as in Strindberg's work.) The production was an artistic success and remained on the repertoire for thirty-three performances. O'Neill sent a telegram with his good wishes for this première which was printed in the program:

> . . . deeply regret due to delay your cable reaching me here too late now to write for opening night program i do wish to convey to everyone connected with studio theatre and the production of all gods chillun got wings my deep appreciation of the honor of having a play of mine chosen to open this new theatre stop can only hope it may justify your faith and its production start the studio theatre on a long life of high artistic achievement stop i remain as ever deeply grateful to the swedish theatre for all it has done for my work
>
> eugene o'neill

This was the last communication of a more personal nature that the Royal Dramatic received from the American playwright.

Pauline Brunius has been criticized for presenting too much light drama, but it can be said in her defense that she had to manage the national theatre (the Royal Dramatic) in time of war and of difficult restrictions. In spite of this, and in spite of the more or less invisible censure of a country trying to be neutral, Mrs. Brunius managed to present a varied repertoire. She succeeded in restoring Olof Molander to the Royal Dramatic, after a period of "exile," with his legendary production of Strindberg's *The Spook Sonata* in 1942. She got a second stage for the theatre in 1945, as we have seen, and did it in the middle of a nationwide building stoppage. After the opening of that stage Mrs. Brunius managed to get the Swedish première rights for O'Neill's latest play, *The Iceman Cometh*, from the Danish publisher Strakosch, who had been O'Neill's representative in Scandinavia for a long time. She accomplished this by a correspondence filled with exaggerations, sometimes even pure lies.

> . . . The Royal Dramatic Theatre has—as you know Miss Bischoff—had all the O'Neill premières first of all the theatres in Sweden, and Molander has directed most of them.

Olof Molander was to be the director, and it was he who, together with the Royal Dramatic's long tradition of O'Neill productions, acted as bait for the rights.

The Iceman Cometh had its well-received European première on the 31st of October 1947 and featured in the large cast were Uno Henning, who had played in Anna Christie a quarter of a century earlier, Olof Sandborg, Hugo Björne, Holger Löwenadler, Hans Strååt, Ulf Palme, and Eva Dahlbeck. The critics were profusely enthusiastic about both the returning playwright and the director and cast. Forty-one performances must be considered a lot if one takes into consideration that the play took four and a half hours in performance time.

I have discovered new information that reveals that O'Neill had two choices in 1946 for the play with which he would make his comeback on Broadway: A Moon for the Misbegotten and The Iceman Cometh. I have recently found a letter dated April, 1964 in the archives at the Royal Dramatic from an American actress, Elizabeth Scott, to Ingmar Bergman, at the time head manager of the Royal Dramatic. Miss Scott states: "In 1946 I was rehearsed for the premiere of Eugene O'Neill's A Moon for the Misbegotten, working with Mr. O'Neill and Dudley Digges on the part [Josie] until the Theatre Guild decided to shelve the play in favor of The Iceman Cometh."

In the spring of 1952 Random House published A Moon for the Misbegotten, at the request of O'Neill, who was in need of money. This was not unnoticed in Sweden, and in the autumn of that year the printed edition was reviewed in a Stockholm newspaper. Two Swedish theatres soon began to show interest: the Royal Dramatic and Malmö's Municipal Theatre. It was the latter theatre that gave the European première—which was called a world première—at the end of March 1953. But this did not disturb Karl Ragnar Gierow, who had then been manager of the Royal Dramatic for a couple of years. He had asked Olof Molander to direct the play and the three major parts had been given to Lars Hanson, Eva Dahlbeck and Uno Henning. The critics had questioned the quality of the new O'Neill play and were even more critical about the production in Malmö. They were very much impressed by the Royal Dramatic's production, which had its première just a month later. Several critics thought they had seen a quite different play. *A Moon for the Misbegotten* was one of Molander's best productions, alongside his interpretations of Strindberg, and the actors interpreted both the comedy and the tragedy which make up the Irishness of the play in the most exemplary manner.

According to Carlotta O'Neill, the playwright's widow, the critics' favorable reviews of the successful Stockholm production of *A Moon for the Misbegotten* reached O'Neill shortly before he died in 1953 and influenced him to give the Royal Dramatic Theatre permission to present the world premières of what would become his posthumous plays: *Long Day's Journey into Night, A Touch of the Poet, Hughie,* and *More Stately Mansions.* Americans probably ask why the historic theatrical premières of these plays took place in Sweden and not in the United States.

There are two main reasons why O'Neill felt obligated to Sweden and the Royal Dramatic. The first is the long history of successful productions of his plays at the Royal Dramatic from *Anna Christie* in 1923 to *The Iceman Cometh* in 1947 (often these were the first European presentations). The second reason is the debt O'Neill stated he owed to the Swedish dramatist, Strindberg. The American playwright acknowledges this debt in his written speech to the Swedish Academy when he received the Nobel Prize for literature in 1936. In 1949 in a telegram to the Royal Dramatic declining an invitation to write something for the Strindberg centenary, O'Neill says: "I regret that the state of my health does not permit me to write as I would wish of this centenary of Strindberg's birth but I must add my name to those thousands who will want to pay him homage and to express again the gratitude I feel for the inspiration of his genius sincerely Eugene O'Neill."

A few months later, the Royal Dramatic requested permission to perform *A Moon for the Misbegotten* as a tribute to the long and firm relationship between this special theatre and the American playwright, but Carlotta O'Neill was, at that time, unwilling to agree to this production, even in Stockholm. In March 1952, one of the Royal Dramatic's young, promising actresses, Gunnel Broström, who was then living in the United States and who would later play Sara Harford in the world première of *More Stately Mansions* in Stockholm in 1962, wrote from New York: "The play by O'Neill is not available. *A Moon for the Misbegotten* is the name, if I am not wrong? Everything has been tried, even the Nobel committee has appealed to Mrs. O'Neill, who is not willing to give up this play, nor O'Neill's last one. The playwright is very ill and his wife has complete right of decision."

The Royal Dramatic continued negotiations with O'Neill's representative in Scandinavia and eventually permission was given for the première in Sweden. When O'Neill died later that year, the Royal Dramatic sent a telegram of condolence to his widow and received a telegram of gratitude from her. A year later, in 1954, the Royal Dramatic made inquiries about the possibility of producing *A Touch of the Poet*. In response, Jane Rubin, Carlotta O'Neill's agent, wrote: "Re: *A Touch of the Poet*—this play is definitely not available for production in this country or anywhere else. Since the play has not even been published copies are not even available for reading."

In the spring of 1954, Dag Hammarskjöld—at that time General Secretary of the United Nations—visited Stockholm and met with his old friend, Karl Ragnar Gierow, who explained the difficulty he had encountered in getting permission to do *A Touch of the Poet*. Hammarskjöld promised to do everything possible to get a positive response from Mrs. O'Neill. At the same time, she had asked her agent to try to get Swedish copies—translations—of O'Neill's plays published in Sweden. The Royal Dramatic arranged a special volume of the unpublished play, *Desire Under the Elms*, and sent it to Mrs. O'Neill together with other published plays.

When Hammarskjöld met Gierow in Stockholm in the fall of 1954, the two friends discussed, among other things, how to continue the effort to break into the treasure house of the posthumous O'Neill. Again, nothing of substance came of this meeting, but in a letter to Gierow dated May 31, 1955, Hammarskjöld states: "I have not forgotten your wish to break up the gates to the O'Neill treasury. I hope you will try it and succeed, thus giving Stockholm a new chance to show what O'Neill's countrymen do not dare to produce."

Two weeks later, Hammarskjöld received a letter from Mrs. O'Neill. He had mentioned Gierow and the Royal Dramatic in an earlier communiqué to her agent. Mrs. O'Neill writes: "This is a strange coincidence. I have intended writing to Mr. Gierow to ask if he would *care* to produce "Long Day's Journey into Night." Later, in a letter to Gierow, she states:

> ... he [O'Neill] would like it to be produced in your theatre in Stockholm. He felt you (and Sweden) understood what he was trying to say and that you would understand the tragedy of the play and what it cost him to write it! I have explained to Miss Rubin, my agent, that there will be no financial returns in this production for her, or me or the Strakosch office [for the Scandinavian rights].

Gierow found an appropriate way to use the royalties that he felt should be returned to the O'Neill estate. He made his suggestion to Carlotta in a subsequent letter: "I do hope, that you don't mind a somewhat different suggestion. Let us subtract from our receipts of this play the usual author's fee and make the sum an O'Neill Stipendium to be given to some of our actors. I shall be very happy, should this idea appeal to you." This was the beginning of the famous O'Neill Stipendium at the Royal Dramatic. It has been awarded annually on O'Neill's birthday, October 16, to actors of this theatre, and it is looked upon as the highest award of theatre in Sweden.

In response to Gierow's question, why the Royal Dramatic was selected to present the world première of *Long Day's Journey into Night*, Mrs. O'Neill says:

> You asked why O'Neill had the desire for your theatre to be the first of all theatres to produce "Long Day's Journey into Night." He felt you would understand the tragic undertones of the play—and not produce it as a sensational melodrama.

—A few weeks before my husband died he dictated a long list of things he *wanted* done—and *not* done. But, under *no* circumstances was it to be produced in the theatre in this country. And he gave me the reason why.

Later, after meeting with Carlotta O'Neill, Gierow came to a conclusion about what he felt must have been O'Neill's reason for not wanting *Long Day's Journey into Night* produced in the United States. The Swedish director writes:

Having been silent for many years, O'Neill, after the war, presented two new plays to the public: *The Iceman Cometh* in 1946 and the next year *A Moon for the Misbegotten*. Neither of them was very well received; *A Moon for the Misbegotten* was a real flop, or next to it. Here, at the Royal Dramatic, *The Iceman Cometh* was a great success, and when, some years later, *A Moon for the Misbegotten* was released and produced by us, it was unanimously hailed as one of its author's capital works and one of the masterpieces of modern drama. Now, at that time O'Neill's illness approached its terminal, and he knew it. He knew that he could never be able to write anything more; his only occupation was to wait for death, while his last works, which he himself considered as fruits of his ripeness, were, in his own country, regarded as barren leaves. Thus dying, himself maybe in doubt of his own judgement, he got news from this far away part of the world, telling him, that after all he might be right. There did exist a theatre, deeply interested in his works and eager to do it all justice, within its own limits. This, I think, is the background to the wish, which O'Neill uttered before his death and which is to us a great honour and an even greater responsibility to accept. . . . Well—I can easily explain why the works of O'Neill are so highly estimated in Sweden, although I can't tell you why they are not in his own country. . . . To us O'Neill is not just a good playwright—sometimes he is not good at all, in my opinion—but he is something rather different and very rare, a real dramatist, born with the secret, the gift and the curse of tragedy. The great line of drama runs, I think, from Ibsen to Chekhov to Strindberg and now to O'Neill, because of their stronger feeling and deeper understanding of human nature, its passion and its conflicts. As you know,

O'Neill himself regarded Ibsen and Strindberg as his masters, and we might be especially trained by those two to recognize O'Neill's qualities, maybe a little better than his countrymen do. But that is certainly nothing to boast of. Strindberg was famous abroad in Europe before he was accepted at home as our greatest dramatist; the same thing happened to Ibsen in his country; just as to Eugene O'Neill in his.

Gierow's conjecture is supported by Carlotta's statement in her letter to him: "The Scandinavian Peninsular is dear to me and was to him (though he never visited it). They kept us going in 1953 when this country wasn't interested in O'Neill!"

This letter raises some questions. Did O'Neill give his wife permission to do *anything* she wanted with the play? In the mid-1940s O'Neill made an arrangement with Random House that the manuscript of *Long Day's Journey into Night* should be kept in a safe until twenty-five years after his death; *then* it could be published, but *never* performed as a play. O'Neill's requests are clearly analyzed in Louis Sheaffer's second book on the dramatist. *O'Neill: Son and Artist*. It would seem to be a strange turn of events if O'Neill changed his mind about his dearest play before he died. Nevertheless, thanks to Carlotta O'Neill and Karl Ragnar Gierow—with much assistance from Dag Hammarskjöld—one of the most touching and profound pieces of literature has taken its rightful place in modern drama.

Another question should be answered: Was O'Neill completely forgotten in the United States in the early 1950s as Carlotta's letter implies? As I have stated previously, the Royal Dramatic had great success with its 1953 production of *A Moon for the Misbegotten*, and news of the favorable reception of the play reached the dramatist before he died. We also know that after the failure of the pre-Broadway tour of *A Moon for the Misbegotten* in 1947, the Theatre Guild and Lawrence Langner and his wife Arnina Marshall—both personal friends of O'Neill—together with Theresa Helburn, attempted to bring this production to New York. The Guild tried to keep its agreements with O'Neill with a production of *A Touch of the Poet* and possibly of *Hughie* as well. Langner endeavored to persuade O'Neill up until 1951, when, as a result of pressure from Carlotta, O'Neill made an irrevocable break with all friends on Broadway.

At the beginning of the new theatre season in Stockholm in 1955, there was a lot of publicity in the newspapers about O'Neill's tribute to the Swedish national theatre, but no preparations for an immediate production of *Long Day's Journey into Night* were undertaken. Karl Ragnar Gierow made his first trip to New York—one of eight he would make —in September. But it was not until November and December that any specific information was released about the upcoming production. The roles of Mary and James Tyrone were already cast—Inga Tidblad and Lars Hanson. Inga Tidblad was at first reluctant to play the role as she had accepted a part in another play, outside of Stockholm, scheduled for a spring production in 1956. Eventually, she agreed to do both plays. No decision had been made about the choice of actors for the two sons, Jamie and Edmund. All of the details for the production of *Long Day's Journey into Night* are discussed in the correspondence between Carlotta O'Neill and Karl Ragnar Gierow—a collection of letters absolutely unique in the history of theatre. The two hundred letters that were exchanged are in the archives of the Royal Dramatic.

As he informed Carlotta in his letter of December 1955, Gierow was having a problem getting the director he wanted for the play. His choice from the beginning was Olof Molander, but this director had a heavy schedule in 1955: Strindberg's *The Dream Play* in the spring and *Advent* in the fall. Molander was the obvious choice because of his previous experience directing O'Neill's plays: *Mourning Becomes Electra* in 1933, *The Iceman Cometh* in 1947 and *A Moon for the Misbegotten* in 1953. He would later direct *A Touch of the Poet* in 1957. New productions of *Mourning Becomes Electra* and Strindberg's *To Damascus*—all three parts—were presented at the Stockholm Municipal Theatre rather than at the Royal Dramatic and reveal Molander's life-long dedication and interest in Strindberg and O'Neill.

In his letter to Carlotta, describing the man who would replace Molander, Gierow states: "Now the helmsman will be a man, Bengt Ekerot by name, a comparatively young stage director but already rather promising, not to say famous, especially for his production of Strindberg's *The Father* (with Lars Hanson)." There is then in his choice another connection between O'Neill and Strindberg. Ekerot had some previous experience with an O'Neill production. He had directed *A Moon for the Misbegotten* in 1953 for a summer tour company with great success. He was to become famous for his acclaimed direction of *Long Day's Journey into Night* and, later in 1958, of the world première at the Royal Dramatic of *Hughie*.

Rehearsals for *Long Day's Journey into Night* began on December 14, but there were interruptions in the first weeks because some of the actors became ill. Gierow received permission from Carlotta to set the date for the world première for the 10th of February, 1956, and not wait for the day of publication of the play in the United States on February 15. Never before had a premiere been followed with such interest as this one, and newspaper people from all over the world came to Stockholm.

On opening night, the Swedish critics were overwhelmed. They praised the production in their reviews the next day:

Theatrical history at the Royal Dramatic. Unique is the word! And that includes all parts of yesterday's performance. You will never more see a theatrical performance of four hours, where nothing else happens than four or five people sitting around the same family table, small talking and drinking whiskey, and where all the members of this family through this simple realistic means of expression reach such self exposure, one after another, that *Ghosts* by Ibsen turns out to be an idyll, and all the dream-play stage craft among streetcars and salesmen in late American drama become unnecessary trinkets and trifles.

If you say that the Royal Dramatic had its royal evening last night, it is not because the royal box was occupied— strange enough—but that on the stage appeared the king and queen of the Swedish theatre, assisted by two of the

50 A EUROPEAN PERSPECTIVE

worthiest successors to the throne. The dramatic world they offered—with the help of a brilliant young director—was a royal present, given to the Royal Dramatic through legacy and will be the last monarch of World Drama of the dimensions of Aeschylus and Shakespeare.

Long Day's Journey into Night proved to be the greatest success in the history of the Royal Dramatic. It ran, with certain intervals, to the fall of 1962—130 performances, a miracle in a Swedish repertory theatre. This production of *Long Day's Journey into Night*, Strindberg's *The Father*— also directed by Ekerot, and *Miss Julie*—directed by another giant of the Royal Dramatic, Alf Sjöberg, were selected to represent the Royal Dramatic and the Swedish theatre on a guest tour to the United States in 1962. The company visited Seattle, Washington, during the World's Fair and New York. The serious critics were enthusiastic, but mostly over Strindberg. One humorous incident occurred which reveals how little some Americans knew about their great native dramatist. At one of the first press conferences in Seattle, an American newspaper man asked what would be offered. The following exchange resulted:

"First we will show *The Father* by our great Swedish playwright, Strindberg."
"Marvelous—and then?"
"*Miss Julie*—also by Strindberg."
"Great—and something else?"
"We will also perform *Long Day's Journey into Night* by Eugene O'Neill."
"Splendid! Is he also Swedish?"

In New York, however, the Swedish company met with more understanding. In an article for the *New York Herald Tribune*, Louis Sheaffer wrote:

The Royal Dramatic will open a week's run—at the Cort— of Strindberg and Eugene O'Neill. . . . The engagement could scarcely be more right, not only because the American regarded Strindberg his literary father in the theatre, but because to the Swedish people O'Neill has remained, ever

since he attained artistic maturity, a living, important
writer. In the years before and after his death in 1953, when
the American theatre came to look upon O'Neill as somewhat passe, more of historical than of present interest, a
crippled potential giant whose infirmities negated his aspira-
tion to size, the Royal Dramatic theatre continued affec-
tionately reviving his works, more than any other theatre
has done.

During the Royal Dramatic's American tour, Lars Hanson was unfortunately unable to act in both Strindberg and
O'Neill for reasons of ill-health and the role of James Tyrone
was given to George Rydeberg. Something of the balance
of the Tyrone family in *Long Day's Journey* was spoiled by
this change.

Between 1956 and 1962 four world premières of O'Neill
plays took place at the Royal Dramatic. The unrepeatable
success with *Long Day's Journey* led to the March 1957
presentation of *A Touch of the Poet*. Olof Molander directed
the play, but by then the long harmonious working relationship between him and Lars Hanson was showing signs
of disintegration. The friction had an effect on the production, which critics found vastly inferior to *Long Day's
Journey*. Hanson, playing Cornelius Melody, seemed detached and at odds with the rest of the company. Sif Ruud
as Nora and Eva Dahlbeck as Sara performed brilliantly.
Unfortunately, this was to be Molander's last production of
an O'Neill play for the Royal Dramatic. *A Touch of the Poet*
was only on the bill for thirty-four performances, which is
the least for any of the plays in O'Neill's bequest to the
Royal Dramatic.

Hughie, which had its world première eighteen months
later in the middle of September 1958, was a much greater
success. Bengt Ekerot produced the one-acter. In the only
speaking part, Bengt Eklund gave one of his best performances in his career at the Royal Dramatic. Eklund's portrayal of Erie Smith captured the dual nature of the character: the outer brash Broadway wise guy and the inner
tragic loner, longing desperately to communicate with another human being. Allan Edwall played the almost totally

silent supporting role of the Night Clerk in a way which avoided making his comic gestures an end in themselves, but instead underlined an intelligent actor's ability to listen. This one-act play has been acclaimed by critics as the best of its genre that O'Neill has written. Altogether, the play was performed sixty-four times at the Royal Dramatic.

Hughie had its première with another short work, an early effort of the dramatist, *The Emperor Jones*, which was finally to be performed at the Royal Dramatic. This was to have been the play that would introduce O'Neill at the theatre in 1922/23. It had been under consideration a number of times over the years, and finally it was done in a new translation. Bengt Ekerot produced the play, but his feeling for realistic dialogue was out of place here. The critics called for a bolder, more experimental interpretation, and O'Neill's great expressionist hit from the beginning of the twenties was totally eclipsed by the more realistic *Hughie*. Anders Ek was left stranded in the title role of Brutus Jones in a badly conceived production which critics compared, to its detriment, with *Hughie*. In the last two performances of the one-act combination, *The Emperor Jones* was deleted and replaced by Strindberg's *The Stronger*.

More Stately Mansions is the second of the two plays which have been saved for posterity from the cycle *A Tale of Possessors Self-Dispossessed*, which orginally comprised nine plays and later eleven. It was to be the last Royal Dramatic production of O'Neill's posthumous works. Between Karl Ragnar Gierow's first journey to New York to discuss *Long Day's Journey* with Carlotta O'Neill, and his last visit to the U.S.A. to help with the printing of *More Stately Mansions* at Yale, he had travelled across the Atlantic eight times. The interest shown by the international press, and especially by the Swedish, was considerable each time, and at least after the first four visits, the manager of the Royal Dramatic was able to give news of a new play from the effects of the dead playwright. In the case of *More Stately Mansions* it was a typewritten copy of an uncompleted draft which Carlotta had "saved" from the author, who thought that only the completed manuscript of *A Touch of the Poet* was worth saving from the great cycle. O'Neill himself was not aware of this fact.

During the years when the Royal Dramatic and Gierow produced O'Neill's posthumous works, Gierow often mentioned the "detective work" which had been necessary to find them. This seems strange, as they were known, not only by the inner circle around O'Neill in the U.S.A. but also by the American press, since the latter part of the forties. The critic Ebbe Linde rightly pointed this out in the Stockholm daily, *Dagens Nyheter*, before the première of *A Touch of the Poet* in the Spring of 1957. Much of the myth about the Royal Dramatic being some sort of unique O'Neill theatre was created during these years. It is beyond doubt that the Royal Dramatic made a great contribution to the production of O'Neill's work for four decades, but it must not be forgotten what other Swedish theatres and, above all, other European theatres were producing of O'Neill's work during the same period. I shall return to this in connection with the concept of an O'Neill tradition at the Royal Dramatic.

It took Karl Ragnar Gierow almost five years to complete an acceptable Swedish stage-version of O'Neill's 1939 draft of *More Stately Mansions*, and the process went through five distinct forms. The play is next after *A Touch of the Poet* in chronological order, and the original prologue refers to the latter play in describing the wake after Cornelius Melody's death. This scene, as well as the original epilogue, was deleted and then replaced by Gierow during the course of his work, as can be seen from a comparison of the five different versions. Finally, presumably to make the work as independent as possible of *A Touch of the Poet*, both prologue and epilogue were deleted and Sara's last lines were revised to round off the play.

The Swedish stage version was the basis for the edition published by Yale University Press in 1964. It has later received considerable criticism in the United States, especially from the Gelbs in their new, revised edition of O'Neill's biography, published in 1973, where the authors criticize Carlotta for having selfishly misused her husband's unpublished works in order to regain some standing after having been forgotten. It is mainly her cooperation with Donald Gallup and later with Karl Ragnar Gierow which is questioned. According to the Gelbs, O'Neill himself would never have allowed *More Stately Mansions* to be printed in the version authorized by Carlotta O'Neill, Gallup, and Gierow. This play was also to be included, along with *Long Day's Journey, A Touch of the Poet,* and *Hughie* in the agreement between Carlotta O'Neill and the Royal Dramatic which gave that theatre the première rights to the four plays in Stockholm and district without paying royalties. Thus Carlotta did not gain anything financially from the Royal Dramatic for this, but when the Royal Dramatic gave a lead, there was a boom in posthumous O'Neill both in the rest of Europe and in the United States. Only six months after the Stockholm première, *Long Day's Journey* was given in New York, even though O'Neill himself had specified that the play was never to be shown in the United States, for wholly personal reasons.

After the première of *More Stately Mansions,* the critics were not generous with their praises, and the reason lay mainly in the play itself. There was a marked surfeit of "rediscovered" O'Neill plays. The production itself, staged by Stig Torsslow, with Inga Tidblad, Jarl Kulle and Gunnel Broström in the main parts, was received very well. The première took place on the 9th of November 1962, and it was performed forty-nine times. But it seems as though everything paled beside *Long Day's Journey*—but that play did have a cast (Lars Hanson, Inga Tidblad, Ulf Palme and Jarl Kulle) that was so unified that it truly became the Tyrone family, with everything well-monitored and blended by the director, Bengt Ekerot. It was something that was quite impossible to repeat.

It has often been maintained—and not only in Sweden—that Sweden and especially the Royal Dramatic were alone in acknowledging O'Neill's dramatic greatness at an early stage. We have seen that this was not the case. The Royal Dramatic was to have introduced O'Neill with *The Emperor Jones* but eventually decided to do so with the more realistic *Anna Christie.* And since 1923 the theatre has continued to put on

O'Neill's more realistic and psychological plays, whilst at the same time—the early twenties—other European theatres were staging the more topical, experimental pieces like *The Emperor Jones* and *The Hairy Ape* in productions by Baty and Pitoëff in Paris, Piscator in Berlin and Taïrov in Moscow. In England small avant-garde theatres had staged both plays from the nautical suite, *S/S Glencairn*, and *Anna Christie* before the Royal Dramatic's production. As has also been mentioned, other Swedish theatres have given well-received O'Neill performances, in many cases, also before the Royal Dramatic.

It was when Karl Ragnar Gierow came to the theatre that the Royal Dramatic came into the limelight, but this was mainly dependent on the opportunities made available by Carlotta O'Neill. The world première of *Long Day's Journey* in 1956 brought the eyes of the world onto the Royal Dramatic, by means of a well-represented international press, followed by articles on the other posthumous plays. These were expansive years, some of the most important in the history of the Royal Dramatic, but one burning question remains: would the Royal Dramatic's reputation as O'Neill's special theatre have been the same today if the playwright's wishes had been followed and *Long Day's Journey* not staged until twenty-five years after his death? Presumably not. But by then the name of Eugene O'Neill would probably have been, if not dead, at least somewhat passé. Carlotta O'Neill realized this and, with the help of Karl Ragnar Gierow's literary and artistic intuition, she created a place in the future for O'Neill by staging his most notable work, *Long Day's Journey into Night*.

In this way we have seen a concept, known as the Royal Dramatic's O'Neill tradition, created. But what does that concept entail? First, there is the simple answer: fourteen different plays by the same author have been staged at the theatre during a period of forty years. But this answer loses all interest if one compares plays by O'Neill's English-speaking contemporaries performed during the same period; ten or so by G.B. Shaw, five by Anderson, who was followed after the Second World War by Saroyan, Tennessee Williams, and Arthur Miller. This is surely a far too one-dimensional view of the concept of tradition.

A tradition, centering around a single author at one theatre, can be influenced from within the theatre itself, as was the case with Strindberg and Olof Molander at the Royal Dramatic. But in O'Neill's case it was mainly during the time when Gierow was manager of the theatre—in itself a long and important epoch, but one with certain special traits. Others within the theatre did not work for this American playwright more than their work at the theatre demanded as has been proven. This was the case with both manuscript-readers and others in advisory capacities.

On the other hand the initiative may come from the outside, in the form of newspaper articles; and we know that those can be fruitful from the case of Gustav Hellström, even if that course of events progressed differently from Hellström's expectations. But after him there is nobody with whom a direct connection can be shown; nobody outside the theatre has directly influenced the repertoire of the Royal Dramatic in favour of O'Neill. Gustav Hellström was also connected with the Royal Dramatic as a translator. Indeed, no other translator has ever offered a work on his own initiative; they have all been done to order, even in the case of Sven Barthel who has rendered all O'Neill's plays, from *The Iceman Cometh* on, into Swedish. Barthel's first O'Neill translation for the Royal Dramatic was *All God's Chillun Got Wings* for the opening of the Studio stage in 1945.

Certain reviewers have without doubt created an interest for O'Neill in Sweden, quite simply by giving information, and may even, to a certain degree, have stimulated a demand for his work at the Royal Dramatic. Anders Österling reviewed the first edition of *Strange Interlude* quite soon after its publication in New York, and paid special attention to O'Neill for many years, translating *Days Without End* in 1934. In 1937 Stig Torsslow was the first in Sweden to publish a retrospective account of O'Neill the dramatist. Torsslow was, at the time, employed as theatre secretary and he may have been supporting his colleagues. Martin Lamm, who also appreciated O'Neill's genius at an early stage, gave the American a relatively large amount of space in his book, *The Modern Drama*, alongside Ibsen and Strindberg amongst others. This work was published in a new, revised edition in 1964, edited by another important O'Neill critic in Sweden, Lennart Josephson, who was one of the first outside of Gallup's circle at Yale to gain access to O'Neill's Work Diary of 1924–1943, as can be seen from the expanded O'Neill chapter in the book; Josephson was to devote a large part of his research to O'Neill and the great cycle. Artur Lundkvist gave his impressions of O'Neill's work in a special chapter in *Atlantic Wind* as early as 1932; Stig Torsslow gives the reference in his publication five years later. Lundkvist was to devote more space to O'Neill in his *Poets and Disclosers in Modern American Literature*, and the picture he paints there is very similar to that of the preface he wrote for the program for the Royal Dramatic's premiere of *All God's Chillun Got Wings* in 1945. In this way one can list all the writers in the daily press and in the magazines who may have influenced the Royal Dramatic's repertoire. But no influences can be satisfactorily proven in the sources at the Royal Dramatic.

In order to get a deeper and more tangible picture of this so-called O'Neill tradition at the Royal Dramatic one must first examine the choice of plays and their production. We have maintained earlier that the Royal Dramatic chose, almost exclusively, the playwright's realistic and psychological works. There must be an explanation for this, and it can be found in the method of acting which had developed earlier— a method founded on the group, instead of on a 'star.' The foundations were laid, according to Olof Molander, during the years when Tor Hedberg was manager at the Royal Dramatic in the late 1910s. The inheritance—this tradition —was carried forward by Molander. It was founded on the use of a minimum of expression and on a sharp psychological focus. Molander propagated this method of acting amongst the actors he collected around him during the twenties, the most notable names being Tora Teje, Lars Hanson, Märta Ekström, Anders Henriksson, Inga Tidblad and Uno Henning. In the case of O'Neill this work found its most powerful expression in Molander's production of *Mourning Becomes Electra* in 1933.

Two years later there came a great breakthrough for Molander's interpretations of Strindberg—in the *Dreamplay* production of 1935. This production was to a great degree founded on Martin Lamm's conclusions in his first important work on the plays of Strindberg in 1924–26. Molander became a friend of Lamm's from the beginning of the thirties and they had a prolonged exchange of letters. Many of the letters are unfortunately unavailable to research as they are sealed until the end of the century in the Royal Library in Stockholm. Lamm interpreted Strindberg's later, more autobiographical, plays wholly in the light of the author's surroundings and this influenced Molander's production of *Dreamplay* to a considerable degree—for example, in the realistic tone in the dialogue. This more or less unverifiable cooperation between Lamm and Molander continued through the years and bore fruit in such productions as *To Damascus. Part I*, 1936, *The Ghost Sonata*, 1942—the same year as Part II of Lamm's second work on Strindberg was published—*To Damascus. Part II*, 1944, *The Highway*, 1949, *Dreamplay* and *Advent*, 1955, *To Damascus. Part I*, 1960, and, lastly, *The Ghost Sonata* in 1962 which played in Paris almost at the same time that *Long Day's Journey* toured the United States—all these plays being staged at the Royal Dramatic. Right from *Dreamplay* in 1935, Molander's productions were given a noticeably religious slant; he was converted to Catholicism in 1945, after an almost ten-year period of preparation.

It must have been the discovery of a connection on the religious plane between Strindberg and O'Neill that gave Molander such an early interest in these two playwrights in particular. It is true that, before *The Iceman Cometh* in 1947, Molander only produced *Mourning Becomes Electra* (1933) at the Royal Dramatic, but one must also take into account several radio productions. In the printed editions of O'Neill's plays at the Royal Dramatic, there are numerous notes made by Molander, even in the plays which he didn't produce personally. All these come from his years as manager of the

Royal Dramatic, 1934–38. After *The Iceman Cometh*, O'Neill and Strindberg intertwine more and more in Molander's productions. Both these playwrights, with their art founded on their own experiences and pitted with love/hate relationships to their God, grew to a lifework for Sweden's great director. As we have seen earlier, the long cooperation between Molander and Hanson began to wear thin during the rehearsals for *A Touch of the Poet* in 1957, resulting in an unsatisfactory production. In 1960 they came together again for a production of Strindberg's *To Damascus. Part I*. After Molander eventually decided to leave the Royal Dramatic in 1963, his last two productions, before he died in the Spring of 1966, were *Mourning Becomes Electra* (1964) and *To Damascus. Parts I–III* (1965), both at Stockholm's Municipal Theatre.

It may be said that it was a pity that Molander's and Hanson's cooperation wore thin before the première of *A Touch of the Poet* in 1957, but perhaps an epoch within the Royal Dramatic was over; a tradition had come to an end. Perhaps a younger generation can create a new one. It has indeed happened with José Quintero's productions in O'Neill's native country, since the mid-fifties. But what about the Royal Dramatic? Well, the autumn season of 1976 started with *A Moon for the Misbegotten* on The Small Stage, a production well-received by both critics and audiences. It was kept on the repertoire in the Spring of 1977. Will young actors and producers open up new roads into the work of perhaps the most noteworthy playwright of our time? That has been the case with Strindberg. Perhaps it will be with O'Neill, too.

On October 2, 1962, the last performance of the six-year run—with intervals—of *Long Day's Journey into Night* was given at the Royal Dramatic. A few days later Karl Ragnar Gierow wrote to Carlotta O'Neill and stated:

> Last Sunday we gave the last performance, sold out and the audience just as moved and shaken as the first night more than six years ago. Six years! It is unbelievable. While the curtain went up and down, Bengt Ekerot was standing beside me in the wings, looking at the stage with tears in his

eyes. I felt the same kind of grateful and proud sadness. I shall never more see the curtain drop for that production.

After seeing many productions of O'Neill's plays at the Royal Dramatic in Stockholm and attending performances in the United States of *A Moon for the Misbegotten* in New York in 1974, and *Ah, Wilderness!* at the Milwaukee Repertory Theatre and *A Touch of the Poet* in New York in 1977, I can say with certainty that the curtain will never finally drop for Eugene O'Neill!

O'NEILL'S SIGNIFICANCE
A Scandinavian and
European View

Timo Tiusanen

Eugene O'Neill was an American playwright who was born in a hotel room ninety years ago and died, rootless and isolated, in a hotel room twenty-five years ago. What is his significance to us? He wrote "words, words, words," or, all in all, some fifty plays. Yet should he not be forgotten by now? We cannot remember what happened in world politics a fortnight ago. Why should we remember him? He belonged to a nation and to an age not inclined to celebrate its own classics or revive the plays of yesteryear. While alive, he was the first dramatist of world renown the United States had produced, yet he was an embarrassment to the American theatre and to a great many American critics and scholars. Now he is in the process of turning into the first classic playwright the United States has produced. Again, he is an embarrassment. How are we supposed to treat our own classics? What is O'Neill's significance to the American theatre or to the Western theatre?

There were people who did not quite know what to think about O'Neill in the years between the wars or after World War II. There are people who do not know what to think right now. On the other hand, there are those who know. At least three approaches to the dramatist have been operative in the 1970s. O'Neill is taken as the emblem of the best achievements, ambitions, and endeavors in the American

61

theatre; his work is appreciated and analyzed as an object of scholarly study; and his major plays are revived, more or less sporadically. These approaches deserve some consideration, and this discussion of them will provide Americans with an objective, outsider's view of how the dramatist is apparently perceived by his fellow countrymen in this decade. I shall deal with generalities as I have already published a detailed discussion of every play in the O'Neill canon.

First, O'Neill represents an emblem for some Americans. A *New York Times* article, which evaluated the 1977–1978 theatre season, announced there would be some two hundred new American plays given a reading or produced. I cannot know how much the O'Neill Theatre Center in Waterford, Connecticut, has contributed to the atmosphere surrounding serious attempts to write plays in this country. The Center has offered a helping hand to over one hundred writers in its fourteen-year history; its annual National Playwrights' Conference was mentioned in the *New York Times* article. The name of Eugene O'Neill seems to work as an emblem. The name of a minor playwright would not have such magnetism and such a unifying and activating effect. This is, without any doubt, part of O'Neill's significance to the American theatre. It is not appropriate for a non-American to judge or analyze the emblematic usage of O'Neill's name in detail. I wish those who use it for any symbolic purpose the best of luck.

On a second level, O'Neill has become an object of study. It is easier for a European to follow the American discussion on O'Neill on the level of new scholarly studies rather than on that of live theatre performances or through the daily press. A shift in emphasis seems to have taken place in O'Neill studies; the approach to the dramatist today differs from that of the 1950s and 1960s. The general orientation has been away from philosophy toward aesthetics and away from psychology toward biography. Let me state that I consider this a healthy change. There did not seem to be new territory to be conquered through philosophical or psychological approaches to O'Neill after the 1960s. He was, after all, neither a professor in philosophy nor an ignorant bum; he was an artist in search of all kinds of equivalents to his powerful feelings of anguish and alienation. He had an appetite for literature—only or mainly to feed his creative imagination. He was most avid as a reader when trying to find his way as an aspiring young playwright. In recent studies, there has been ample new evidence on these points and on the importance of close family relations in his work. I am full of admiration for several monumental studies. Americans have recognized the various social, historical, cultural, and intellectual trends that connect him with his background. Yet there seems to be a fairly general consensus that we need still another approach to O'Neill, both on the stage and in scholarly study. A few remarkable American scholars are beginning to pay serious attention to another important question: how significant was O'Neill as a writer for the stage?

To me, this is a most relevant question. No man is a hero in the eyes of his valet, it is said; few men succeed in being heroes in the eyes of their biographers. Never mind what kind of fellow O'Neill was; in the middle of a tempestuous life he somehow succeeded in writing a canon of remarkable plays, and these plays should be our first and foremost concern. It is amazing how little has been made of O'Neill as a conscious and determined writer for the stage in recent years and in several studies extremely remarkable in other respects. How is it possible that so little emphasis has been put on O'Neill's literary and theatrical structures in the native country of New Criticism? Is there still a Puritan prejudice alive in America against the theatre—and another against O'Neill as an analyst of "low" characters?

August Strindberg was not a pleasant individual, to put it mildly. Yet his canon of plays and other works has merited thorough study and analysis by an army of scholars. The same should apply to O'Neill. It has been a necessary task for O'Neill scholars to try to interview every eyewitness to his life. Has not this task now been finished? Have we not gathered most of the materials needed for our next journey, that towards a total conception of O'Neill as a playwright? It is necessary to probe the relation between a playwright and the stage. At this time O'Neill is undergoing the process of becoming a classic of his age. This is an easy enough process for a poet or a novelist; as the times have changed, it has been possible to establish Walt Whitman and Herman Melville as great American men of letters. This is not an easy process for a playwright.

A playwright needs the stage. He needs it while alive; he needs it after his death. The plays of our age, of any age, are born or stillborn on the stage. The stage is the only delivery room for them. The significance of O'Neill will be seen and kept alive only with the help of an always evolving stage practice. A classic play is subjected to a variety of dramaturgic and staging methods throughout the changing fashions of the times. We cannot even start finding out whether O'Neill is a classic of our age if we are not careful to submit him to such a process.

It is the third and final approach to O'Neill, the actual production of his plays, that deserves special consideration here. There have been several remarkable revivals of his major plays in recent years. I know that the American educational theatre has played a significant role in keeping O'Neill alive, both on the stage and in scholarly discussion. This is fine, but I do not think it is enough. An institution, an O'Neill Theatre and Institute, should be established to produce the plays over and over again. This theatre-institute would encompass all three approaches discussed here: the emblematic use of his name, scholarly interest, and productions of his plays.

Several European countries have long-established traditions in treating their theatre classics. This is an area where European scholarship might be of help in this country. There is even a word in the all-embracing English language for that process: "classicize." The dictionary identifies the word as "chiefly British." Why shouldn't Americans begin using that foreign word? Why not classicize O'Neill? He is worth it. Yet a word of warning is needed: "classicizing" a playwright does not mean mummifying him. It means a sound middle road between negligence and glorification; it means keeping him alive, not through the artificial respiration of reverential revival but by paying him respect in the only way acceptable to O'Neill's ghost: by finding ever new relevances for his plays. For him, life meant writing; for his plays, meaningful production is essential for life. The United States is, by and large, a country without a dramaturgic tradition; that is, a tradition of adapting the great classics of bygone ages. Dramaturgy is no alchemy, no black magic that might turn base metal into gold. It is an artistic craft like playwriting or stage directing. It can be practiced, criticized, and taught. It can shape marvels of sculpture out of suitable raw material. There are such materials in the O'Neill canon.

Adapting a play means, of course, a risk taken. Yet a similar risk is taken every time a play is produced. If an adaptation fails, this does not destroy the play; the original script remains safely on the shelves. If the adaptation succeeds, the play, or perhaps a new approximation of O'Neill's original vision, comes alive in the theatre. It might be especially advisable to touch O'Neill's dialogue with a light hand and try to do something with his use of the vernacular. There is nothing as old as yesterday's newspaper—except yesteryear's slang. O'Neill has spoken to his audiences in Germany, Sweden, and Finland and on the European continent in the 1950s and in the 1970s. When a play is translated, it is natural to resort to present-day slang, not to antiquated usage. Why should not O'Neill capture the American spoken idiom of the 1970s? This work could be done by a native dramaturgic midwife with a sensitive ear and hands. I would like to see a number of plays revived, either as adapted versions or as they were originally written. Some of them are fairly far from the mainstream: *The Abortion, Shell Shock, The Straw, The Hairy Ape, The Great God Brown, Strange Interlude.* These experiments should not be executed just to follow the whim of some scholar but to give new generations of theatregoers an opportunity to see how a script behaves on the stage. O'Neill's potential audience could be multiplied by a wise and considered use of television—perhaps even television in the classroom. In Europe, a theatre laboratory without an audience has been the dream of many a man of the theatre in this century. Some think that the experiments should take place without an interfering audience. In my opinion, perference should be given to a theatre laboratory with an audience.

What, then, would such a laboratory tell us about O'Neill's significance? If I may anticipate some of the findings, I should like to guess that part of the adverse criticism of O'Neill's use of language will be proved unjustified. There is an element in his dialogue not captured by the traditional approaches of literary analysis. This element is movement. There is a constant pendulum movement between several polarities in O'Neill's dialogue; between such polarities as fear and and laughter, love and hatred, tragedy and comedy, aversion and sympathy, search and finding, heroism and baseness, self-deception and honesty. The result of this movement is a grotesque, grand language of the stage, even in the apparently most traditional or realistic of his plays. This is the feature that makes O'Neill modern even today, in this new age of drama after Samuel Beckett. And it is a feature that can be seen and heard only on the stage, as a part of a continual encounter between a classic playwright and his interpreters, during our long day's journey into the theatre of tomorrow.

In short, O'Neill's significance is based on two magnificent truths. He created his own personal theatre or stage language, and he conveyed significant statements about the condition of modern man by means of that language. Theatre language is not only something attached to the written page. It is an audiovisual and artistic language that needs to be spoken, lest it die. The stage of live theatre is the only place where this language can be spoken. The Scandinavian countries and Germany have done what can be reasonably expected from them to keep a crucial body of modern classics of world drama alive; Sweden has done even more. Will Americans choose to listen to that language, now and in the days to come? In America, O'Neill was praised to death while he was not yet mature, either as a craftsman or as a perceiving human being; and he was silenced to death after he had completed his incomparable masterpieces. If there is a balance of payment between O'Neill and the American theatre, this balance must be in O'Neill's favor.

O'NEILL IN ENGLAND—FROM ANNA CHRISTIE TO LONG DAY'S JOURNEY INTO NIGHT 1923–1958*

Clifford Leech

What I offer here are reminiscent reflexions about O'Neill productions in England in the days of my youth (did I ever have a youth, I wonder?). I will provide some personal observations on those early productions, primarily in London, in the 1920s and '30s, a time when the work of this major dramatist was not fully appreciated in his own country. I want to comment on two qualities found in O'Neill and his work that will be treated at length later by American scholars: his Puritanism and mysticism. After a brief reference to them now, I shall not use the words "Puritan" or "mystical." These words did not mean much to us in England in the time when I was a belligerent undergrad and then an increasingly belligerent grad student. We defined "Puritanism" as a disease that started in approximately the first Elizabeth's time and lingered on in England even to the days of our own parents. Do not be foolish; we are over all that now.

* Editor's note: Clifford Leech died before completing this essay. A colleague, William Blissett of the University of Toronto, stated that the English critic, on the day before his death, discussed with great enthusiasm this unfinished work, his renewed interest in the playwright, and his involvement in the O'Neill projects of his friends in the States. This fragmentary essay is typical of Leech; it is scholarly, humorous, spirited. As perhaps his last critical commentary, and certainly the coda to his work on the dramatist, it deserves a permanent place in O'Neill scholarship.

Probably the worst thing we English ever did to our then compatriots was to allow the Mayflower to sail west. The captain of that unhappy vessel had been told to sail round the North Coast of Scotland, to keep well away from North Sea shores, and then to disgorge his freight at Amsterdam. "Here's your New Amsterdam," he could then say, and tell them to get ashore. It wouldn't have done much harm to the Dutch, for they had Puritans enough already and could absorb a few more. Alas, we let the poor ship take the hapless rebels where they wanted to go, and the result is all around us. The disease tainted even that Irishman, Eugene O'Neill, who is still largely a Puritan. If he had ever been aware of this condition, I think it would have made him want to vomit. Of course, he was deeply aware of Puritanism and felt the need for a paring down, in some of his last plays, though not in *The Iceman Cometh*, a rebellion against the rebellion of the flesh. In that sense, but only in that sense, we English are Puritans even now although we love the delights of the flesh more deeply than do most Americans, who are still intellectually brought up to repudiate them. When Americans and Englishmen get together, this is often a source of embarrassment. We often say things that provoke the silent response, for Americans are much better-mannered than we are. "Of course, that is right, but how can you say it in public?"

"Mystical" is another matter. We in England and on the European continent have had our own mysticism: people who have gone through experiences which make them feel that they have come into contact with an "ultimate reality!" Pascal most splendidly illustrated this when, for a particular entry in his diary, he would write against a particular date and time the word "Feu!" We admired that; we took it as an historical event, but we didn't believe in it. There was an experience all right, but not one of ultimate truth; it was simply—and grandly—one of transcendent (dare I use an American word?) by-passing of the everyday self, emerging into a sense of discovery. We understood "discovery," for Aristotle had taught us that, but we knew that every discovery was provisional.

Now let us look back to what we in England thought

about O'Neill in those comparatively early days. We saw him, not as a mystic, but as a man hankering after mysticism, after anything to replace the Roman Catholicism he had lost. We saw him as a man haunted by those chaps and girls on the Mayflower and their descendants. But all of that didn't seem to matter much. What did matter was his sense of how human beings behaved in relation to their ancestry, to each other, and to their immediate environment. And we worshipped him. Why was it that the first play I ever directed was *The Rope*, my own choice? Why did I recommend that the L.S.C., an unofficial dramatic society for the University of London, of which through a series of accidents I found myself president, put on *The First Man*, which nearly bankrupted us? In both instances these were probably the first performances ever in England.

For us then O'Neill was primarily neither a Puritan nor a mystic! He was a "naturalist" in the French sense, the heir of Ibsen and Flaubert and Zola. We didn't know much about contemporary puritanism in those days, and it is still something of a shock to an Englishman when he first visits the States and finds puritanism still flourishing, all the way from the small community to the world of scholarship. Doubtless we have lived too cloistered a life. We thought, wrongly, that O'Neill was "placing" puritanism historically in *Desire Under the Elms*; we came to find it endemic. It has come to represent the opposite extreme to violence and is only just conceivably preferable to that. But there were other reasons why O'Neill was close to us. First, there was his attachment to the continental European theatre, notably Strindberg and, though he denied this, to Toller and Kaiser, who in those days were among the dramatists we were most attached to. My belief is that the fascination that so many young English people felt was linked with their groping knowledge of German Expressionist drama and their cultural attraction to the States, which was indeed strong. I still had that feeling of excitement when I first saw Manhattan in 1958. *O tempora!* Then the United States of America constituted a wonderland for us. We couldn't go there, for we English academics were poor. It wasn't until 1958 that, through the courtesy of the Folger

Library, I made my first visit across the Atlantic, seeing as many plays in New York as I could in the brief while I spent there in route. We knew that America was a capitalist country, but we also knew that it was still the "New World," the place we wanted to see above all—rivalled only by the Soviet Union, where O'Neill's early anti-capitalist plays were done. Even the Russians recognized his power to stir the masses.

I discovered O'Neill's universal appeal during the Second World War when I made a long sea-journey by merchant-ship from Liverpool to West Africa, where I was to take a plane to Cairo. The voyage brought to mind a film I had seen in the 1930s: John Ford's *The Long Voyage Home*. Taking the title of one of the plays, it incorporated all of the S. S. Glencairn group. The London critics damned it as "arty," and certainly Ford used a lot of soft focus and soft anguish. Well, I didn't know, for life at sea was as foreign to me as it was for the bastardly little critics. One evening when we were in harbour at Freetown Sierra Leone, a few of us passengers were harning together (as the Australians say) with some members of the crew, and a young third mate said he had seen Ford's film and realized that the screen had given him a faithful picture of what his own life was like. He was hardly articulate, but on this occasion he made me think.

Anna Christie was O'Neill's greatest success in the West End in the twenties. I can remember reading an advertisement in a London newspaper which began with "Would you let your daughter see *Anna Christie*?" I saw the first United Kingdom production of *Strange Interlude* twice and that staggered along for a time as a *succès d'estime*. *Mourning Becomes Electra* at an enterprising theatre near the West End did better. But the real hold that O'Neill had was at experimental theatres, most notably the Gate Theatre Studio (which the Second World War killed) and in many adventurous and amateur dramatic companies.

We went to see every O'Neill play we could. The place where we saw the plays was primarily the Gate. That was a tiny theatre with a full stage. The auditorium held about 140 people. That led to an extreme degree of intimacy between players and spectators. Distinguished performers appeared there (I was told for three pounds a week). There, as still a student, I saw *Welded, Desire Under the Elms* (with Flora Robson), *All God's Chillun Got Wings.* Later in other theatres there were performances of *Desire, All God's Chillun* (with a black actor), *Strange Interlude, Mourning Becomes Electra,* and then after a long interval *The Iceman Cometh* and *Long Day's Journey into Night.* On my second visit to *Desire,* A. P. Rossiter was my guest, and he was appropriately taken with it. London!, and later the provinces; enthusiasm for O'Neill continued, and *The Iceman Cometh* and *Long Day's Journey* found their way to distinction on the English stage.*

* Clifford Leech's last words here were: "special significance of *Iceman's* success."

PLATONIC LOVE IN O'NEILL'S *WELDED*

Egil Törnqvist

Composed in the fall of 1922 and the spring of 1923, *Welded* is one of O'Neill's most autobiographical plays. Not only were O'Neill and his wife Agnes at that time of exactly the same age and more or less of the same appearance as the central characters of the play, Michael and Eleanor Cape, but their marital problems apparently resembled those which drive the Capes to separation and reunion.[1]

The autobiographical nature of *Welded* does not, of course, exclude the possibility—or even probability—of literary influence. Thus the title of the play and its scenes of marital struggle have caused several critics to regard *Welded* as a poor imitation of such Strindberg plays as *The Father, The Link,*[2] and *The Dance of Death.* George Jean Nathan points out:

> What O'Neill had in mind in the writing of *Welded* was, unquestionably, a realistic analysis of love after the manner of Strindberg's *Dance of Death.* What he planned to show was that a deep love is but hate in silks and satin, that suspicion, cruelty, torture, self-flagellation and voluptuous misery and torment are part and parcel of it, that it constantly murders itself and that its corpse comes to life again after each murder with an increased vitality, and that once a man and a woman have become sealed in this bond of hateful love they are, for all their tugging and pulling, caught irrevocably in the trap of their exalted degradation.[3]

When finishing *Welded,* O'Neill himself referred to *The Dance of Death* as an admirable example of the "real realism" he wanted to explore.[4] This is what Nathan has in mind when he claims that the play was written "after the manner" of Strindberg's drama. The kinship between the two plays is unmistakable—although an even better case, to my mind, could be made for *Comrades* with its professional rivalry. Equally striking, however, are the differences. As Nathan's own description of the theme in *Welded* reveals, O'Neill is decidedly more idealistic and romantic than his Swedish predecessor. That he is also, in this play, inferior to Strindberg as a craftsman—a circumstance which Nathan takes pains to demonstrate—should be obvious to anyone.

Nathan's use of the label "realism" in connection with *Welded* is unfortunate. It is true that O'Neill had himself used this term when speaking to Nathan about the play, but he then used it in an unconventional sense. In a letter to the critic, dated May 7, 1923, he writes:

> To point out its (*Welded's*) weakness as realism (in the usual sense of that word) is to confuse what is obviously part of my deliberate intention.
> Damn that word, "realism"! When I first spoke to you of the play as a "Last word in realism," I meant something "really real," in the sense of being spiritually true, not meticulously life-like—an interpretation of actuality by a distillation, an elimination of most realistic trappings, an intensification of human lives into clear symbols of truth.[5]

What Nathan did not point out was that O'Neill manifestly stated that when writing *Welded,* he was trying to get back "to the religious in the theatre."[6] Presumably Nathan, who was later to denounce such religiously oriented plays as *Dynamo*[7] and *Days Without End,*[8] disliked the religious aspect. Had he considered *Welded* from this point of view, he would have found that the "analysis of love" in the play is less Strindbergian than Platonic.

That O'Neill was familiar with Plato may safely be assumed. His profound interest in the Greek conception of

life, aroused or further stimulated by his reading of
Nietzsche's *The Birth of Tragedy*, is well known.[9]

In *The Symposium* Plato expounds not one but several
theories on the nature of love. Three of these are relevant
in connection with *Welded*: that of Pausanias, of Aristophanes, and of Socrates or, to be scrupulous, of Diotima.

Pausanias makes the important, though crude, distinction between *Aphrodite urania*, spiritual or heavenly love, and
Aphrodite pandemos, physical or common love. The latter
goddess he considers "far younger than her heavenly counterpart." Characteristic of the baser kind of love is that "it
prefers that its objects should be as unintelligent as possible,
because its only aim is satisfaction of its desires" (p. 46).[10]

In *Welded* Michael Cape's desire is directed towards two
women: his wife Eleanor and a prostitute. Eleanor is thirty
years old, tall; her face is

> dominated by passionate blue-gray eyes, restrained by a
> high forehead from which the mass of her dark brown hair
> is combed straight back. The first impression of her whole
> personality is one of charm, partly innate, partly imposed
> by years of self-discipline. (p. 443)[11]

This is obviously a portrait of O'Neill's wife Agnes.[12]
But it is more than that. Stature, intelligence, charm, passion,
self-discipline—these traits visualized in Eleanor's appearance—are also characteristic of *Aphrodite urania*. Michael's
love for Eleanor is thus an expression of the spiritual nature
of his love. Fusing Platonic and Christian ideas, he sees marriage as a sacrament:

> a consummation demanding and combining the best in each
> of us! Hard, difficult, guarded from the commonplace, kept
> sacred as the outward form of our inner harmony! (p. 448)

The common love—*Aphrodite pandemos*—is not for them!
Or so Michael believes until he discovers that Eleanor (as he
mistakenly imagines) has dragged their ideal "in the gutter"
by an act of adultery. Longing for revenge and spiritual
suicide, he now tries to outdo the "traitress" at her own

game, seeking the company of a woman of the gutter. The prostitute looks quite different from Eleanor:

> The WOMAN is fairly young. Her face, rouged, powdered, penciled, is broad and stupid. Her small eyes have a glazed look. Yet she is not ugly—rather pretty for her bovine, stolid type—and her figure is still attractive. . . . (p. 471)

This is obviously a representative of *Aphrodite pandemos*, fleshy, young and unintelligent. It is significant that the Woman, except for her small, dead eyes, so different from Eleanor's,[13] is physically attractive. Like the love she represents, the prostitute is a pretty shell covering spiritual death, a symbol rather than a human being; as Michael puts it:

> You're a symbol. . . . You're the suicide of love—of my love —of all love since the world began! (p. 475)

So far Michael has adhered to Pausanias' simple black-and-white pattern. Having exchanged his former, spiritual love for the vulgar love of the world, he is ready to lay himself down "among the swine" (p. 474), thereby making the murder of his higher love complete. It is at this point that his eyes open to the fact that the prostitute, far from being a monster of lust and greed, is actually a human being, capable of both love and wisdom. Despite her outward appearance, the spark of heavenly love can still be found in her. Michael realizes that her servitude to "the baser sort of men," to use Pausanias' phrase, involves suffering and sacrifice and that her prostitution may thus be seen not as a "suicide of love" but, on the contrary, as signifying love of mankind,[14] or at any rate of the pimp who takes her money and beats her up, but to whom she feels "welded" just the same. Michael returns home, his faith in the power of love restored.

Love, says Diotima, is neither a god nor a mortal but a *daemon* or spirit through whom God deals with man (p. 81). Translated into Christian terms this means that love is neither divine nor human but angelic.

When Eleanor attempts to climb John's stairway to the bedroom up above, where she intends to kill her love for Michael by committing adultery, she is prevented from doing

so by a vision. At the top of the stairs she sees Michael the
way he was standing a little earlier, waiting for her to come
to the marital bed. Eleanor's hallucination is depicted both
as an outer phenomenon and as an inner experience. "An
angel with a flaming sword" John calls it, referring to
Michael's name. The angel, Eleanor tells him, was in her
heart. Both agree that the vision she has had is a divine token
of the strength of her love for Michael.

The Capes' love for one another is seen from two
slightly different, but not conflicting, viewpoints which may
be labeled the Aristophaneic and the Socratic one.

To Aristophanes, love—not necessarily sexual love as
Freud later would have it—is the basic human urge. To
explain why this is so, he assumes that originally "each human being was a whole, with its back and flanks rounded to
form a circle" (p. 59). But Zeus, angry with the insolence of
men, yet unwilling to extinguish them, decided to enfeeble
them by cutting each of them in two.

> Man's original body having been thus cut in two, each half
> yearned for the other half from which it had been severed.
> When they met they threw their arms around one another
> and embraced, in their longing to grow together again. . . .
> (p. 61)

> It is from this distant epoch, then, that we may date the
> innate love which human beings feel for one another, the
> love which restores us to our ancient state by attempting to
> weld two beings into one and to heal the wounds which
> humanity suffered. (p. 62)

Michael's description of the genesis of love, Raleigh correctly
suggests,[15] is a scientific—science being the mythology of our
time—restatement of Aristophanes' view:

> It began with the splitting of a cell a hundred million years
> ago into you and me, leaving an eternal yearning to become
> one life again. (p. 448)

Suppose, Aristophanes continues, that Hephaestus would
visit a loving couple as they sleep together and declare:

> . . . I am ready to melt and weld you together, so that, in-
> stead of two, you shall be one flesh; as long as you live you
> shall live a common life, and when you die, you shall suffer
> a common death, and be still one, not two, even in the next
> world. (p. 63f.)

"No one would refuse the offer," Aristophanes adds. The
reason for this universal desire for oneness, he concludes, is
that we long for our lost half, our primordial state of wholeness. What then are we to do in our desperate plight? The
consolation Aristophanes offers is this: try to find "a proper
mate" and you can, in a measure, return to the blessed
original condition. Occasionally Michael has experienced
this blessed state together with Eleanor and he believes, with
Aristophanes, that this momentary sense of oneness points
both backwards to a primordial condition and forwards to a
future situation, so that our development, being circular, in
fact copies our original form; he says to his "proper mate":

> . . . with you I become a whole, a truth! Life guides me back
> through the hundred million years to you. It reveals a be-
> ginning that I may have faith in the unity of the end.
> (p. 488)

Scenically O'Neill tried in various ways to illustrate the
theory of the primordial whole, which has been cut in two
and longs to become complete again. Thus the play begins
and ends by showing the two halves—Michael and Eleanor—
in a tender embrace, expressing, in Aristophanes' words,
"their longing to grow together again." The metaphysical
significance of the embrace is indicated in the lighting.
Throughout the play Michael and Eleanor are each surrounded by a circle of light. The two circles at once visualize
Aristophanes' primordial man and Michael's cell split in two.
Forced to function separately and autonomously, the halves
have lost the harmony and perfection of the whole and self-
protectively surround themselves with *"auras of egoism"* (p.
443). Yet when the halves come together in a loving embrace, when the circles of light coalesce and become one, the
original oneness and harmony are restored. Aristophanes'
dictum that only love can overcome our separateness is thus

scenically dramatized. The notable difference between the couple's initial and final embrace is that the latter is preceded by a mutual cross gesture, indicating Michael's and Eleanor's recognition that true oneness can only be attained through mutual sacrifice, through a life *in imitatio Christi.*

In the draft, Michael's final words, a comment on Eleanor's gesture—"the great cross—love of mankind"— reveal that he considers the Passion the supreme example of love. Why did O'Neill omit these words? Perhaps for artistic reasons: the suggestiveness of the cross gesture is lost and its significance reduced if we are explicitly informed of its meaning. Perhaps for ideological reasons: Michael's words might easily give the audience a false impression—as *Days Without End* later did—that *Welded* is an argument for Christianity.

We have met the word "weld" twice in Aristophanes' speech. Moreover, the two embraces just referred to visualize the Capes' attempts "to weld two beings into one." The play title, we may conclude, should primarily be understood in a positive sense;[16] as Michael says in the draft version: "Welded, not bound by a tie! We've realized the ideal we conceived of our marriage."

Possibly O'Neill also had another meaning in mind. In the draft Michael talks about "the magic fire that welds flesh and spirit into a symbol of the eternal fusing of love and beauty." Although this meaning is never made explicit in the play, it is implied in the final embrace with its fusion of the cross—the spirit—and the coalescing circles—the two made one flesh.

Just as the light circles visualize Aristophanes' philosophy of evolution, so the stairway that appears in all the acts and most prominently in the first and third, set in the Cape studio apartment, seems to be derived from Diotima's imagery. The right way of becoming initiated into the mysteries of love, says Socrates, quoting Diotima, is

> to begin with examples of beauty in this world, and using them as steps to ascend continually with that absolute beauty as one's aim . . . until from knowledge of various kinds one arrives at the supreme knowledge whose sole object is that absolute beauty. . . . (p. 94)

> Do you not see that in that region alone where he (man) sees beauty with the faculty capable of seeing it, will he be able to bring forth not mere reflected images of goodness but true goodness, because he will be in contact not with a reflection but with the truth? (p. 95)

In *Welded* O'Neill seems to dramatize this idea. In the first act Michael attempts to bring Eleanor up the stairway, but she rebels against the "Grand Ideal" he wants their marriage to be and cannot bring herself further than to the foot of the stairs. In the following act both of them experience "knowledge of various kinds," which brings them closer to one another and makes her accept his Platonic gospel. In the final act it is she who takes the lead up the stairs. When the curtain falls they have both reached the top of the stairway; their love is purged; their idealistic "old dreams" are back again, sublimated.

To O'Neill, as to Diotima, love in its highest manifestation is a love for "the absolute beauty" beyond the phenomenal world. By striving to ascend to the region where he can divine the absolute beauty, man affirms what is noblest in him and makes himself worthy of the love of his fellowmen and of God. To O'Neill, as to Diotima, all higher love between human beings stems from the impulse that prompts them to seek truth, beauty, God. Inspired by mutual affection, Michael and Eleanor together set out on this search as the play closes. Their love is essentially Platonic.

The object of love, says Diotima, is procreation, for this is "the nearest thing to perpetuity and immortality that a mortal can attain" (p. 87). But the procreation can take different forms. For the majority the creative instinct is physical and results in children:

> but there are some whose creative desire is of the soul, and who conceive spritually, not physically, the progeny which it is the nature of the soul to conceive and bring forth. If you ask what that progeny is, it is wisdom and virtue in general; of this all poets and such craftsmen as have found out some new things may be said to be begetters. (p. 90)

Michael's and Eleanor's marriage is childless; he is a play-wright, she an actress. Both thus belong to the spiritually creative minority. Once we are aware of the Platonic signifi-cance of their outer circumstances, we are able to see more than professional rivalry in such an exchange as this:

> CAPE (*furiously*): Good God, how dare you criticize creative
> work, you actress!
> ELEANOR (*violently*): You deny that I create—? Perhaps if
> I'd have children and a home, take up knitting—!
> (p. 459)

The professional pride should not be dismissed as empty vanity. Nor should Eleanor's contempt for the life of a house-wife be taken as a statement of a bluestocking. The point O'Neill tries to make—that to both of them spiritual crea-tivity is a life necessity—is essentially nontopical. When the Capes discover that they can both be spiritually creative—Michael as a playwright, Eleanor as his "mother"—they can have faith in a life together. On this mystical note of equi-librium regained the play ends.

To sum up: The theme and form of *Welded* can best be understood in the light of Plato's philosophy of love, as propounded in *The Symposium*. Pausanias' distinction be-tween a heavenly and a worldly love is at the root of the play and is concretized in its two female parts: Eleanor and the prostitute. Aristophanes' theory of the primordial whole is echoed in Michael's cellular "philosophy" and dramatized in the two light circles that surround the Capes. The play title, which relates to this theory, appears *verbatim* twice in Aris-tophanes' speech and may well have been derived from Plato's dialogue. Diotima's view of higher love as a God-sent spirit has its symbolic counterpart in Eleanor's angelic vision, while her escalatory gradation of love from physical to spiritual desire is dramatized in the finally ascended stairway and in Eleanor's spiritually attained maternity. Other parallels re-lating to plot and character—in either work the action spans the time from evening to dawn; Alcibiades' "loud knocking at the street door" (p. 96) may be compared to John's threefold knocking at the front door (p. 449), etc.—further demonstrate the kinship between *The Symposium* and O'Neill's play.

In view of these correspondences it seems safe to conclude that *Welded* is not primarily, as Nathan suggests, "a realistic analysis of love after the manner of Strindberg's *Dance of Death*." An "analysis of love" it is—but in the Platonic tradition.

NOTES

[1] Cf. C. Bowen, *The Curse of the Misbegotten: A Tale of the House of O'Neill* (New York, 1959), p. 144.

[2] See L. Lewisohn's review of the first production in *The Nation*, April 2, 1924, reprinted in O. Cargill *et al.*, *O'Neill and His Plays: Four Decades of Criticism* (New York, 1961), p. 163.

[3] *The American Mercury*, May 1924. Quote from the reprint in A. Downer, *American Drama and Its Critics* (Chicago, 1965), p. 81.

[4] See Arthur and Barbara Gelb, *O'Neill* (New York, 1962), p. 520.

[5] Quoted from A. Caputi (ed.), *Modern Drama*, New York, 1966, p. 449. In an undated letter to Mike Gold, probably written about the same time, O'Neill significantly avoids the word "realism" and calls the play "an attempt at the last word in intensity in truth about love and marriage"; quoted from Gelb, p. 521.

[6] Gelb, p. 520.

[7] *The American Mercury*, March 1929, pp. 368–373.

[8] *Vanity Fair*, March 1934, pp. 42, 49f.

[9] John Henry Raleigh is the only critic, to my knowledge, who has mentioned Plato in connection with O'Neill's work. This is done in a brief but illuminating comparison between the parabolic cave in *The Republic* and Harry Hope's saloon in *The Iceman Cometh*. See *The Plays of Eugene O'Neill* (Carbondale and Edwardsville, 1965), p. 166f.

[10] All quotations from *The Symposium* refer to W. Hamilton's translation in the Penguin Classics series, first published in 1951.

[11] All quotations from *Welded* refer to *The Plays of Eugene O'Neill*, II (New York, 1955).

[12] Cf. the photographs in the biography by the Gelbs.

[13] About the latter the draft adds: "The eyes are mirrors reflecting an instantaneous emotional reaction to each thing seen. But, for the most, they look within & frankly shadow forth the quick words of her soul." The longhand draft of *Welded* is in Princeton University Library.

[14] Cf. the prostitute Cybel's compassionate love-making in *The Great God Brown*.

[15] *Op. cit.*, p. 11.

[16] When Clark states (p. 91) that the Capes "are 'welded,' indissolubly linked together," and Falk (p. 85), similarly, claims that they are " 'welded,' rather than wedded, by a mutual dependency which they both fight," they are attaching a misleadingly negative, Strindbergian meaning to the word. B.H. Clark, *Eugene O'Neill: The Man and His Plays* (New York, 1947), Doris Falk, *Eugene O'Neill and the Tragic Tension: An Interpretive Study of the Plays* (New Brunswick, N.J., 1965).

THE LASTING CHALLENGE
OF EUGENE O'NEILL
A Czechoslovak View

Josef Jařab

From the early 1920s to the present, Eugene O'Neill has been considered a major world dramatist in Czechoslovakia. When reports of his accomplishments and, not long after, his plays reached Prague and other cultural centers in the newly established Republic of the 1920s, O'Neill was regarded as the first American playwright who was a modernist rather than a mere contemporary. The distinction was, of course, of vital importance. It brought the dramatist into the company of Pirandello and Shaw, while at the same time it made him appear a follower of Ibsen, Strindberg, and Wedekind as he was, in his own way, replacing these elder masters. This does not mean that O'Neill was praised for everything he wrote, that he was extolled or just welcomed by everybody within and without the professional community here; but he did make a strong and immediate impression on those with a creative mind who sought new grounds for the theatre.

One such person, who was attracting great interest in Prague cultural life, was Karel Hugo Hilar, an independent, dynamic, and, for many, rather controversial director from the Municipal Theatre in Vinohrady who was put in charge of the drama section of the National Theatre in 1921. Hilar was a man who had his own ideas about staging a play, and he had "no use for the habits and manners of the current theatre," which he thought was incapable of going beyond a conventional reflection of surface reality. For Hilar the real was identical with the very essence of experience. To create it as a director, he made use of his earlier reading of works using symbolism, his naturally expressionistic vision of man and man's social existence, and, finally, of his own knowledge of life. No wonder he felt a strong affinity with the American playwright whose early plays reflected a man with similar impulses. Hilar "found himself" in the dramatic work of O'Neill, as one critic years later rightly observed.

In 1922 when he was involved with the expressionistic stage experiments of Molière and Marlowe and the triumphant production of the masterpiece of the national expressionist drama, *The Insect Play*, by the Čapek brothers, Hilar was, understandably enough, drawn especially to *The Emperor Jones* and *The Hairy Ape*. (William A. Brady's invitation to Hilar to direct the New York production of *The Insect Play* in 1922, unfortunately, never materialized—for rather trivial technical and bureaucratic reasons.)

Today it is almost impossible to determine who deserves more credit—Hilar or the erudite dramaturge, František Götz—for taking the initiative to bring O'Neill and other modernist playwrights to our theatre stages. Götz, who was not really in favor of the expressionist movement and later proved to be a bitter critic of its "destructive" effects on drama and theatre in general, became, nevertheless, a co-translator of *The Hairy Ape*. The translation of *The Emperor Jones* was done by Frank Tetauer, an O'Neill enthusiast, who was responsible for the Czech texts of the majority of O'Neill's plays staged here during the first four decades. However, some time elapsed before Hilar received adequate translations of these two plays, and it was not until 1925 that Prague audiences became acquainted with the American dramatist. The failure of *The Hairy Ape* in the Prague "Deutsches Theater" in the preceding year might explain why *The Emperor Jones* was presented at the National Theatre on a double bill with a less experimental play, *In the Zone*. Another reason could have been the changes in the cultural atmosphere. The "vogue of expressionism" seemed to be over, and the impact of *The Emperor Jones* would probably have been even greater had it come some three years earlier. This impressive production was directed by Karel Dostal, with Václav Vydra playing the leading role and Vlastislav Hofman designing the haunting scenery. The play ran only four nights, yet audiences were given their first real O'Neill experience.

The Hairy Ape was not presented again in Prague until 1934. It had, however, been staged earlier in Moravia. In 1927 it was performed in Olomouc, a historical university town, and two years later in an experimental theatre studio in Ostrava, a large industrial center, where the strong social aspects of the play were stressed. In this discussion of expressionistic productions, it should be stated that the racial play, All God's Chillun Got Wings, has only been staged once in this country—in 1926. The play was translated and directed by Rudolf Walter.

At this point, a critical observation should be made about the nature of O'Neill's and Hilar's expressionist thinking. Neither the American dramatist nor the Czech director, whose interest he aroused, ever fully identified with or subscribed to the more abstract and extreme forms of expressionism as practiced by some in German drama and theatre. The bonds with realism (whatever they may have called it) were never severed, neither in motivation nor in aim. What else could Hilar have had in mind when he praised O'Neill for his "rediscovery of Henrik Ibsen" in the time, as he saw it, of "general disorientation in dramatic art"? And when Hilar was compared with the Berlin director Leopold Jessner, Miroslav Rutte stressed, above all, the fact that the Prague stage manager "remains earthly and concrete even in his metaphysics; he is always closer to a naturalistic symbol than to a vague scheme." It is revealing, too, that Hilar felt urged to defend O'Neill's Ibsenism along with the American playwright's artistic individuality, which had been questioned by Herbert Ihering in his pamphlet, "Die getarnte Reaktion." Neither Hilar nor O'Neill adhered to rigid concepts; both saw the potential and the limitations of the expressionistic method in dramatic art; and each, in his own way, in a different field and under dissimilar conditions, kept open the possibility for further development.

The American dramatist retained some of the expressionistic devices in works described as naturalistic, and even, in his final period, realistic. The subtlety of his use of the aside as objectified interior monologue and of the mask as a device to deal with various layers of reality and to distinguish reality from "pseudo-reality" would call for a special study. Here I am thinking not so much of the obvious illustrations —*Strange Interlude, The Great God Brown,* and *Lazarus Laughed*—but rather *Mourning Becomes Electra* and the later masterpieces—*Long Day's Journey into Night* and *Hughie.* An indication of O'Neill's genius and prescience is that some of the technical innovations in his plays which might have been unusual, even shocking, yesterday may be seen and accepted as conventional today, being not obtrusive but dramatically effective.

Similarly, Hilar accomplished through his expressionistic experiments a modernization of the traditional realistic staging and acting techniques in the Czechoslovak theatre. When in the later 1920s he defined his new artistic program as a subdued reaction to the exaltation of the postwar period, his "civilism," as he chose to call it, did not disregard the achievements of the previous years. On the other hand, Hilar was also worried that his critical remarks concerning expressionism might look like a total withdrawal; and he therefore avoided the term "realism"—although critics used it freely in reference to his work, adding to it epithets like "new" or "constructive," thus manifesting both continuity and progress. And so, being the creative and imaginative director and producer that he was, Hilar gradually loomed as an authoritative predecessor and stimulating rival for the "youngsters" (E. F. Burian, Jindřich Honzl, Jiří Frejka and others) who were soon to represent the nation's theatrical avant-garde. O'Neill's work continued to present a vital challenge in this productive atmosphere.

Between 1925 and 1928 the drama ensemble of the National Theatre staged three O'Neill plays: *Desire Under the*

Elms, Anna Christie, and *The Great God Brown,* all directed by Karel Dostal, Hilar's devoted disciple. The production of *Desire Under the Elms* in Prague was its European première. This was to become O'Neill's most enduring play in this country (to this time, some twenty productions). *Anna Christie* is the second most frequently produced play (presented about a dozen times). *Desire Under the Elms* enjoyed greater theatrical success than *Anna Christie* in the mid-twenties and has remained the more popular of the two plays over the years. *Desire Under the Elms* is obviously a much better play, but there seem to be other reasons for its appeal to audiences in Czechoslovakia. One is its theme and subject matter; the property and landowning issue in a family drama is reminiscent, no doubt, of a tradition in our national literature, both dramatic and fictional. In contrast, the theme of the sea in *Anna Christie* is, for the islanders that we are, practically unknown and is quite often associated with romantic ideas and superficial exoticism. "Dat old devil sea," therefore, could hardly ever come through in the play in all "her" imminency as shaper of human fate. Yet, I assume, it is also important to realize that *Anna Christie* is no *Riders to the Sea* and that the emotional and cognitive pleasure of true tragedy is missing here altogether. In a current production of O'Neill's drama at Olomouc (first night in February, 1979), the only scene that emerges as real and convincing is Anna's revolt against both her father and lover in Act Three—a manifestation of genuine feminism. The rest of the play is reduced to more or less affective melodrama; and this is an element that is found in all productions—including Dostal's of 1926, however good the quality of acting might have been.

Echoing the tragedies of Euripides, *Desire Under the Elms* provides a final effect of Aristotelian catharsis in the story of the New England Puritans who find themselves confined by their possessive—both materialistic and sexual—desire. Karel Dostal presented a model production that has apparently never been repeated. He achieved what he stated was his goal: a harmonious blending of social and psychological aspects of the human experience in its "synthetic density." One critic in reviewing the National Theatre presentation stated that O'Neill's "devotion to reality" created an atmosphere in the play which spiritualized the physical. A. Heythum's original "illusionist-constructivist" stage setting—which was the earliest example of its kind—and the dynamic acting, especially the memorable performance of Leopolda Dostalová as Abbie, contributed to the powerful effect.

Later productions of *Desire Under the Elms*, both in Prague and in the provincial towns (where theatre companies have been especially fond of it—for the obvious rural features), stressed one or the other of the major conflicts in the play. This polarity of interpretation is reflected even in the wavering between two versions of the translated title: one making a reference to "Farm," the other to "Desire," under the elms. Of particular interest in the historical record is the 1946 production of the play—the first O'Neill presentation in Prague after World War II. A newly founded company, the Realistic Theatre, decided to use this famous "peasant tragedy" in its repertory (along with John Steinbeck's *Of Mice and Men*, to give another interesting example) as a test to determine the effectiveness of the manifesto to produce popular theatre for the masses. Staged by Karel Palouš, this *Desire Under the Elms* was interpreted as a work of poignant social criticism; however, "desire" was depicted as pure "greed," and the play lost some of its dramatic poetry. Nevertheless, it had a run of forty performances—many more than the eleven of the highly-praised National Theatre production of 1925.

In 1928 in the fourth attempt to present O'Neill to the theatregoers of Prague, the director Karel Dostal discovered that *The Great God Brown* was a difficult play to stage. According to the playwright's own statement, this work "does succeed in conveying a sense of the tragic mysterious drama of Life revealed through the lives in the play." Such, of course, was the intention; and it should be said, in all fairness, that O'Neill came quite close to achieving his stated purpose in this drama. However, the author's ambitious "exercise in unmasking" the various forms of reality also reveals a mechanical quality in his structuring and restructuring of the dramatic characters and the plot. The same aspect is evident in his attempt to present the tragedy of modern man as something comprehensible through the Nietzschean concept of Apollonian-Dionysian duality and dichotomy. Here it must be pointed out that some of the German philosopher's unclear concepts found their way into the play of his American admirer. Yet, the drama offers interesting and suggestive reading.

The real trouble starts when the play is staged, and a director tries to utilize the experimental devices in the text—especially the masks. To avoid some of the crudeness of the literal application of the masks on stage in a realistic context, Dostal emphasized the element of fantasy and the symbolic message of the play, thus anticipating, surprisingly enough, one of O'Neill's own requirements for staging it which he states in his notes on the use of masks some four years later.

For the audience of the National Theatre, however, the abstractly stylized production of *The Great God Brown* remained nothing but an "interesting failure." It could not be said that the drama was a great success when it was staged again in 1965. In addition to overcoming the awkward technical difficulties involved in the use of masks, the director had to struggle to present a balanced interpretation of a play whose scheme was magnified to such unrealistic proportions that William Brown and Dion Anthony ceased to function as complementary elements of painfully imperfect humanity; they were no longer counterparts but black and white contrasts. Obviously, this was the result of a political interpretation which the company at Vinohrady, then called The Czechoslovak Army Theatre, had already applied three years earlier to its production of *Marco Millions*. Questions were raised by contemporary reviewers as to whether the two plays had been adequately staged and whether O'Neill's William Brown and Marco Polo should be presented as stereotyped satirical examples of social vices in bourgeois society. The answer to both is negative.

By this time it must have been clear that O'Neill was not to be made over into a manifest political writer without grave distortion of the complexity and artistic integrity of his work. In addition, any attempt to make him one only lessened the spontaneous effect of social and political elements already actually and potentially present in his plays. It has often been stated that O'Neill was not a consistent social thinker; but it seems to be of equal importance to realize that his views of social life and historical events and developments do not originate as much from conceptual reasoning (not even in his more "abstract" plays) but rather from the author's imagistic obsession with human nature and his interest in its basic characteristics and manifestations. This observation may be less evident in a play like *Marco Millions*, but a failure to recognize it could result in a separation of allegorical and decorative externals from their true and original motivations. Indeed, this is what has happened to several productions of *Marco Millions* staged throughout Czechoslovakia; and the very first one—the European première of the play, in fact, at the Vinohrady Theatre in 1930—was no exception. Under the direction of Jan Bor, the company presented a showy performance devised to lure large audiences—good professional acting and an attractively designed set by the renowned Vlastislav Hofman. Five years later the European première of *The Fountain* was presented by the same company, director and designer and in a similar manner—pompous, exotic, ostentatious. *The Fountain* lacks action and proved to be a disappointment to the dramatist himself, as his biographers state.

The company, perhaps inspired by the personal effort of the translator and dramaturge of the theatre, Frank Tetauer, appeared to have as its goal to increase the public's knowledge and understanding of O'Neill, a most praiseworthy objective. In the competition to stage the first production of the masterpiece of O'Neill's early period, *Mourning Becomes Electra*, Vinohrady lost to Hilar's National Theatre; and, in retrospect, this can be considered an unquestioned gain for the modern Czech theatre. No one would have wanted to miss the "American Electra" under Hilar's own direction as it came to represent the culmination of his work in the theatre and proved to be the most memorable of the encounters with Eugene O'Neill in Czechoslovakia during the 1920s and 1930s.

However, before Hilar produced the tragedy in which he wished to express "the pathos of modern times," he tested the potential of his "civilism" in the staging of *Strange Interlude* in 1930. The director's interest in this basically paradoxical experiment of O'Neill, in which he sought to dramatize the stream of consciousness, was stimulated this time not by the expressionistic but rather the realistic quality of the play. Hilar called *Strange Interlude* a "drama of physiological reality," and while he recognized the psychoanalytical function of the monologues, he wanted the conscious to conquer the subconscious and had all the inner dramatic conflicts softened and moderated.

The text of the play was effectively cut to half its original length. Hilar omitted the more reflective passages that would, in his opinion, interfere with the rhythmical progression of the action. The performance was quiet, the general mood conciliatory. Nina's longing at the end of the play—"to be in love with peace together—to love each other's peace—to sleep with peace together—to die in peace!" —and her statement of being "so contentedly weary with life" were interpreted both symbolically and literally. The casting of Anna Sedláčková and Karel Vávra, two unemotional actors, helped Hilar achieve his original aims. The means used were economical; to distinguish between the "speaking" and "thinking" lines no masks or contrasts in lighting were employed, only realistic changes in facial expression. (One can visualize an effectual television production of the play as, by nature of the experiment, the text of *Strange Interlude* fits somewhere between drama and epic where the art of film belongs.) All in all, Hilar's presentation of O'Neill's unusual play was done in style; the result was a perfect realization of the director's idea. One enthusiastic reviewer saw in it "simplicity made monumental."

Yet, Hilar, just when he had brought the principles of "civilism" to excellence, realized that they could become a restraint if adopted indiscriminately. Thus, at last, the synthetic period of Hilar's work in and for the theatre was under way. O'Neill's *Mourning Becomes Electra* was to be his artistic and personal testament. As Miroslav Rutte wrote later in his study of the director, "When the door of the Mannon mansion banged ominously at the end of the play, it was not Electra only who vanished into the house of death; unseen there, joining her, was the shadow of Karel Hugo Hilar." The play opened on December 8, 1934 and four months later a memorial performance was given in honor of the director, who had died at the age of forty-nine.

The term "synthetic," as it refers to Hilar's last period, implies maturity in method reached through his experience with naturalism, expressionism, "civilism" and realism; but it also pertains to his continuous effort to bridge the gap between the true pathos of the Greek age and the meek sensibility of his own time. What other dramatist could have suited Hilar better than Eugene O'Neill? The fact that he staged *Oedipus Rex*, with great care and personal involvement, shortly before he turned to *Mourning Becomes Electra* is significant. Moreover, the presence of the personal element in the work of both the American author and the Czech stage manager is another interesting feature they had in common. O'Neill is known as the most autobiographical among playwrights, and Hilar, as much as a director can, also shares this attribute, as his biographer M. Rutte suggests.

Although *Mourning Becomes Electra* was shortened, the number of characters reduced, and the theme consciously modernized, the play did not lose its dramatic impact. On the contrary, using his experience and artistic instinct, the director made the nightmarish story of the Yankee Mannons, with all their neuroses of contemporary humanity, reverberate with the truth he found in Aeschylus. Neither the reviewers nor the audiences failed to recognize this achievement, especially with the powerful, but controlled, acting of Olga Scheinpflugová (the wife of Karel Čapek) as Lavinia, and Leopolda Dostalová as Christine reinforcing the impression of complexity.

With Hilar's production of *Mourning Becomes Electra*, our long relationship with O'Neill seemed to have reached its high point. It was to be interrupted by a sad occurrence. The grave events after the Munich "Agreement" of September 1938 put an end to Czechoslovak independence; the spirit of free national culture was maimed and eventually suppressed. In the censored theatre repertories, there was no room left for the Nobel Prize winning dramatist. After a rather surprising premiere of *Days Without End* in the Slovak National Theatre in Bratislava in 1939 and three not too exciting O'Neill productions in Prague (*S.S. Glencairn*—with *In the Zone* significantly missing), Plzeň and Ostrava in the following year, there was silence.

Although in the immediate postwar period the American playwright was presented sporadically on stages all over the country, a revival of real interest did not occur before the early 1960s. But even then, the situation should not be judged by mere statistics, as Jindřich Černý warns in his article, adequately titled "Our Long Journey to O'Neill." Naturally, some of the numerous productions of those years were more interesting or more successful than others; most of them tried out new translations which were supposed to make the prewar O'Neill sound more conversational and up-to-date. For the younger generation of Czech and Slovak directors, actors, and stage designers, the encounters with the challenging American dramatist doubtlessly offered a fruitful experience; but to re-establish a close rapport with him, some of the more sensitive among them felt that a novel, more creative approach was needed.

The introduction of O'Neill's later plays—those of his "second dramatic career"—proved to be the way to accomplish this. Of seminal importance in this respect was an earlier essay, "The Autobiographical Motif in Eugene O'Neill's Work," by Jan Grossman, a stage manager and translator, written in 1957. The ideas expressed in this essay were restated some years in a provocative O'Neill monograph by Milan Lukeš who formulated a working principle—the autobiographical element in O'Neill's dramas conduced towards a deeper knowledge and understanding of both private and social reality conveyed through particulars aspiring after universal meaning. Yet it seems to be a paradox that the dramatist's greatest achievement in this sense is *Long Day's Journey into Night*, a domestic tragedy using his own biographical experience as straight subject matter. Grossman was the first to familiarize us with the play and to analyze it; but his essay, which may have launched the renewal of general interest in the American playwright, as Jindřich Černý maintains, did not succeed in bringing this particular work promptly to the stage. It was the State Theatre at Ostrava with the director Radim Koval who achieved the breakthrough in 1966. Koval presented the Tyrone-O'Neill drama in powerful simplicity; however, because of the outstanding acting of Zora Rozsypalová, it became primarily Mary's story. The play was staged by Juraj Svoboda at the Slovak National Theatre in Bratislava two years later with a more balanced cast.

Long Day's Journey into Night is an exceptional modern play with dimensions of true tragedy. In terms of artistic honesty, formal perfection, and linguistic accomplishment, it remains O'Neill's most enduring work. From the dedication of the play and—even more important—from the play itself, we can sense the aesthetic and, consequently, moral triumph of the playwright's ordeal. Like Melville when he completed *Moby Dick*, O'Neill must have felt "spotless as the lamb" after the difficult task was over. O'Neill was so convinced of its worth that he did not have to see this play staged. When it was finally presented after his death, not only did it unveil much about the private lives of "all the four haunted Tyrones," but it also forced readers, theatregoers, and, above all, critics to re-evaluate the man's whole work from a new perspective—with *Long Day's Journey into Night* as the starting point. Some things looked different; some started to make more sense. One example is the play, *Ah, Wilderness!*, of 1933. What always seemed to be a rather illogical exception in the body of O'Neill's work, at most a comedy written for relief, all of a sudden looked like a meaningful counterpart to the domestic tragedy—a daydream of happy family life that was never to become more than a visionary fancy. It was easy to make a comparison when these two plays, consciously or by mere chance, were offered in the same theatre season at the State Theatre in Ostrava. Earlier, in 1966, a lively performance of *Ah, Wilderness!* was staged at the Realistic Theatre in Prague.

Meanwhile, productions of O'Neill's other late plays were staged in various theatres. Some of them were merely interesting; others were really exciting. *The Iceman Cometh* at the Realistic Theatre in 1967 falls into the former category. The ensemble, with Jiří Dalík as director, was obviously facing a difficulty similar to the one Eric Bentley encountered when he helped stage the play in Zurich; the scenes were too static, and there was no way to make them dramatically dynamic. The play should not be staged as if it were *The Lower Depths* transferred to America; in fact, there may be fewer true similarities between the two often compared plays than we like to think, as the Russian critic, A. Romm, has suggested recently.

The two productions of *A Touch of the Poet* in 1970 and 1972 were only average; but *A Moon for the Misbegotten* received two very good stagings—in Prague at Vinohrady in 1969 and in the Petr Bezruč Theatre of Ostrava in 1978. Audiences greatly enjoyed the hilarious humanity of father and daughter, Phil and Josie Hogan. Again one is astonished by the wide range of O'Neill's characters and moods. At times Phil and Josie looked like visitors from an Irish peasant folk drama by Synge; and then, a few minutes later, gentle and nostalgic poetry hovered over the stage. Stanislav Remunda's production in Prague managed to capture the poetic qualities of the play, but the more recent one in Ostrava became fragmented the moment Jim Tyrone comes into focus.

Truly exciting is the current production of *Long Day's Journey into Night* at the Prague Drama Club (Činoherní klub). In the small, informal theatre where there is very little space between stage and audience, an atmosphere is created that does not allow those present to remain mere observers; it absorbs them into the action. Under the sensitive direction of Ladislav Smoček (who used his own brilliant theatrically effective translation of the text), all of the Tyrones invite the "spectators" into the ultimate privacy of their lives to share in their dreams and reveries and to see how they use any means—drugs, alcohol, illusions—to escape the reality that has trapped them. The splendid acting of Josef Somr, Jiřina Třebická, Petr Čepek, and Josef Arbhám makes all the rich semantic texture of their lines come alive—the actual meanings of their words filled with ironic implications; the fact that hatred and love are at times not only compatibles but inseparables; the natural unity of the tragic and comic elements; and, finally, the phenomenon of American Irishness with its psychological, cultural, and social effects. The short appearance of Libuše Šafránková as Cathleen is so convincing as to make her view of life a viable alternative to that of the Tyrones.

There are a few things in the performances (and in the play, for that matter) that one could seriously criticize; for example, Edmund occasionally giving the impression he knows he is going to survive and "become" Eugene O'Neill.

The central notion of the play, however, the one that seems to rise from the "fogs" within and without us—that to live with other people and to love them calls for "understanding and forgiveness"—dawns on all the characters by the end of the long night. *Long Day's Journey into Night* at the Drama Club is vintage O'Neill with a message that is provocative because it is relevant and vitally important to all of us. It also proves that the pessimism inherent in O'Neill's work and personality is not an unchallengeable condition—that it can be altered by accomplishment as the author himself must have found in the catharsis of creation. This is not the only aspect of O'Neill that strikes one as Melvillian; others include the aesthetic use of the sea; the notion that "truth uncompromisingly told will always have its ragged edges"; and the ensuing fear of formal perfection, or, finally, the conviction that poetry should be put to a wider, i.e. "practical use." As Melville's best poetry is to be found in his fiction, O'Neill's finest lyric efforts are inherent in his dramatic art. It is not so much the poetic quality in his plays but rather the *poetry of the theatre* that has distinguished him and made him a genuine and devoted experimentalist as well as a strong influence in modern drama both in America and abroad. Because O'Neill came to Czechoslovakia as a modernist, first in the 1920s and then again in the 1960s, he can still be our contemporary, and we can continue to get constant pleasure and inspiration from his work.

O'NEILL PRODUCTIONS IN CZECHOSLOVAKIA 1925 TO 1979*

1925	*Desire Under the Elms* (European première) *The Hairy Ape*
1926	*The Emperor Jones* *Anna Christie* *All God's Chillun Got Wings* *In the Zone*
1927	*The Hairy Ape*
1928	*The Great God Brown*
1929	*The Hairy Ape*
1930	*Marco Millions* (European première) *Strange Interlude*
1934	*Mourning Becomes Electra* *The Fountain* (European première)
1939	*Days Without End* *S.S. Glencairn Cycle* (without *In the Zone*)
1946	*Desire Under the Elms*
1962	*Marco Millions*
1965	*The Great God Brown*
1966	*Long Day's Journey into Night* *Ah, Wilderness!*
1967	*The Iceman Cometh*
1968	*Long Day's Journey into Night*
1969	*A Moon for the Misbegotten*
1970	*A Touch of the Poet*

* Compiled list of plays and their production dates provided by Josef Jařab. List is not complete, but it does indicate that all of O'Neill's major plays have been staged in Czechoslovakia.

1972 *A Touch of the Poet*
1978 *A Moon for the Misbegotten*
1979 *Long Day's Journey into Night*
       Anna Christie

SELECTED BIBLIOGRAPHY

Boor, Jan. *Dialektika dejín divadla* (Dialectics and the History of the Theatre). Bratislava: Tatran, 1977.

————. "Západní literatury a dramaturgia slovenských divadel v rokoch 1945–1965" (Western Drama in Slovak Theatres from 1945 to 1965). *Slovenské divadlo*, XIV (February 1966), 231–242.

Burian, Jarka M. "E. F. Burian: D 34–D 41." *The Drama Review*, XX, 4 (December 1976), 95–116.

Černý, Jindřich. "Dlouhá cesta O'Neilla k nám" (Our Long Journey to O'Neill). *Divadlo* (September 1966), 50–59.

Deák, František. "Structuralism in Theatre: The Prague School Contribution." *The Drama Review*, XX, 4 (December 1976), 83–94.

Götz, František. *Zrada dramatiků. Studie o soudobém světovém dramatě* (Betrayal by the Dramatists: An Essay on Contemporary World Drama). Prague. Václav Petr, 1931.

Grossman, Jan. "Autobiografický motiv v díle Eugena O'Neilla" (The Autobiographical Motif in Eugene O'Neill's Work). *Divadlo* (June 1957), 655–662.

Hilar, K. H. *Čtvrt století české činohry* (Twenty-Five Years of Czech Drama). Prague: Dramatický svaz a Družstevní práce, 1936. The volume presents contributions by Miroslav Rutte, Jan Sajíc, Frank Tetauer, František Götz, Edmond Konrád, Vlastislav Hofman, and Jiří Frejka.

————. Prague. Národní muzeum, 1967. Papers from a conference at the National Museum in January 1966. Of special interest are the contributions by Josef Träger, František Černý, Milan Obst, Karel Bundálek, and Jaroslav Švehla.

Honzl, Jindřich. *K novému významu umění* (On the New Meaning of Art). Prague: Orbis, 1956.

Kneževič, Debora Julii. *Eugene O'Neill na pražském jevišti* (Eugene O'Neill in the Prague Theatre). Thesis submitted at Charles University, Department of Theatrical History and Theory, 1978.

Lukeš, Milan. *Eugene O'Neill, osobnost v dramatu* (Eugene O'Neill: Personality in Drama). Manuscript dated 1972, in the library of the Theatrical Institute, Prague. In a supplement a list of productions of O'Neill's plays in Czechoslovakia and a bibliography of their reviews is given (completed by Naděžda Gajerová).

Rampák, Zoltán. "Československá divadelná avantgarda 20. a 30. rokov" (The Avant-garde in Czechoslovak Theatre of the 20's and 30's). *Slovenské divadlo*, XIV (March 1966).

Romm, A. *Amerikanskaya dramaturgia pervoj poloviny 20 veka* (American Drama of the First Half of the 20th Century). Leningrad: Isskustvo, 1978.

Tetauer, Frank. *Drama i jeho svět* (The World of Drama). Prague: Václav Tomsa, 1943.

O'NEILL IN POLAND

Marta Sienicka

This year—1979—the Polish stage should celebrate the jubilee of its first encounter with Eugene O'Neill. Fifty years ago, on November 22, 1929, Teatr Nowy in Warsaw presented *Anna Christie*, a production which marked the beginning of the strange relationship between the Polish audience and the great American playwright. The relationship started slowly, waned for a twenty-four-year period when O'Neill experienced almost total theatrical and critical oblivion, and then unexpectedly and suddenly exploded in the 1960–61 season into a violent and short-lived love-hate affair, marked by the most typical feature of a youthful infatuation—immaturity, and finally settled into an understanding and lasting co-existence.

Only four of O'Neill's plays were staged in Poland before World War II: *Anna Christie*, *All God's Chillun Got Wings* (translated as *Black Ghetto*), *The Emperor Jones*, and *Desire Under the Elms*; yet his iconoclastic greatness and originality were immediately acknowledged. In 1936, when introducing that year's Nobel Prize winner for literature to the Polish reading public, Roman Dyboski—an eminent scholar and anglicist—wrote: "O'Neill, like Walt Whitman, dazes us with the chaotic richness of his texture and frequently shocks us with brutality of the form of his expressions and drastic

101

flouting of all traditional conventions: moral, social, or dogmatic."[1]

There were several reasons for the twenty-four years of what I have termed as "almost total oblivion": first of all, the war and its aftermath; then in the early fifties an unpropitious political a mosphere. During this period only a few essays on American drama and theatre appeared, emphasizing the art of O'Neill in its American context, his uniqueness, pre-eminent position, and achievement.[2] Since 1956, as Polish cultural life was making up for what it had missed and theatres were pulsating with a new vitality, *Dialog*—a newly established monthly devoted to modern drama—has been providing the Polish reading public with masterpieces of world drama. And thus O'Neill was finally resurrected in Poland. Between 1956 and 1960 six translations of his plays were made available by *Dialog: Long Day's Journey into Night, A Touch of the Poet, A Moon for the Misbegotten, Hughie, Mourning Becomes Electra,* and *The Hairy Ape.* Yet the dramatist's return to the Polish stage was being delayed, partly because of some difficulties created by Carlotta O'Neill. Karl Ragnar Gierow of the Royal Dramatic Theatre in Stockholm intervened to resolve the problems; and O'Neill made a comeback—indeed royally—in an avalanche of 1960–61 premières.[3]

Practically every major city in Poland had its premiere of an O'Neill play in that theatrical season, the first one being the production of *A Moon for the Misbegotten* at Teatre "Wybrzeże" in Gdynia on October 29, 1960. Subsequently, four other theatres (in Warsaw, Kraków, Wrocław, and Lublin) staged this work which, incidentally, until now is the most popular of O'Neill's plays among Polish directors (seven productions). Nine Polish premières were presented during the extraordinary one-season renaissance: five productions of *A Moon for the Misbegotten;* two of *Long Day's Journey into Night* (Kraków, Katowice); and two of *Desire Under the Elms* (Warsaw, Kraków).

In the following season the euphoria of the directors began to subside; there were only four premieres in 1961–62: three of *Anna Christie* (in Łódź, Bydgoszcz, Częstochowa) and one of *Mourning Becomes Electra* (in Kraków). *Anna Christie* was done again in Warsaw, but this was the only O'Neill production offered in the 1962–63 season. Since then, O'Neill's presence on the Polish stage has become less glamorous, yet apparently permanent. In the late 1960s and early 1970s Polish directors seem to have been greatly attracted to *Long Day's Journey into Night.* Two theatres (in Wałbrzych and Łódź) staged it during the 1968–69 season, and Zygmunt Hübner thrilled theatregoers with his memorable production of this play at the Teatr Współczesny in Warsaw in 1972. In 1976 the *Iceman*, finally, came to Warsaw, movingly interpreted by Gustaw Holoubek at Teatr Dramatyczny. The most recent production of O'Neill in Poland was that of *Long Day's Journey into Night* in Wrocław in 1977–78.

In all, there have been over thirty productions of O'Neill plays in Poland. Unfortunately, they included only eight titles. *A Moon for the Misbegotten* holds the record as the play most frequently staged with *Long Day's Journey into Night* in second place (six productions), followed by *Desire Under the Elms* and *Anna Christie* (four productions each), and then *Mourning Becomes Electra, The Iceman Cometh, All God's Chillun Got Wings* and *The Emperor Jones*. It should, moreover, be stated that *Long Day's Journey into Night, Mourning Becomes Electra,* and *A Moon for the Misbegotten* have reached nation-wide audiences: the first was adapted for radio, and the other two were given special television productions (in 1965 and 1971 respectively). Apart from the pre-war production of *The Emperor Jones* none of O'Neill's experimental dramas were introduced to the Polish audience (dramatists included); and, unfortunately, an incomplete, if not one-sided, image of him has emerged in this country. Yet, one can realistically hope for the exposure of more facets of O'Neill's achievement in the future, in view of the Polish première of *The Iceman Cometh* in 1976 and considering the fact that sixteen of his plays have already been translated into Polish; plays not cited previously include: *Lazarus Laughed, The Great God Brown, The Moon of the Caribbees,* and *More Stately Mansions.*

No famous foreign dramatist has provoked such a gamut of emotional reactions, extreme judgments, and even personal arguments as did O'Neill—the writer and visionary—among Polish theatre specialists, critics and reviewers. It seems that in most other cases the critical attitude has been consistent with an established point of view. Celebrities—also relatively recent ones like Arthur Miller, Tennessee Williams, Edward Albee, and Arthur Kopit—are received favorably, if not with the admiration due to the great ones; and if the daggers of criticism are drawn, they are pointed at the directors, actors, and stage designers rather than at the writers themselves.

What, then, has been "the trouble with O'Neill," to quote the title of a revealing article by Grzegorz Sinko,[4] who represents a moderate voice and sensible approach in the violent dispute over O'Neill's renaissance in 1960–61? It should be pointed out that the "trouble" cannot be attributed to any single factor; it is complex in nature and covers several sets of problems: first, the question of the reception of O'Neill as a writer possessed or obsessed by a vision; the relevance of this vision to the Polish audience and critics; and the difficulty of a full, or at least adequate, understanding of his work in this country. What should be considered—perhaps before anything else—concerns the very essence of his existence in Poland: the quality of the Polish translations of his texts and the accuracy of their theatrical interpretation. Two things should be noted in any analysis of Polish reception of the dramatist. O'Neill's fame as the father of American drama and the greatest experimentalist in the American theatre was an established fact and the work of his followers produced before any of his plays was performed on Poland's post-war stage. This factor and the lack of variety in the O'Neill Polish repertoire could, at least partly, account for the mixed reaction among critics. The O'Neill that has been rather monotonously produced and re-staged represents, on the surface, heavy naturalistic traditional drama; and its psychological, poetic, and symbolic subtleties require, first of all, a profound understanding on the part of translators and the people of the theatre.

The understanding reviewers of the first productions in the early 1960s consistently stressed the universal character of O'Neill's psychological values and the profound truths about human nature and existence revealed in his work. Wojciech Natanson, a famous theatre specialist, hailing the return of O'Neill, indicates the direction of a proper interpretation: "a contemporary American turning to O'Neill participates in a journey to the sources of contemporary artistic thought." He then asks:

> But is it possible for a foreigner to make profitable use of this journey? . . . Here and there one already hears voices deprecating the author of *Desire Under the Elms* as having no values whatsoever for us. It seems that one has to find some permanent values in his work and to distinguish them from the temporal ones.

Natanson believes that psychological values age more slowly than formal experiments.[5]

Emphasizing the symbolic quality of *Long Day's Journey into Night*, Zofia Karczewska-Markiewicz sees the whole of O'Neill's work as "a journey to the bottom of the human soul" and its utmost revelation as the discovery that "the hell is within us."[6] Highly praising both the play and its production in Kraków, Leonia Jabłonkówna says:

> This play has a mysterious power which raises it infinitely above other American plays written in a similar mood. . . . This peculiar power . . . grips the onlooker; filled with pain, disgust, protest, he, nevertheless, gets involved in the life presented here. . . . O'Neill's heroes awaken our great sympathy; they are extremely close to us . . . as "sinners without guilt," victims of a cruel fate. That is why *Long Day's Journey into Night*—in spite of its external attributes as a realistic psychological play—is elevated in our experience to the ultimate heights of tragedy.[7]

Similarly, Roman Szydłowski, discussing the 1972 Warsaw production of *Long Day's Journey into Night*, appreciates the play's universal appeal since "it carries a prodigious load of human truth, and for this simple reason the play is worth staging."[8]

There was, however, an extreme minority strongly opposing O'Neill's genius. Ludwik Flaszen, commenting on the Kraków production of *A Moon for the Misbegotten*, says: "I am surprised by the theatre which in search of bad plays has to reach across the Atlantic, since similar plays— boring and wallowing in verbosity, in which muddy lyricism competes with high-handed principality—can be found, with a little dose of good will, closer at hand."[9] And Zygmunt Greń, discussing the same production, saw the play itself as "banal, shallow, muddy like pond-water at the end of a hot summer," and he went on to suggest that the only way of making O'Neill palatable to the modern audience was to present him farcically

> as great theatrical fun . . . as a pure conglomeration of all depths and violent feelings. . . . There is nothing in the play but a pure, abstract structure which is filled by the actors not with life but with discipline. . . . Even when granted the best efforts of the actors and producer, we won't ever be touched by their maniac, lunatic visions; we won't believe them; we won't be concerned.[10]

Perhaps a word of explanation will help in understanding the real nature of these attacks. As Natanson suggests in his essay, "O'Neill's Return," the cauldrons of hatred stirred here were not brewed for O'Neill plays specifically or their particular staging, but rather for psychological drama in general. Incidentally, Ludwik Flaszen has, for a long time, been a devout apologist of Grotowski's theatre and for many years its literary director.

Quite a large number of critics took what might be called a "middle road." Well aware of the development of world drama since the time these plays were written, they place O'Neill in what seems to be a correct perspective. Treating him as a traditional, old-fashioned playwright, they nevertheless not only acknowledge his influential achievement and his position in 20th century drama, but, what is more important, as do the indiscriminate eulogists, they also point out his universal values. Claiming that he shares his

views with the majority of the public and critics, Julian
Stawiński writes:

> . . . a famous dramatist, perhaps he was the father of Ameri-
> can theatre, but, basically, he is an old-fashioned writer and
> today his morbid, nauseous sinking into the slough of psy-
> chology is just a lamentable anachronism.

He then comments on the revival of interest in O'Neill both
in the United States and in Western Europe, makes a dramatic statement that but for O'Neill there is nothing genuine
in American drama, and concludes by saying that "the O'Neill
plays will be a permanent part of the standard repertoire of
Polish theatres."[11] Grzegorz Sinko, taking a European view,
says: "In spite of its undoubtedly permanent values, O'Neill's
theatre may cause difficulties in today's Europe, which spring
not only from its exotic texture."[12]

In a more recent discussion, Maciej Karpiński em-
phasizes the profound and tragic truth of *Long Day's Journey
into Night*, and, at the same time, warns contemporary
producers of the immense difficulties awaiting them in O'Neill
plays, and advocates caution and the profound reading of the
plays. The critic points out that "O'Neill appeals to [modern]
sensibility in a slightly 19th century fashion; from the arsenal
of human misfortunes, he digs out those to which we have
already managed to grow immune."[13]

Apart from the universal appeal of O'Neill's vision of
the human condition, which equals that of Ibsen, Strindberg,
or Dostoevsky, some critics noted his peculiar relevance to
the Polish audience. More than once he has been compared
to Conrad on the grounds that the artistic visions of both
men were similarly affected by their sea experiences. Natanson, on the other hand, saw a definite analogy between the
drives and motivation of the characters of *Desire Under the
Elms*, their struggle for the possession of land, their idea
of emigration, and the situation in Poland in the second
half of the 19th century as portrayed by Sienkiewicz or
Świętochowski.[14]

Insofar as one can infer from the subjective views of

critics and reviewers, the general audience received O'Neill, on the whole, favorably. Wojciech Natanson seems to be the most outspoken in this matter. Recalling his impressions of the general ambiance of the theatre during a performance of *Desire Under the Elms,* he wrote: "Authentic theatre lovers, who are not easily influenced by shallow classifications or pretentiousness, in contrast to first night audiences, listened with great attention to the confessions made by Nina Andrycz who played the role of Abbie Putnam."[15] The same play could provoke different critical opinions, but it seemed to evoke a similar favorable response by the audience.

One critic, Jaszcz, considers *Anna Christie* to be a very weak play; yet he acknowledges its extreme popularity and, calling it "a classical melodrama," foresees that "it will constantly appear [on our stage], willingly produced by directors and even more willingly played by the actors."[16] Discussing *Anna Christie* "after 40 years," August Grodzicki claims that the play has withstood the passage of time with great difficulty; "it does not move us any more and some characters are irritating. . . . O'Neill did not go beyond the limits of 'small realism.'" Yet, like the previous critic quoted, Grodzicki admits that this play may be liked and "may even find a grateful audience."[17]

The essential difficulty in attaining a full, and sometimes even adequate, comprehension of O'Neill in Poland lies, undoubtedly, in our different cultural background, which makes him "exotic" to the Polish audience. (This invites more general reflections on the problem of reception of any foreign literature and/or culture by sensibilities alien to it, for which, however, there is no place here.) Let me then limit my remarks to "the trouble with O'Neill." What some directors and the general audience miss in their productions and reading of O'Neill (and other American authors) is, in the first place, the concept of Puritanism in all its cultural and psychological ramifications. This oversight is greatly attributable to our descent from a Catholic tradition. As a matter of fact, even American Catholicism with its specific Puritan coloring (as in Flannery O'Connor) seems, for the most part, heretical to an average practicing Catholic in Poland. No wonder, then, that the New England Puritanism, so devastatingly present in so many O'Neill plays, has disappeared from their Polish interpretations.[18] Freudianism too, so profoundly permeating not only O'Neill's vision but the American imagination in general, as well as American social and cultural life, has never absorbed the average Pole to the extent that is quite "natural" to the average American.[19] It is, then, another aspect of O'Neill's exoticism. Furthermore, Freudianism deprived of the Puritan dimension in a Polish rendering of *Desire Under the Elms* seemed not only exotic but shallow and cheap.

The inability to grasp the significance of the distinctly American social and psychological implications of the texts accounts, in part, for the frequent misunderstanding or deletion of the symbolic and poetic qualities of O'Neill plays. A statement made by an advocate of the "impoverished" O'Neill illustrates this: "The general public [obviously meaning the Polish public] may be interested only in O'Neill the realist; however, it is difficult to get rid of his 'horny mysticism.' "[20] A critic with the opposite view, chiding Teatr Narodowy in Warsaw for its shallow interpretation of *A Moon for the Misbegotten*, writes: "The emphasis falls on realism. . . . The total absence of the poetic aspect of the play adumbrates its intentions." The reviewer also notes a certain passivity in the performance, which he found inconsistent with the nature of the play.[21] There is a considerable amount of criticism of the superficiality of productions and acting. More often than not producers and actors are blamed for the misinterpretation or lack of understanding of O'Neill's vision.

Another difficulty in staging O'Neill in Poland springs from our temperamental disparity and the more practical differences of our daily lives. That the Poles are unable, or do not know how, to play the roles of Americans is an accepted fact and is sometimes used as a critical complaint. Commenting on the Kraków production of *Mourning Becomes Electra*, Jerzy S. Sito observed that "General Mannon's

office resembles the office of a President of a County Council
[somewhere in Poland] rather than an arena in which Evil
fights against Good, Absolute against Reality."[22]

Finally, a serious responsibility for bringing the "true"
and authentic O'Neill to Poland rests on the translators
whose job, as has been stressed frequently, is exceptionally
difficult. Many specialists in the field of theatre claim that in
order to translate O'Neill properly, one has to be a poet and
dramatist; mere translational skills are far below the actual
requirements of O'Neill's vision and language.[23] The trouble
begins with the titles, especially in view of considerable dis-
crepancies between their actual symbolic meanings, carrying subtle suggestions as to the possible interpretations of
the plays, and the implications of the Polish versions. There
have been more well-founded critical remarks on the absurdity of some renderings of the titles than comments on
the whole texts of the plays. And, indeed, the title for *A
Moon for the Misbegotten* has appeared, so far, in four
different versions, none of them adequate, with "misbegotten" being translated as "unhappy," "lost," or "stray." In
two cases the moon "shines" as if showing the way out. Thus
the notion of fatal determinism, so crucial in this play, is
considerably toned down.[24]

The three existing versions of the Polish title of *Long
Day's Journey into Night* have been considered nonsensical.
In fact, they lose the notion of the journey altogether; one
preserves both "day" and "night," while the other two concentrate on the end of the day or twilight. There have also
been disputes over the translation of *The Iceman Cometh*.
The literal one (existing also in the German) has been found
less than revealing. Suggestions have been made to substitute
"Death" or "Icy Death" for the "Iceman."

A translation of the full text of *Desire Under the Elms*
has been criticized for its lack of syntactical resemblance to
the original, its standard Polish being inconsistent with
O'Neill's stylistic conventions.[25] The translation of *Long
Day's Journey into Night*, on the other hand, has been found
totally abortive. Zofia Karczewska-Markiewicz is of the opinion that

the stylized sophisticated simplicity born out of the author's
strivings has been understood by the translator as simple-
mindedness. The Polish text appeared [to the critics] as
vulgar and deprecating the literary value of the original.

She adds that, as a consequence, "the gaudy naturalism of the
translation has weighed upon the production which was
preserved in the same tone."[26]

Jerzy S. Sito has been the most ardent critic in the whole
dispute. Reflecting on the sudden 1960–61 O'Neill "craze"
in an article—significantly entitled "O'Neill Buried Alive,"
he exclaims: "So far O'Neill's art has been warped in five
successive premieres and now we are being threatened with
further repressions." Slightly exaggerating, he also condemns
all the existing (in 1961) translations of O'Neill as "attempts
at home-made rendering of O'Neill dialogue with total disregard for the actual language—O'Neill's single defense
against accusations of shallowness, melodrama and anachronism." And these were precisely the major accusations of
critical reviewers of O'Neill in Poland. Perhaps part of the
blame should, then, be put on the translators.

To conclude this superficial and impressionistic presentation of the complex relationship between the work of
O'Neill and the Polish theatre and audience, I want to add
that the 1960–61 renaissance which has sometimes been
called "unhealthy" was, in point of fact, evidence of a serious
striving towards understanding. In the obvious, shall I call
it slavic, enthusiasm with which so many theatres at the
time—having been finally granted the opportunity—tried
their artistic competence, the real O'Neill suffered a great
deal. Yet, he only fell victim to immature admiration. Since
then, the Polish theatre has gained experience in staging
O'Neill and has rectified the early blunders. Practically all
productions, though not so numerous, have been widely
praised by the critics for the maturity of the directors' concepts and the excellence of acting.

In contrast to practical criticism of actual productions
of O'Neill plays, which by its very nature has been much more
alive to the dramatist's progress in Poland and, therefore, to
his work, scholarly works devoted to them are not so numer-

ous. Parenthetically, let me add that American literary studies in Poland have only recently been established formally (in the early 1970s) and in a very limited capacity. Not more than a dozen Poles have earned a Ph.D. in American Literature in the whole country, only one specializing in O'Neill. Thus Halina Filipowicz-Findlay is the author of the only book on O'Neill in which she presents the man and his work. She has also written three essays in which she discusses O'Neill's concept of fatality, determinism and free will and compares *Beyond the Horizon* and Hauptmann's *Vor Sonnenaufgang*—dream and death.[27] Other analyses by Polish scholars deal with O'Neill's experiments in dramatic technique,[28] his Irish background,[29] his affinity with Irish drama,[30] and his naturalism.[31] Andrzej Falkiewicz, in one of his essays in his book, discusses O'Neill's treatment of the myth of Orestes as a continuation of a literary tradition since Aeschylus.[32]

Unlike Ibsen, Strindberg, Czekhov, or Hauptmann, O'Neill reached Poland too late and in too traditional a form to exert a creative influence on our drama. At the time of his return, we were being surprised by our own grotesque Mrożke; we were going back to the 1920s and 1930s into the incredible, lunatic world of the theatre of S. I. Witkiewicz, watching the gradual birth and growth of Grotowski's apocalyptic vision, participating in the waiting for Godot, sharing the anger of the young Englishmen and even begging to fear the old dame—Virginia Woolf; we also witnessed the Sartrean struggle between The Devil and God, to mention just a few events and tendencies in the life of Polish theatres and to suggest the sources of possible and more recent influences.

Yet, though there is little possibility that O'Neill will ever directly influence the Polish drama, he will undoubtedly remain permanently present on our stage; and this very presence may prove, in some way, formative to the Polish sensibility since—to use the words of a critic: "there is in him the same kind of unruly greatness which the people of the French Enlightenment, with all their negation, had to acknowledge in Shakespeare."[33]

NOTES

[1] Roman Dyboski, "O'Neill," *Przegląd Współczesny*, No. 176 (1936), p. 1.

[2] Ryszard Ordyński, Amerykańska twórczość dramatyczna" (American Drama), *Teatr*, No. 3–4–5 (1948), pp. 18–20.

Tadeusz Grzebieniowski, "Teatr i dramat amerykański" (American Theatre and Drama), *Łódź teatralna*, No. 3 (1949), pp. 12–14.

————, *Dramat i scena amerykańska* (Warszawa: PWN, 1954), p. 20.

[3] Wojciech Natanson, "Powrót O'Neilla" (O'Neill's Return), *Teatr*, No. 6 (1961), pp. 8–11.

[4] Grzegorz Sinko, "Kłopoty z O'Neillem" (The Trouble with O'Neill), *Nowa kultura*, No. 20 (1961), p. 4.

[5] Natanson, p. 8.

[6] Zofia Karczewska-Markiewicz, "W 'pieke' O'Neilla" (In O'Neill's 'Hell'), *Życie Warszawy*, No. 37 (1961), p. 8.

[7] Leonia Jabłonkówna, "Obsesje i obsesyjki" (Obsessions and Little Obsessions), *Teatr*, No. 13 (1961), pp. 7–9.

[8] Roman Szydłowski, "Piekło życia rodzinnego" (The Hell of a Family Life), *Trybuna Ludu*, No. 254 (1972), p. 8.

[9] Ludwik Flaszen, in *Echo Krakowa* (February 21, 1961), quoted after Natanson, op. cit.

[10] Zygmunt Greń, "Księżyc dla zbłąkanych" (Moon for the Stray), *Życie literackie*, No. 9 (1961), p. 8.

[11] Julian Stawiński, "O anachroniżmie teatru O'Neilla" (On the Anachronism of O'Neill Theatre), *Współczesność*, No. 12 (1961), p. 9.

[12] Sinko, p. 4.

[13] Maciej Karpiński, "Długi zmierzch" (A Long Twilight), *Literatura*, No. 33 (1972), p. 12.

[14] Wojciech Natanson, "W cieniu architektury teatralnej" (In the Shadow of Theatrical Architecture), *Życie literackie*, No. 10 (1961), p. 7.

[15] Natanson, "Powrót O'Neilla," p. 9.

[16] Jaszcz, Review of *Anna Christie*, *Trybuna Ludu*, No. 10 (1963), p. 6.

[17] August Grodzicki, "Po 40 latach" (After 40 Years), *Życie Warszawy*, No. 8 (1963), p. 4.

114   A EUROPEAN PERSPECTIVE

[18] cf. Jerzy S. Sito, "Piekło dla ludzi dorosłych" (Hell for Grown-ups), *Teatr*, No. 7 (1963), pp. 8–9.

[19] Sinko, p. 4.

[20] Jaszcz, "Czyżby nowy festiwal" (What, A New Festival?), *Trybuna Ludu*, No. 58 (1961), p. 5.

[21] "B.W.," "Nieszczęśliwi" (The Unhappy), *Teatr*, No. 13 (1961), pp. 22–23.

[22] Sito, op. cit.

[23] cf. Stawiński, op. cit. and Sinko, op. cit.

[24] cf. Jerzy S. Sito, "O'Neill żywcem pogrzebany" (O'Neill Buried Alive), *Polityka*, No. 13 (1961), p. 7.

[25] Sinko, p. 4.

[26] Karczewska-Markiewicz, p. 8.

[27] Halina Filipowicz-Findlay, *Eugene O'Neill* (Warszawa, 1975), p. 295.

Halina Filipowicz, "Fatalizm, determinizm a wolna wola w sztukach Eugene O'Neilla" (Fatality, Determinism and Free Will in Eugene O'Neill Plays), *Kwartalnik neo filologiczny*, No. 17 (1970), pp. 325–331.

————, "The Idea of Fatality in Eugene O'Neill's Plays," *Anglica Wratislaviensia* (1972), pp. 51–61.

————, "Dream and Death in Gerhart Hauptmann's *Vor Sonnenaufgang* and Eugene O'Neill's *Beyond the Horizon*, *Anglica Wratislaviensia* (1974), pp. 69–83.

[28] Ewa Aumer, "Eugene O'Neill's Experiments in Dramatic Structure and Stylization," *Anglica Wratislaviensia* (1972), pp. 37–49.

[29] Wanda Krajewska, "Irlandzkość Eugene 'a O'Neilla" (Eugene O'Neill's Irish Background), *Przegląd humanistyczny*, No. 4 (1966).

[30] Irena Przemecka, "Eugene O'Neill and the Irish Drama," *Kwartalnik neofilologiczny*, No. 18 (1971), pp. 2–9.

[31] Krystyna Przybylska, "O'Neill zbuntowany naturalista" (O'Neill—Naturalist in Revolt), *Dialog*, No. 5 (1970), pp. 110–121.

[32] Andrze j Falkiewicz, *Mit Orestesa* (The Myth of Orestes), (Poznań, 1967).

The above list of Polish scholarly publications on O'Neill is not complete. It is meant to show only a sample of the directions of Polish O'Neill scholarship.

[33] Sinko, p. 4.

THE USE OF THE SHORT STORY IN O'NEILL'S AND CHEKHOV'S ONE-ACT PLAYS
A Hungarian View of O'Neill

Peter Egri

I

The last decades of the nineteenth century and the turn of the twentieth century saw a growing sense of instability and restlessness in Europe. Old, seemingly firmly established ideas and ideals disintegrated; new social and artistic aims were set; all values came to be reinterpreted both in society and art. Manifestations of a new social, moral, and psychological reality abounded: the expanding monopolies; the wholesale industrialization and mechanization of life; the experience of large-scale alienation; the clash between philistinism and idealism; the conflicting and complementing trends of realism enriched with modern aspirations (Ibsen); naturalism (Hauptmann); impressionism and symbolism (Hofmannsthal, Maeterlinck, Yeats); paradoxical aestheticism (Wilde); transition from naturalism to expressionism (Wedekind, Strindberg); the modern realistic aspirations of intellectual satire (Shaw); lyric tragicomedy (Chekhov); and social, socialist activism (Gorky). The mass destruction of human, moral, and material values during World War I, the tectonic historical earthquakes of revolutions and counter-revolutions, the depression, the threat of fascism, the victory of antifascism, the fight between totalitarianism and antitotalitarianism, the accompanying chorus of new artistic and dramatic schools showed a sharpening of conflicts and justified the presentiment of the earlier writers and artists of the inevitable rearrangement of values.

The vigorous expansion of civilization in the United States after the Civil War, the unparalleled spread of industrialization, the dynamic drive of monopolies, and the social and cultural contradictions inherent in the process created an extremely favorable climate for a dramatic approach in literature. Working in different periods and genres, such diverse writers as Herman Melville, Theodore Dreiser, Ernest Hemingway, William Faulkner, Robinson Jeffers, Ezra Pound, and T. S. Eliot showed, in varying degrees and ways, a dramatic awareness of a new human predicament. It is little wonder that in the period following World War I this general dramatic quality of life and culture found a natural expression in the medium of the serious drama, which quickly and inevitably assumed national and international significance through the work of Eugene O'Neill. His individual talent, social position, psychological make-up, and search for values combined into an ideal unity to give voice and ingenious expression to those tensions inside himself that proved to be the equivalents of outer, objective contradictions.

The never-ceasing fascination and the hold that O'Neill's genius and art have had on European dramatists and audiences can, I think, be explained in this way: he summed up, developed further, synthesized and Americanized general social trends, historical processes, human aspirations, moral and psychological dichotomies, and, as a result, European dramatic forms, with vigor, originality, and evocative power. Just as American social developments can be viewed as an enhanced, increased continuation *and* a qualitatively new phase of trends found in European societies, American dramatic tendencies can also be considered as a carrying on *and* a meaningful and functional alteration of European dramatic forms. In different ways and degrees this is true of all four major American twentieth century dramatists: O'Neill, Miller, Williams, and Albee. O'Neill's continuing popularity in Europe is equally based on his similarity to, and dissimilarity from, his European predecessors. This applies to his relationship to Ibsen, Strindberg, Kaiser, Gorky—and Chekhov, a connection occasionally and sporadically referred to but so far unexplored and unstudied systematically. The examination of any of these relationships is bound to shed light on the problem of continuity and discontinuity, and therefore on the question why O'Neill has been so much esteemed all over Europe ever since his plays became known in this part of the world.

It is in this context that the present essay undertakes to analyze the Chekhov-O'Neill relationship, laying special stress on the dramatic function of the short story design in the overall pattern of Chekhov's and O'Neill's one-act plays. The connection between the short story and the drama is both generic and genetic. It is generic in the sense that both genres constitute a story; concentrate the narrative; seek out contradictory phenomena in life; and display the dialectic of contingency and necessity, phenomenon and essence, appearance and truth with a dynamic turn.

Although the short story represents a minor epic, focussing particular or even accidental traits, whereas the drama presents a literary genre traditionally juxtaposed with the epic and throwing into relief what is general and necessary, the generic relationship is unmistakably there. The short story is anything but a story that is short. If it could be defined that way, the term "long short story" would be an absurdity; in fact, a contradiction in terms. Although the short story is usually restricted in length, it is not identical with a short narrative. The aesthetic difference is derived precisely from the presence and genre-constituting role of a dramatic element which usually comes to the surface by means of a conspicuous change in the course and direction of the action.

This generic rapport between the short story and the drama explains the striking similarity one can find in Boccaccio's delineation of large groups of his *novellas* and Aristotle's description of *metabasis* and *peripeteia*, i.e. important elements of a dramatic plot. It is noteworthy that in all the ten *novellas* of *The Decameron*'s second day "stories are told of those who after passing through various adventures reach a happy end they had not hoped for"; in all the ten short stories of the fifth day, "tales are told of those lovers who won happiness after grief and misfortune"; but in all the ten tales of the fourth day, "tales are told of those whose love had an unhappy ending."[1] Is this not a case of *metabasis*, a change of fortune from bad to good, or from good to bad; is this not an instance comparable to *peripeteia*, a reversal, "a change of the situation into its opposite" that Aristotle speaks of in *The Poetics* characterizing simple and complex dramatic plots, respectively? [2]

I am not, of course, arguing that a short story is, in fact, a scaled down drama and that the drama is a magnified short story. The difference between the two genres is not one of size, but essentially one of kind. The emphasis in the short story on the particular and the accidental and in the drama on the general and the necessary constitutes a qualitative difference, even if both genres reach the category of the specific, which unifies, indeed synthesizes, the particular and the general.[3] Aristotle was certainly right in condemning an episodic plot in the drama; a short story as a whole is but an episode. He was also justified in stressing the dramatic importance of the probable and the necessary (especially in tragedy). In a short story the possible is more conspicuous than the probable, and the necessary does not prevail over the action but only flares up for a moment, frequently in an accidental turn which Aristotle disapproved of in a dramatic (tragic) plot.[4]

This qualitative difference in the artistic focus of the short story and the drama explains the deviation in approach as well. Both the novel and the drama, each in its own way,

> aim at comprehensiveness, completeness in their depiction of life; in both of them the many-sided play of action and reaction round the most pressing questions of the age produces a gallery of human types, contrasting with and complementing each other and taking their rightful places on the state of events. The novella, on the contrary, starts with an isolated case and does not go beyond it; . . . it can dispense with the details of people's origins and connections

and the situations in which they act. It can set in motion without need or preliminaries, and it can omit any precise, full-scale settings.[5]

In spite of these qualitative differences between the short story and the drama, with the foregoing restrictions, reservations and qualifications, we may still maintain that the specific feature of the short story among the minor epic genres is its dramatic charge.

This generic connection has its genetic aspect as well. Every genre category can be considered a formal crystallization of historically conditioned, recurring life-contents and attitudes, and every generic relationship embodies correlations of such human contents in the historical process. The relationship between the short story and the drama changes from age to age, from author to author, and even from work to work; indeed it has no fewer modifications than examples. Yet three especially significant types can be isolated.

In type one, the elementary dramatic impulse of the short story grows energetically into an elemental dramatic pattern. The result of the process is a change in kind, i.e. genre: the short story develops into the drama. An early and classic example for this trend can be observed in the Boccaccio-Shakespeare relationship. In his *Decameron* Boccaccio created an elastically pulsating generic framework which—*mutatis mutandis*—can also be recognized in Maupassant's, Chekhov's, Hemingway's or Tennessee Williams' short stories. This type of short story points, with dramatic gesture, to an individual trait, but, in doing so, it flashes up some universal facet; it calls attention to a chance feature or event, but for a significant moment it offers a short glimpse of some inevitable motive. The dramatic tension between the two contrasted poles is discharged at the apex of the action. A characteristic case in point is the falcon story (the ninth *novella* of the fifth day), whose theme is summarized by Boccaccio: "Federigo degli Alberighi loves, but is not beloved. He spends all his money in courtship and has nothing left but a falcon, and this he gives his lady to eat when she comes to visit him because there is nothing else to give her. She learns of this, changes her mind, takes him as her husband, and makes him a rich man."[6]

This seminal dramatic effect is rooted in the general social conditions of the early Renaissance. At the incipient stage of the bourgeois development, non-dramatic literary forms were characterized by an elementary dramatic quality expressing the embryonic outer and inner contradictions the new class experienced. The magnificent cathedral of Dante's *Divine Comedy* in its monumental total structure is not of a dramatic nature, but in some of its scenes, especially in Hell, a dramatic gesture or conflict does crop up. In the Petrarchan sonnet form the octave and the sextet are contrasted in a manner not unlike the way in which the structural units in Boccaccio's short stories are opposed. The *volta* in the sonnet and the turning point in the short story betray a compatible dramatic interest.

It was in the late Renaissance that the increase in dramatic quality within non-dramatic genres led to an extraordinary and unprecedented flourishing of the drama itself. Although the incessant growth of dramatic interest can also be witnessed in the development of the Italian Renaissance which produced such masterpieces as Michelangelo's sculptures, paintings, and sonnets, still the trend reached its most pronounced form in the most advanced country of bourgeois development, Elizabethan and Jacobean England. In her book, *A reneszánsz ember* (Renaissance Man), Agnes Heller points out with good reason that the whole climate of contemporary English culture was characterized by a dramatic inclination. In England

> it is the drama which becomes the dominant genre of the Renaissance. The English Renaissance saw the collapse of an old world and the birth of a new one. Its dramatic quality and "openness" to the future are responsible for the fact that of renaissance cultures it was precisely in England that the contradictions of capitalism were recognized *in a foresight*, at the very moment of its birth, as it were. . . . Thinking these contradictions through makes the dramatic quality universal, even in the works of those whose field was not

the drama at all. Thus the dramatic quality can be discerned not only in Morus' speeches but also in Bacon's *Novum organum*.[7]

It goes without saying that the peak of this development is Shakespearean drama, which in its world historical aspect, can be considered an epilogue to the Wars of the Roses, an interlude to the Absolute Monarchy, and a prelude to the bourgeois revolution of the 17th century. It was this extraordinary concentration of social contradictions of a truly world historical magnitude which made it possible for Shakespeare's genius to consummate the dramatic trend inherent in renaissance culture. The motives in his plays, directly or indirectly, reach back and relate to those in Boccaccio's stories (that of *The Merchant of Venice* to the first tale of *The Decameron*'s tenth day, of *All's Well That Ends Well* to the ninth tale of the third day, of *Cymbeline* to the ninth tale of the second day). With this very gesture, Shakespeare also laid his finger on the generic leap the early Renaissance short story took into late Renaissance drama, a latent and isolated dramatic quality bursting into a violent and full dramatic explosion.[8]

This course of development would seem to have been reversed at the turn of the 20th century. Whereas in the Renaissance the short story was expanding into the drama, in naturalistic and symbolistic trends the drama was moving towards the short story. The sense that old social patterns became outmoded and new sets of values were emerging, the awareness of a new phase of social alienation, and the uncertainty about the motivation and direction of social development led to the fragmentation of the artistic outlook, which, in turn, promoted the fragmentation of the dramatic structure into naturalistic episodes, impressionistic sketches, or symbolistic states of mind and mood. The secret play of unknown forces created an irrational atmosphere in which the workings of Fate appeared to lonely individuals as unpredictable examples of unaccountable accidence.

The affinity of the drama to the short story is manifest in Hauptmann's naturalistic play, *Drayman Henschel*, which is, in fact, an elaboration of his early short story "Bahnwärter Thiel" (Signalman Thiel); it is conspicuous in a number of Hofmannsthal's fine impressionistic and symbolistic, poetic one-acters with balladesque overtones (*Yesterday, The Death of Titian, Death and the Fool, Madonna Dianora*),[9] as well as in his "The Woman Without a Shadow," originally a short story and later a libretto to Richard Strauss' opera; and it is most striking in Maeterlinck's sensitively symbolistic playlets (*The Intruder, The Blind, Interior,* etc.).

These two genetic types of relationship between the short story and the drama seem to bear out G. Lukács' statement: "The novella makes its appearance either as the harbinger of some new conquest of reality by large-scale forms, narrative or dramatic, or else at the close of a period, by way of a rearguard or postlude."[10]

If, however, we examine the works of Chekhov and O'Neill, it becomes fairly obvious that they do not fit in with either of these two categories. The reason why Lukács's observation cannot be mechanically applied to them is that Lukács, while he also refers to the drama, is naturally interested chiefly in the historical and artistic correlation between the short story and the novel and the pioneer role of the short story with Boccaccio and its rearguard function with Maupassant, Conrad, and Hemingway in relation to the fiction of Balzac, Stendhal, Flaubert, and Zola. Nor does the difficulty simply lie in the fact that by highlighting the general and the necessary, the dramatist must find it especially problematic to recede to the isolated world of the short story which, as it has already been underlined, stresses the particular and the accidental. The relationship between the short story and the novel is not identical with the contact between the short story and the drama. Lukács mentions that the terms "pioneer" and "rearguard" do not describe the many-faceted historical rapports, even in the field of the epic.

The chief reason why Chekhov's and O'Neill's oeuvres call for a separate group is that, while they do have significant points of contact, and on occasion even partially overlap with the first and the second categories, they, in fact, synthesize those polar possibilities into a new kind of dramatic unity. While in type one the short story grows and changes into the drama and in type two the drama moves towards or recedes into the short story, in Chekhov's and O'Neill's art the short story becomes organically integrated into the dramatic pattern.[11]

II

There are numerous ways the integration is achieved, but some uses of the short story in Chekhov's and O'Neill's plays seem to deserve special attention. In both playwrights' oeuvres the short story and the one-acter are closely related in that the turning point of the short story and the culminating point of the short play converge or coincide.

In Chekhov's early work a case in point is the link between the story, "A Defenseless Creature" (1887), and the playlet, *The Anniversary* (1891). The story concerns a certain Shchukina whose husband has been ill for five months and been dismissed from his job. When she finds that his employer had deducted twenty-four roubles and thirty-six kopecks from his salary, Shchukina visits "His Excellency" Kistunov, an influential man in a bank and asks him for redress. Kistunov does his best to point out that he represents a private bank and that Shchukina's husband had worked for the Army Medical Department; she should, therefore, turn to that department. Neither Kistunov nor his clerk can fend her off; exhausted and exasperated, Kistunov gives Shchukina the sum she has demanded out of his own pocket.

A similar situation occurs in *The Anniversary*; part of the dialogue in the story has been taken over word for word. The farce re-presents what the story represents. The change of the title from "A Defenseless Creature" to *The Anniversary* or *The Jubilee* indicates a shift of emphasis from a funny incident to (or rather towards) a satirical comedy. The theme is also expanded by the introduction of a festive occasion, the fifteenth anniversary of the establishment of the N. Mutual

Credit Bank which is going to celebrate its jubilee in a grand manner.

The characters and the characterization are also modified. Shipuchin (the dramatic continuation of Kistunov) is not merely an influential clerk but is, in fact, the chairman of the bank. The satirical slant of the comedy is mainly derived from the double standards of his attitude: he loves to deliver pompous speeches, but he leaves it to his clerk Khirin to put in the facts; he feels deeply honored to be presented with an address and a silver tankard, but it was he himself who wrote the address, had it bound; he also bought the tankard—the shareholders would never have thought of that. If Kistunov as Shipuchin becomes more pompous and empty-headed, Shchukina, now called Merchutkina, appears in a somewhat more favorable light.

The conflict inherent in the short story and explicit in the play becomes sharper in the latter. In the story, at the opposite poles of the clash, we find a gout-ridden man afflicted with nervous exhaustion, and a misguided, stubborn and silly woman who, while she calls herself a defenseless creature, drives the victim of her attack half-mad. In the play, Merchutkina's obsessed insistence leads to the unmasking of a false notability and ruins a sham anniversary. In "A Defenseless Creature" when Kistunov pays the woman the 25 roubles which someone else owes her, he seems to act foolishly, trapped by an importuning fool. In *The Anniversary* when the rich bank director, trying to get rid of her, gives the poor woman the same sum of money, his act still maintains a measure of nonsense, but it also suggests (rather than puts) a quiet question about the righteousness of a social order in which it is right to pay 45 roubles for the binding of an address to be presented to oneself, but it is wrong (nonsensical) to donate 25 roubles to a woman whose husband is ill, out of work, short of money, and docked unexpectedly. Can not Merchutkin and Merchutkina be considered the victims after all? Is there no connection between the richness of the Shipuchins and the poorness of the Merchutkins? Isn't this state of affairs a greater nonsense than Merchutkina's indiscriminate demands?

Chekhov, to be sure, does not answer these questions; he does not "make a point." His method is one of juxtaposition, not one of didactic comment. But this sort of juxtaposition constitutes a dramatic conflict which uses, extends, intensifies, and modifies the incipient antithesis of the short story. The payment of the banker for what he does not owe becomes part of ruining a false anniversary: the turn of the story leads to the peak of the play.

A similar relationship can be observed between a number of other short stories and short plays by Chekhov: "In Autumn" (1883) which was dramatized as *On the High Road* (1885); "Kalchas" (1886) which suggested the one-acter with the same title and was later modified into *Swan Song* (1887–8); "One Among Many" (1887) which came to dramatic life in *A Tragic Role* (1889–90); the three tales: "The Wedding Season" (1881), "Marrying for Money" (1884), and "A Wedding with a General" (1884) which were integrated into the one-act play *The Wedding* (1889–90); and "The Night Before the Trial" (1886) which in the 1890s was partly given a dramatic form with an identical title but ultimately remained unfinished.

Moreover, even in such one-acters as are not directly dramatized short stories, the quality of the dramatic summit is closely related to a short story-like turn (*The Bear*, 1888; *The Proposal*, 1888–9; *Tatyana Repina*, 1889; and all the six versions of *Smoking Is Bad for You*, also translated as *On the Harmfulness of Tobacco*, 1886–1903).[12]

The generic affinity between the epic turn of a short story and the dramatic zenith of a short play is also characteristic of Conrad's and O'Neill's work. It appears very clearly in the complex relationship of Conrad's story, "The End of the Tether" (1902), O'Neill's one-act play *Warnings* (1913), and his short story "S.O.S." (1918).

Published in the volume *Youth: A Narrative and Two Other Short Stories*, "The End of the Tether" was considered by Conrad a short story. At the heart of the narrative we certainly find the outlines of a short story: Captain Whalley going blind, being forced by financial pressures and his love for his daughter Ivy to remain the captain of the ship Sofala even after losing his eyesight, the running of the ship upon a reef, its sinking, and Whalley's refusing to leave her and essentially committing suicide are the motifs and motives of a short story. The complexity of the story, however, opens up epic dimensions, sweeping beyond the limits of a short story and approaching the genre of a short novel. The numerous references to Captain Whalley's better days, to his earlier trips, the introduction of a number of types: the mean and shrewd shipowner and first engineer Massy; the upstart first mate Sterne; that drunkard of a second engineer, Jack; the dutiful and docile Malay Serang; and the benevolent and sympathetic planter Van Wyck need more epic space than a simple short story can afford and supply.

Conrad's story also has a strong dramatic drive and an ever increasing dramatic tension due to the sharpening conflict between individual effort and fateful circumstances, manly stature and physiological defect, human frailty and its disastrous consequences, the excess of love resulting in an ominous concealment of a dangerous weakness, the clash of mean calculation (Massy) and paternal passion (Whalley), the opposition of selfish ambition (Sterne) and selfless devotion (Whalley). The dramatic explosiveness of Conrad's work makes itself felt on the stylistic plane as well when Mr. Van Wyck compassionately responds to Captain Whalley's intimations about his concealed deafness with: "We shall share the guilt then," Whalley desperately retorts: "Nothing could make mine less." Their speech sounds like a dramatic dialogue.[13]

O'Neill's *Warnings* bears a number of striking similarities to Conrad's "The End of the Tether." The central figure of the playlet, James Knapp, though no captain, is the wireless operator of the S.S. Empress, and in this capacity he plays a crucial part in the safe sailing of the ship. Losing his hearing, he, too, is afflicted by an illness fatal for his work. Like Captain Whalley, Knapp is also compelled to carry on with his work because of financial pressures and his emotional ties to a woman, in this case his wife Mary, whose reproaches torture him beyond endurance and make him undertake just one more trip. He, too, keeps his defect in secret. The voyage could have been as uneventful as many former ones for Knapp, but the S.S. Empress hit a derelict and sank just as the Sofala had been wrecked on a reef and gone under. Knapp realizes his responsibility as did Whalley, and rather than accept his captain's invitation to take to the lifeboat, he takes his own life. So many similarities in the plot seem to justify Travis Bogard's observation to the effect that "the play's central situation was quite possibly suggested to O'Neill by Joseph Conrad's 'The End of the Tether.' "[14]

The deviations between Conrad's story and O'Neill's play are no less illuminating. Showing the influence of his youthful experiences and his early naturalistic leanings, O'Neill diminishes Whalley's heroic stature; Knapp manifests only the weaknesses of Whalley. Material and biological determination play an increased role in *Warnings*. Whalley used to be a ship owner, and, even after losing his fortune, he is Massy's partner with his £500; Knapp is a pauper whose large family will starve if he gives up his job. While Ivy owns a boarding house, Mary owes the grocer and the butcher, and her penny-pinching existence has made her a prematurely old and nagging wife. Whalley has been ruined by his blindness *and* the vile calculation of Massy, who, hoping to receive money from the insurance company, deflects the ship's compass; Knapp's disaster is caused by his deafness alone.

Since a physiological mischance of this kind necessarily throws into relief the fateful operation of chance, concentrating the tragedy on this element serves to underline in the play the accidental, short story-oriented turn of Conrad's narrative within the dramatic form. Conrad, on the other hand, while underscoring the importance of the accidental, also gives prominence to traits defying chance. Motivating Captain Whalley's refusal to leap from the sinking ship into the ocean, he writes: "People sucked down by the whirlpool of a sinking ship do come up sometimes to the surface, and it was unseemly that a Whalley, who had made up his mind to die, should be beguiled by chance into a struggle."[15] There is character and nobility in this stance of facing necessity. In Knapp's suicide the main motive is accepting personal responsibility and psychological collapse.

Thus Conrad wrote a tale with short story-slanted turns and a dramatic sweep in it; and O'Neill composed a play isolating and enhancing the dramatic aspect in Conrad's plots, dramatizing the short story-inspired turns in the nucleus of the narrative, and even stepping up the accidental quality of these turns. O'Neill's detailed scenic descriptions and epically elaborate exposition in Scene 1 also add to the short story character of the play.

Under the circumstances, it is little wonder that O'Neill rewrote his one-act play as a long short story in "S.O.S." Since it is as yet unpublished, it needs a more detailed discussion.[16] Written at the end of 1918, after the United States had entered World War I in April, 1917, and the Germans had declared unrestrained submarine warfare, "S.O.S." transplanted the original plot of the play to a new historical soil. Its central character, John Lathrop, led the life of a silent, average telegrapher in a small town called Acropolis. He had been living for twenty years in Mrs. Perkins' boarding house until one day he surprised the local gossip-makers by marrying a middle-aged spinster, Susanah Darrow. She was the daughter of a captain, who crushed her ambition to marry and succeeded in keeping her to himself. After his death, she was no less lonely than John; loneliness then was the foundation of their love and marriage. John even gave up drinking for her sake. Their peaceful happiness was disturbed by John's losing his job at the local telegraph company. In his attempt to avoid living on his wife's income, he became meticulous in his work, grew self-conscious, and, for this very reason, committed mistakes. People kept complaining about his blunders, and finally the company decided to fire him.

After a long search, John finally found a job as a wireless operator on board the ship S.S. Rio Grande, winning the esteem of the captain and the crew after several voyages. All went well until the couple experienced a double disaster. Susan lost the small income she had inherited from her father, and John was becoming deaf. A doctor in New York told him that occasionally he might regain his hearing, but his temporary recovery could not stop the process of becoming totally deaf, an event which was to occur a few weeks later. Susan went back to Acropolis to sell her house, and John decided to make one more trip on the S.S. Rio Grande, hoping that his affliction would not overtake him before the completion of the last voyage. Their financial situation necessitated his continuing in his job. After all, the doctor himself held up the hopeless hope that he may have been mistaken in his diagnosis, and even asserted that some unforeseen event, e.g. a great and sudden physical shock, might change the case. John set out on his last voyage at a time when the Germans were starting an unrestrained naval war against their enemies. When the Rio Grande was sailing home, she came within the range of a German raider. John did not hear the warnings sent out by American coast posts to turn back, and the S.S. Rio Grande was captured and sunk by the German warship.

Taken as prisoners, the crew of the Rio Grande looked upon John with anger and contempt. The German commander, learning that John was the unwitting cause of his capturing the American ship, maliciously permitted him to walk about freely on the raider. When another American cargo ship appeared on the horizon, the raider's gun was fired with John lying in its close proximity. The tremendous crash of the cannon overpowered him with its noise, covered him with gunpowder, and frightened him almost to death, but it also gave him back his hearing. His humiliation had long turned into mad anger which filled him with obsessed energy. Under cover of darkness, he stole to the room of the German radio operator, stabbed him to death, and sent out S.O.S. signals using the wireless. An American cruiser, the New Orleans, received his message. Being compelled to justify himself, John went among the crew of the Rio Grande and informed the captain of his actions. Soon the Germans discovered the corpse of their operator, and the commander ordered the execution of John. He was shot and lowered into the sea. When the American cruiser arrived, the

German raider was forced to surrender. John was now viewed as a man who, out of shrewdness and patriotic feeling, pretended to be deaf and gave his life to capture a dangerous German raider. He was called a national hero by New York newspapers and was lovingly remembered by his wife.

The similarities between *Warnings* and "S.O.S." are so numerous that the latter appears to be the adaptation of the former; in both works a ship is sunk as a consequence of her radio operator going deaf; the operator knows this might happen, but being short of money and afraid he may lose the esteem of his wife, he fails to take his doctor's advice and ventures out on just one more trip. Understanding his responsibility for the destruction of his ship, the operator loses his earlier self, becomes desperate, and finds his death.

The dissimilarities between O'Neill's play and long short story are due in part to changed historical conditions and to the consequences of the change in genres. In *Warnings* the ship sinks because she hits a derelict; in "S.O.S." she goes under because a German raider captures and sends her to the bottom. In the short story, World War I provides the background to convey an additional meaning to the events. In "S.O.S." O'Neill seems to have been interested in the contrast between appearance and reality, a theme looming large in his later plays. The newspapers depicted John as a great national hero, whereas in reality he was but a grey, simple, timid and lonely man whose seclusion was only heightened by his getting deaf. In the play, the realization of responsibility leads the operator to suicide, while in the short story it drives him to a mad action of retributive murder which is tantamount to following the logics of the war; unwittingly he saves his countrymen and—with grotesque irony—becomes after his death a celebrated heroic figure.

The change in genre also involves significant modifications. In *Warnings* the sailors are on board ship while it is sinking, making the event actual, sharper, and dramatic. In "S.O.S." the crew is watching from the German raider when the Rio Grande is submerging. The play contracts events into a single disastrous action, while the long short story has some epic room to give a broader picture of antecedents, circumstances, surroundings, and graduality. The gradual unfolding of Lathrop becoming desperate and insane, i.e. the psychological process, inherent in his fate, deserves special notice. In the play there is one accidental turn of a biological nature in the action (the operator losing his hearing); in the long short story, there are two such turns (his losing and regaining his hearing). The latter event reinforces and intensifies the effect of the former since its chance character is stronger, and its occurrence rate is obviously smaller. This is in agreement with the generic nature of the drama and the short story, respectively. At the same time both accidental events flash a light on the workings of necessity: Lathrop's losing his hearing caused his humiliation which—even if he was not immediately aware of it—represented the cruelty of war; and his recovering his hearing made it both possible and necessary for him to accept and adopt the logics of war: to kill and—by way of an ironical by-product somewhat anticipating Orin's case in *Mourning Becomes Electra*—to become a hero for the wrong reasons.

It should be noted, however, that in spite of all these generic differences between *Warnings* and "S.O.S." there operates a strong tendency working, as it were, crossways: lending a short story-like quality to the drama and a dramatic trait to the short story. In the play the fact that the action turns around a chance event (however strong its fateful disaster-character may be) gives the plot much of the nature of the short story. The prolonged genre picture in the exposition of the play strengthens this impression. In the short story, the character of the threat (the deliberate hostile action of the German warship seeking out British and American ships to destroy them in a state of war) is more necessary than it is in the play (hitting a derelict).

The enhanced dramatic tension in the long short story can be accounted for by the fact that O'Neill wrote a great many plays after *Warnings*, and by the time he had put "S.O.S." to paper, he had developed an increased sense for the dramatic quality even in stories. The very outbreak of the war also provided him with a dramatic framework more fateful, organic, and necessary than the vicissitudes of a ship on the sea. This is the way in which Conrad's story—obviously much finer than either O'Neill's *Warnings* or his "S.O.S."—gave a dramatic impulse to the young playwright's one-acter which, in turn, inspired his highly dramatic long short story.

A number of other one act plays by O'Neill have a narrative origin. *Bound East for Cardiff* (1914) goes back to Conrad's novel *The Nigger of the Narcissus* which O'Neill read in 1911.[17] *Fog* (1914) shows parallels with Chaucer's *Canterbury Tales*. In the Prioress's Tale the crying of a dead child leads the rescuers to their destination. "That O'Neill had read Chaucer is doubtful; nevertheless a source tale may be suspected for his story."[18] O'Neill's later destroyed one act comedy *The Dear Doctor* (1915) was based on a short story which in its turn had been pirated from a vaudeville sketch.[19] *In the Zone* (1916–17) is strongly related to Conan Doyle's short story, "That Little Square Box."[20] *The Dreamy Kid* (1918) was started as a short story. O'Neill completed about a page in this form feeling it would throw into greater relief the psychological split in the young Negro. Later, however, he was showing visible signs of dramatic concentration. Agnes Boulton remembers having seen his eyes darken, then become intense; he began "to pace the floor as the dramatist in him took over. . . . And as Gene talked, something else in him began to overcome the psychological aspect of the story."[21] In the summer of 1918 O'Neill modified and elaborated on Agnes Boulton's narrative "The Captain's Walk," adding the idea of treasure, gold and a map showing where the treasure was hidden. The result was the one act play *Where the Cross Is Made* (1918) later expanded into the four act play *Gold* (1920).[22] *The Hairy Ape* (1921) was also first composed as a short story in 1917.[23]

The generic proximity of the short story and the one-acter is also striking in O'Neill's other playlets which do not demonstrably hang together with actual short stories, i.e. in *A Wife for a Life* (1913), *The Web* (1913), *Thirst* (1913), *Recklessness* (1913), *Abortion* (1914), *The Movie Man* (1914), *The Sniper* (1915), *Before Breakfast* (1916), *The Long Voyage Home* (1916–17), *The Moon of the Caribbees* (1916–17), *Ile*

(1916–17), *Shell-Shock* (1918), *The Rope* (1918), and partly *The Emperor Jones* (1920).[24]

Thus in his early one act plays O'Neill, like Chekhov, incorporated features typical of the short story. It might be argued that apart from this generic and general point of contact, there is not much Chekhovian quality in O'Neill's youthful one-acters. In spite of the pervasively lyrical mood of short plays like *The Moon of the Caribbees*, this is, of course, essentially correct. Besides the element of natural continuity to be observed in any writer's development, are there many "Chekhovian" properties, in terms of his truly characteristic great late plays, in Chekhov's one act plays? Very few, it would seem. *The Anniversary* is not much less removed from *The Cherry Orchard* than *Warnings* is, or, for that matter, than *Warnings* is from *Long Day's Journey into Night*. The artistic distance may be of a different kind, but it is hardly shorter.

It was chiefly in O'Neill's late masterpiece *Hughie* (1941) that the integration of the generic features of the short story and the short play was coupled with a Chekhovian atmosphere.[25] The very conflict in *Hughie*, without being influenced by any particular story or play by Chekhov, evokes the social and psychological climate of a number of his short stories and dramas in general by being derived from the tension between the contrary reactions of two equally empty souls of their spiritual waste: one apathetic and resigned (the Night Clerk), the other boastful and superior ("Erie" Smith). Like so many of Chekhov's characters, both figures live in loneliness, isolation, and alienation. The Clerk feels distressed and detached wondering *"what anything has to do with anything—then gives it up."*[26] Erie Smith owes a lot of money to dangerous strong guys who may beat him up. Though a good mixer, he is lonely and full of uncertainty, as his desperate and unsuccessful attempts to establish some sort of communication with the Night Clerk and his condescending attitude of the wisecrack betray.

There is only one solution for alienation: a lying pipe-dream, to quote the recurring leitmotif of *The Iceman Cometh* which is similar in many respects to *Hughie*. Thus,

again taking up and elaborating on one of Chekhov's chief
concerns, *Hughie* is also a study of illusion and reality.
Reminiscing about Hughie, Smith recalls the way in which
the earlier Night Clerk led a kind of second life through
Smith's stories.

> The bigger the story the harder he'd fall. He was that kind
> of sap. He thought gambling was romantic. I guess he saw
> me like a sort of dream guy, the sort of guy he'd like to be
> if he could take a chance. I guess he lived a sort of double
> life listening to me gabbin' about hittin' the high sports.
> Come to figger it, I'll bet he even cheated on his wife that
> way, using me and my dolls.[27]

That this is not a mere invention of a teller of tales can be
deduced from the manner in which even Charlie Hughes,
Hughie's namesake and successor, and a much more difficult
person to be made interested in anything, becomes alive
when he learns that Smith knows Arnold Rothstein, the
great gambler. He is the "Big Ideal" for him; when he
imagines himself playing with and beating Rothstein, a
*"Beatific vision swoons on the empty pools of the Night
Clerk's eyes. He resembles a holy saint, recently elected to
Paradise."*[28]

Erie Smith is also a vulgar dreamer of vulgar dreams. In
one of his long interior monologues (disguised as dialogues)
he confides to the inattentive Charlie that by cheering up
Hughie he was cheering up himself: "Yeah, Hughie lapped
up my stories like they was duck soup, or a beakful of
heroin. . . . And, d'you know, it done me good, too, in a way.
Sure. I'd get to seein' myself like he seen me."[29]

The two kinds of self-deception meet in Smith's account
to Charlie of how he placed a big wreath of roses in the shape
of a horseshoe on Hughie's tomb with forget-me-nots around
the top, printing the inscription Good-by, Old Pal. "Hughie
liked to kid himself he was my pal. . . . And so he was at
that—even if he was a sucker."[30] Whether this really happened or was just another lie, it expresses a human relationship based on the mutual need for illusion. A similar and
similarly illusory contact is established between Smith and

Charlie after both have arrived at the extreme point of vacuity, inner barrenness, and dejection, and when—at what appears to be the critical moment of the tragi-comic thrust of the play and a true short story-like turn in its dramatic action—Smith and Charlie start gambling with dice with the money Smith gives Charlie to have something to win from him.[31] The game of chance involves a degree of human solidarity and personal warmth and also indicates an illusory substitute for Smith's and Charlie's former failure to bring about meaningful communication, setting up the evil duality of facing emptiness or escaping into make-believe.

The story-character of the play is also increased by O'Neill's great emphasis on describing the physical appearances of people and their surroundings. Thus O'Neill does not fail to mention that the Night Clerk's face is *"long and narrow, greasy with perspiration, sallow, studded with pimples from ingrowing hairs."*[32] The detailed descriptions of outer noises in the street also contribute to the epic, factual elaboration of the play. Since, however, they always indicate the deviation of Charlie's attention from Erie's words, they also show the intensification of a dramatic tension between Erie's attempt to communicate and the passive resistance of the Night Clerk. Thus even passivity obtains a dramatic intensity. This is only increased by the added dynamics of events Charlie's desperately bored mind associates with the noises: the passing of the fire brigade evokes his desire that the whole city should burn down; the footsteps of policemen arouse his wish that something big should happen, etc. The extraordinary strength of the emotional equivalent of street noises in Charlie's mind gives them a lyric significance, too.

O'Neill's liberal stage directions and descriptions are very accurate, and not infrequently they strike the reader as a kind of running commentary whose epic aspect is on occasion enhanced by the fact that they are unplayable. We can read, e.g. about the Night Clerk that *"It is years since he cared what anyone called him. So many guests have called him so many things. The Little Woman has, too. And, of course, he has, himself. But that's all past."*[33]

Passages of this kind, however, have different aspects to them as well. They are not only epic representations of past events but also have the function of rendering the stream of consciousness of Hughie, as if their proper form were a first person statement only incidentally put into the third person. In this sense, they have lyric overtones enhanced by symbols; they also function dramatically as the recalcitrant drag of indifference working against Smith's intention to establish a relationship. Practically the whole of the play is the juxtaposition and confrontation of Erie Smith's loud and Charlie's silent monologues. The Night Clerk's groping and receding thoughts and feelings are clearly interior monologues. Smith attempts a dialogue, but until the very end, he fails to break through to Charlie, and what he says is more of self-expression spoken aloud than information conveyed to the Night Clerk. On occasion, he is admittedly "slipping back into narrative."[34] At a certain point he even gives up his endeavor to engage Charlie's attention: *"Erie begins talking again but this time it is obviously aloud to himself,* without hope of a listener."[35] His speech increasingly follows the pattern of "the dialectics of the soul," as Chernyshevsky, the inventor of the term, characterized the interior monologue.[36]

Nevertheless the presence and increased importance of a lyric charge and epic elaboration in O'Neill's use of the interior monologue does not result in *Hughie* in a lyric or epic disintegration of the drama. A number of elements demonstrate the essentially dramatic and modern realistic use of the interior monologue in *Hughie*: Smith's bullyingly loud and overpowering monologue and Charlie's timid, embryonic, and vacuously resigned silent free associations; the expression in, through, and by the monologues of the relationship of the patron—who is always right—and the Night Clerk—who, by the policy of the hotel, is supposed to welcome even the smuttiest jokes and personal questions of the patrons; Smith's interior monologue disguised as an external dialogue; the occasional tragi-comic evidence of the self-obsession of the two men; Smith's failure to keep up the appearance of his interior monologue as a normal dialogue; and the eventual establishing of an illusory communication on the basis of gambling with lent money, an end towards which the stream of consciousness is oriented and where it comes to an abrupt end.

A similarly dramatic and realistic use of the interior monologue can be encountered in the last act of Chekhov's lyrically charged and symbolically heightened play, *The Sea Gull*. The Chekhovian form of the interior soliloquy—which unites the traditional dramatic monologue employed in the one act plays and in *Ivanov* with the manner of expression typical of the free association pattern to express and underline essential and real dramatic truth—makes it possible that illusion and its real alternative could be opposed with spontaneous naturalness and dramatic force.

In her day-dreaming Nina says to Treplev: "I am a sea gull. . . . No, that's not it. I am an actress. . . . Do you remember you shot a sea gull? A man came by chance, saw it and, just to pass the time, destroyed it. . . . A subject for a short story."37 Then while her stream of consciousness is drifting scraps of memories of Trigorin's words, she is already proceeding to the insight which may redeem her from the enclosed world of her illusions without letting her fall victim to the false, vain and empty splendor of an actress like Arkadina:

> Now I know, I understand . . . that in our work—in acting or writing—what matters is not fame, not glory, not what I dreamed of, but knowing how to be patient. To bear one's cross and have faith. I have faith and it all doesn't hurt so much, and when I think of my vocation I am not afraid of life.38

The distant hope and tentative faith expressed in these words are peculiar to Chekhov expressing his future-oriented social perspective. This made it possible for him not only to experience but also to transcend a world of illusion. At the time of writing *Hughie*, O'Neill did not possess such a perspective. His social ideals belonged mainly to the past of his youth; for the future he had but a hopeless hope. But even this was enough to hold up the ideal of preserving human integrity as a point of reference and a yard-stick of value, and to know and show illusion as illusion and reality as reality. This discriminating power enabled him, too, to treat even a highly extended form of the interior monologue realistically and dramatically and to synthesize, like Chekhov, the lyric and the epic into the dramatic, to integrate the short story and the short play into a revealing and moving dramatic unity.[39]

The parallelism of Chekhov's and O'Neill's art is not so much a case of direct and immediate influence as one of typological convergence prompted by a similarity of experience, attitude, and outlook. Such a view can also be supported by the circumstance that although O'Neill became acquainted with Chekhov's works as a young man, it was chiefly in his late period, when he put up a desperate fight to search out even elementary traces of human autonomy in an alienated world, that Chekhovian traits in O'Neill's are multiplied and—as a formal, structural equivalent—the organic integration of short story-like motifs into an overall dramatic design became perfect. Thus the Chekhov-O'Neill rapport is one of the major and significant relationships in the American dramatist's international cultural contacts. At the same time, O'Neill's originality is obvious in the way in which he adopted whatever suited his own dramatic purpose in the Chekhovian trend of the drama.

NOTES

[1] Giovanni Boccaccio, *The Decameron*, translated by Richard Aldington (Garden City, 1930), pp. 51, 262, 204.

[2] Cf. Aristotle, *The Poetics*, translated with an Introduction by G. M. A. Grube, *Aristotle on Poetry and Style*. Chapters X, XI (New York, 1958), pp. 20–21.

[3] Georg Lukács, "Über die Besonderheit als Kategorie der Ästhetik," Probleme der Ästhetik, Werke, Band 10 (Neuwied und Berlin, 1969), pp. 669–786. *Die Eigenart des Ästhetischen*, Werke, Band 12, 2. Halbband (Neuwied und Berlin, 1963), pp. 226–66.

[4] Aristotle, *The Poetics*, Chapter IX, p. 20. This does not, of

course, mean that the drama excludes accidence. It only subordinates it to necessity. This is true even of tragedies (the handkerchief in *Othello*), and especially true of comedies.

⁵ Lukács, "Solzhenitsyn and the New Realism," *Marxism and Human Liberation*, edited and with an introduction by E. San Juan, Jr. (New York, 1973), pp. 199–200.

⁶ Boccaccio, p. 305.

⁷ Agnes Heller, A reneszánsz ember /Renaissance Man/ (Budapest, 1967), p. 46.

⁸ How late Renaissance Italian short stories could grow into Shakespearean plays is exemplified by tales in Cinthio's *Hecatommithi* ("Disdemona and the Moor" and "I and Epitia," the latter first dramatized by Cinthio himself) and Shakespeare's *Othello* and *Measure for Measure*.

⁹ Michael Hamburger is certainly right in pointing out that "the splendid early story, 'Das Märchen der 672. Nacht,'" is "intimately related to the poems and the playlets." Hugo von Hofmannsthal, *Poems and Verse Plays*, edited and introduced by Michael Hamburger, with a preface by T. S. Eliot (New York, 1961), p. xxxiii.

¹⁰ Lukács, pp. 198–99.

¹¹ Chekhov's fame grew gradually in the United States. 1908 saw the publication (in New Haven) of *The Cherry Garden* in the translation of Professor Max S. Mandell of Yale, who wrote an enthusiastic introduction to the text. In 1912 it was followed by a volume of *Plays* translated with an introduction by Marian Fell (New York); in presumably 1916 a second series of *Plays* was published, translated and introduced by Julius West (New York).

The Russian playwright's dramas were gradually being produced on the American stage, too. In 1905–6 Paul Orlenev included Chekhov in his program when he performed Russian plays in New York and Chicago in Russian. Productions in English of Chekhov's one act farces by Little Theatre amateur groups followed in New York and Chicago in 1913 and elsewhere quite soon. In 1915 the Washington Square Players, a group which staged O'Neill's plays, presented Chekhov's one-acters and in 1916, in a more ambitious step, performed *The Sea Gull*. Between 1920 and 1960, Eva Le Gallienne was trouping with Chekhov's plays and increased considerably the dramatist's fame.

Evidence shows that all these developments did not leave the young O'Neill untouched. While he was at Harvard in Professor G. P. Baker's English 47 Workshop (1914–15), O'Neill was often listening to the talk of a classmate, William Lawrence, a radical Russian exile "who had seen Alla Nazimova's troupe perform in New York a few years earlier." He "told O'Neill about the troupe's background . . . they presented in Russian plays by Gorky, Ibsen, Chekhov, and Dostoevski." /Arthur and Barbara Gelb, *O'Neill* (New York, 1962), p. 277. The Gelbs also describe a conversation that took place in the ramshackle saloon-hotel nicknamed "the Hell Hole," in New York, sometime in 1917, between O'Neill and "Slim" (James Joseph) Martin, another patron of the place. When Martin asked what O'Neill meant by symbolism, the young playwright exemplified the term by Chekhov's *The Cherry Orchard* and *The Sea Gull* (p. 352). In 1924 O'Neill remarked: "The most perfect plotless plays are those by Chekhov" /"O'Neill Talks About His Plays," in Oscar Cargill, N. Bryllion Fagin, and William J. Fisher (eds). *O'Neill and His Plays* (New York, 1970), p. 111/.

Critical references to the Chekhov-O'Neill relationship tend to acknowledge the significance of the similarities and parallels or meaningful contrasts to be found in the two dramatists' works. But even if appreciative and perceptive, they seem to be scanty, scarce and scattered: George Jean Nathan, "Review of the 1946 Production of *The Iceman Cometh*" (1946), in John Henry Raleigh (ed.), *Twentieth Century Interpretations of the Iceman Cometh* (Englewood Cliffs, 1968), p. 29. Henry Hewes, "Hughie" (1958), in Cargill et al., op. cit., p. 225. Timo Tiusanen, *O'Neill's Scenic Images* (Princeton, 1968), pp. 270, 337. Egil Törnqvist, *A Drama of Souls: Studies in O'Neill's Super-Naturalistic Technique* (New Haven, 1969), p. 13. Travis Bogard, *Contour in Time: The Plays of Eugene O'Neill* (New York, 1972), pp. xiii, 10, 187, 314.

12 It is remarkable that in his letter of September 8, 1891 to A. S. Suvorin, Chekhov summarizes the synopsis of a play which reads like the summary of a short story: "Death gathers men little by little, he knows what he is about. One might write a play: an old chemist invents the elixir of life—take fifteen drops and you live forever, but he breaks the phial from terror lest such carrion as himself and his wife might live forever." Chekhov, *Letters on the Short Story, the Drama and Other Literary Topics*, selected and edited by Louis Friedland (New York, 1966), p. 118.

13 Joseph Conrad, "The End of the Tether," in *Youth: a Narrative and Two Other Stories* (Leipzig, 1927), p. 279.

14 Bogard, p. 24.

[15] Conrad, p. 307.

[16] The typescript of "S.O.S." can be found in Houghton Library at Harvard University, Cambridge, Massachusetts; a photocopy is available in Bancroft Library at the University of California, Berkeley.

[17] Bogard, pp. 38–39, cf. pp. 34–42.

[18] Ibid., p. 27.

[19] Ibid., p. 52.

[20] William Godhurst, "A Literary Source for O'Neill's 'In the Zone,' " *American Literature*, XXXV (Jan. 1964), pp. 530–34.

[21] Agnes Boulton, *Part of a Long Story* (Garden City, 1958), p. 176.

[22] Ibid., p. 192.

[23] Louis Sheaffer, *O'Neill: Son and Playwright* (Boston, 1968), p. 389.

[24] Martin Lamm expresses the view that although O'Neill "has written practically nothing but plays, his gift is for narrative. The one-act plays of his youth are evocative short stories, and his mammoth dramas are half-novels." *Modern Drama* (New York, 1953), p. 325. Accepting this view is, of course, not to deny the dramatic function of the epic aspects of the plays.

[25] Henry Hewes in his review of the 1958 world premiere of *Hughie* at the Royal Dramatic Theatre in Stockholm wrote in the October 4, 1958 issue of the *Saturday Review*: O'Neill's "technique is somewhat Chekhovian, and he keeps the play happily free of any important plot." Cargill et al., *O'Neill and His Plays*, p. 225.

[26] O'Neill, *Hughie, The Later Plays of Eugene O'Neill*, edited and introduced by Travis Bogard (New York, 1967), p. 276.

[27] Ibid., p. 283, cf. p. 285.

[28] Ibid., pp. 287–88.

[29] Ibid., p. 284.

[30] Ibid., p. 286.

[31] For the short story aspect of *Hughie* compare: Arthur Gelb, "Dream and Live," *New York Times* (19 April 1959), section VII, p. 5. John Henry Raleigh, *The Plays of Eugene O'Neill* (Carbondale, 1967), pp. 212, 280.

[32] O'Neill, *Hughie, The Later Plays*, p. 263.

[33] Ibid., p. 279, cf. pp. 268, 274, 281, 282.

[34] Ibid., p. 280.

[35] Ibid., p. 285.

[36] N. G. Chernyshevsky, "L. N. Tolstoy, Dyetstvo i otroche-

stvo," 1856, "Voyennye rasskazy," 1856, *Izbrannie literaturno-kriticheskie, statyi* (Moscow, 1953), pp. 291–95.

[37] Chekhov, *The Sea Gull* (translated by Constance Garnett), *Nine Plays of Chekov* (sic!) (New York, 1973), p. 53.

[38] Ibid.

[39] Besides the convergence or coincidence of the turning point of the short stories and the culminating point of the one-acter, three other forms of integrating the short story into the dramatic pattern are conspicuous in Chekhov's and O'Neill's plays:

1. The cascade—connection of short story-oriented dramatic units in multiple-act plays (Chekhov's *Platonov* and *Ivanov* and O'Neill's *Servitude* and *A Moon for the Misbegotten* as well as a number of other plays betraying naturalistic, symbolistic, romantic and expressionistic influences).

2. Building up the conflict of a multiple-act play with a short story-like turn at the dramatic zenith (Chekhov: *The Sea Gull* and *Uncle Vanya*; O'Neill: *A Touch of the Poet*).

3. Total integration in a mosaic structure (Chekhov: *Three Sisters* and *The Cherry Orchard*; O'Neill: *The Iceman Cometh* growing out from the early short story "Tomorrow," and *Long Day's Journey into Night*.)

O'NEILL PRODUCTIONS IN HUNGARY
1928 TO 1978*

1928   *The Hairy Ape* (A szörös majom)
        Uj Színpad, Budapest

1929   *Strange Interlude* (Különös közjáték)
        Vígszínház, Budapest

1934   *Ah, Wilderness!* (Ifjúság)
        Vígszínház, Budapest

1937   *Mourning Becomes Electra* (Amerikai Elektra)
        Nemzeti Színház, Budapest

        Days Without End (Mindörökké)
        Vígszínház, Budapest

* List compiled by András Benedek, Dramaturgist of the Hungarian National Theatre.

1946   *Desire Under the Elms* (Vágy a szilfák alatt)
        Nemzeti Színház, Budapest

1947   *Anna Christie* (Anna Christie)
        Pesti Színház, Budapest

1963   *Long Day's Journey into Night* (Hosszú út az éjszakába)
        Nemzeti Színház, Budapest

        Mourning Becomes Electra (Amerikai Elektra)
        Vígszínház, Budapest

1964   *Mourning Becomes Electra* (Amerikai Elektra)
        Nemzeti Színház, Pécs

        Desire Under the Elms (Vágy a szilfák alatt)
        Katona József Színház, Budapest

1965   *Hughie* (Ejszakai portás)
        Irodalmi Színpad, Budapest

1966   *A Moon for the Misbegotten* (Boldogtalan hold)
        Szigligeti Színház, Szolnok

1967   *More Stately Mansions* (Költö és üzlete)
        Nemzeti Színház, Pécs

        Mourning Becomes Electra (Amerikai Elektra)
        Csokonai Színház, Debrecen

1968   *Mourning Becomes Electra* (Amerikai Elektra)
        Kisfaludy Színház, Györ

        A Touch of the Poet (Egy igazi úr)
        József Attila Színház, Budapest

1969   *Long Day's Journey into Night* (Hosszú út az éjszakába)
        Csokonai Színház, Debrecen

1970   *Mourning Becomes Electra* (Amerikai Elektra)
        Nemzeti Színház, Miskolc

        Long Day's Journey into Night (Hosszú út az éjszakába)
        Szigligeti Színház, Szolnok

1971   *The Iceman Cometh* (Eljö a jeges)
        Vígszínház, Budapest

1973   *Marco Millions* (Marco Polo milliói)
        Nemzeti Színház, Pécs

1974   *A Touch of the Poet* (Egy igazi úr)
        Katona József Színház, Kecskemét

Desire Under the Elms (Vágy a szilfák alatt)
József Attila Színház, Budapest

1975 *A Moon for the Misbegotten* (Boldogtalan hold)
Katona József Színház, Kecskemét

1977 *Long Day's Journey into Night* (Hosszú út az éjszakába)
Pesti Színház, Budapest

1978 *Strange Interlude* (Különös közjáték)
Nemzeti Színház, Budapest

Long Day's Journey into Night (Hosszú út az éjszakába)
Vígszínház, Budapest

ONE HUNDRED PERCENT AMERICAN TRAGEDY
A Soviet View

Maya Koreneva

The development of American literature at the beginning of the twentieth century was profoundly influenced by the social upheavals of the period among which World War I and the Russian Revolution are of utmost importance. American art was revitalized by great social changes and, as a result, American writers paid more attention to the fundamental principles on which society was based, striving to explore the roots of conditions at the time when mankind was facing annihilation. On the other hand, the evolution of American literature in the 1910s and 1920s was marked by a search for values that could help the individual resist the dictates of a hostile world—those values that would be opposed to the norms of stagnant bourgeois society whose spiritual sterility was becoming increasingly obvious. Few American artists of this period could repeat Isadora Duncan's words: "Adieu, Old World! I would hail a New World."[1] But the intensity of their search, in its turn, inevitably made their attitude toward society more and more critical and widened the horizons of American literature.

American drama was not untouched by the great changes that characterized the country's artistic life at that time and was itself undergoing the most important phase of its development—its formation as a branch of national literature (drama meant then O'Neill primarily). By this time American literature had so matured that there was no longer any need for its critics to take an apologetic stance about its level of sophistication as compared with the literature of Europe. Moreover, processes going on in its depths prepared its rise in a not so distant future that was to ensure it a leading role in the years between the First and Second World Wars. Emergence of American drama was, as a matter of fact, a part of this rise, opening new perspectives before it. This, naturally, made the situation extremely difficult for the newborn drama since only sufficiently well-developed literary forms could be equal to demands it had to satisfy. The latter did not impede the progress of drama but rather encouraged it, virtually stimulating its striving for perfection.

Like his great contemporaries F. Scott Fitzgerald, T. S. Eliot, Theodore Dreiser, Wallace Stevens, and later on Faulkner, Hemingway, and Wolfe, who explored the possibilities within other literary forms, O'Neill presented the America of his day in his plays. The scope of problems treated in his dramas even during one decade was indeed remarkable. The dramatist seemed to touch on every aspect of American life, and each play meant a discovery, a new achievement of American theatre as a whole. Among the subjects O'Neill chose to present in his dramas are social injustice and the conflict of races, which the playwright delineated in a highly original form; the conflict of capital and labor, to borrow a term from sociology; the problem of "man versus machine," growing ever more significant as America progressed along purely industrial lines; and the tragedy of a world war. A theme the playwright appears to be preoccupied with, for it recurs in O'Neill's dramas of different periods, is the hostility of bourgeois society, imposing dull utilitarianism through the tyranny of the moneybag, to art and artist, to the spiritual aspirations of man in general.

Of special importance for O'Neill's dramatic world is his tragic view of life. Neither in reality, as he saw it, nor in the future, which he envisioned for America, did the playwright discern anything that could resist the pressure of a hostile world or triumph over it in the end. Therefore, despite the variety in presentation of the conflict in particular plays, there is always man's clash with the world, fate, life at the center of O'Neill's drama in which man is almost always doomed to defeat.

Critics often accused O'Neill of groundless pessimism, of deliberate distortion of American life, of unjustified concentration on its dark aspects and gross exaggeration. As far back as 1922, in connection with the production of *The Hairy Ape*, a polemic took place between the playwright and a critic who asserted that tragedy was incompatible with the American character. Protesting his view of American life and history, O'Neill said:

> Suppose some day we should suddenly see with the clear eyes of a soul the true valuation of all our triumphant brass band materialism; should see the cost—and the result in terms of eternal verities! What a colossal, one hundred percent American tragedy that would be. . . . Tragedy not native to our soil? Why, we are tragedy, the most appalling yet written or unwritten![2]

Years later in an interview in 1946, when he was asked about his cycle *A Tale of Possessors, Self-Dispossessed*, O'Neill said that it depicted the "drive toward material progress and the spiritual degeneration of the American people" and added:

> I am going on the theory that the United States, instead of being the most successful country in the world is the greatest failure. It is the greatest failure because it was given everything, more than any other country. Through moving as rapidly as it has, it has never acquired any real roots. Its main idea is that everlasting game of trying to possess your own soul by the possession of something outside of it, too.[3]

These statements, made years apart, show that the playwright maintained such views throughout his life. It may be worth examining what he considered to be the cause of American tragedy. For him, it was neglect of spiritual values due to the subordination to base purposes of a materialistically oriented society. O'Neill's view of reality determined his artistic aim as such; the dramatist saw it as creation of modern tragedy. He tried to realize it in his earliest significant plays—a group of one-act sea plays of 1916–17, the *Glencairn* cycle. The first performance of one of these, *Bound East for Cardiff*, by the Provincetown Players on July 28, 1916, may be regarded literally as the birth of American drama.

O'Neill uses somber colors for his picture of hard seafaring life, of the troubles and burdens sailors have to bear day after day. Their wearisome labor and severe hardships are intensified by an oppressive fear of the unknown. Tension caused by the constant presence of danger is relieved in violent outbursts, fights, and riots. O'Neill does not try to make life more beautiful, nor his characters nicer or nobler. Yet there is not the slightest condescension, typical of a bourgeois attitude to people of lower strata, in his portrayal of a poverty-stricken, utterly helpless and ignorant man of the masses driven entirely by instincts. The playwright does not make a snobbish judgment about his rough characters endowed with primitive, purely animal emotions. Thus, O'Neill's approach to the central object of art—man— was truly innovative from the very beginning. That was what allowed American drama to make the gigantic leap that took it over the abyss dividing craftsmanship and art. He rejected the restrictive principle of separating "lofty" things from "low" ones and thus relieved American drama of its fear of life. Without any doubt, the freedom it acquired was due largely to O'Neill's introduction of the aesthetics of realism into American theatre.

But it was not only the gloomy, the ugly, the terrible which he could see and depict. He appreciated the beauty of natural human relations, recognizing the eternal value not subject to inflation of such qualities as courage, vigor, honesty, compassion and camaraderie hidden under a rough surface. The wonderful objectivity of an artist who embraced principles of realism also manifested itself in this approach. For O'Neill, ideals of justice and beauty were not empty words, but he looked for them in life itself, not outside it. That is why his sea plays are not mere sketches of ugly everyday existence; that is why the cycle itself reaches its peak in *The*

Moon of the Caribbees, full of poetry rarely seen on the stage and showing the truly humane nature of O'Neill's work.

O'Neill displays great virtuosity in characterization, all the more astonishing in a young playwright since he could have but a limited space at his disposal, considering the number of characters. Individual portraits reveal accurately grasped and carefully chosen psychological, social, and national features. Taken together, his cast of sailors represents a live, organic, and dynamic single unit. However, the dramatist treats them *en masse,* as parts of the crowd. With all their individual characteristics, the individual himself has not yet separated from his environment; on the contrary, it is in the environment that he is most fully realized. Hence, in the sea plays, the emergence of the protagonist was impossible in principle, although the characters, of course, differ widely in vividness of presentation; and their individual features are far from identical.

What makes O'Neill's first tragedy so specific and original is that his tragic vision is embodied not in the individual fate of the protagonist but in the common lot of the whole group. Thus, O'Neill has come to express in his sea cycle what one may call the idea of *universality* of tragedy, something not quite understood at that time. In the young playwright's dramas, the idea itself could not yet be realized in its ideal or final form. O'Neill made it an integral part of his dramatic structure, but he excluded the individual from his picture of reality—which is why his early plays could not be said to have reached great psychological insights or philosophical depths. The playwright was most effective in conveying his tragic vision through the atmosphere he created on the stage. His last and greatest plays, *Long Day's Journey into Night* and *The Iceman Cometh,* were to become a perfect embodiment of the idea of *universal tragedy.* It took O'Neill a lifetime to discover the route that brought him to them.

As for the plays that followed the sea cycle, it seems that the playwright chose to forget his discovery, for he moved in the opposite direction. Nothing in them appears to remind us of the principle of universal tragedy on which the sea cycle

was based. This impression, however, is somewhat mis-
leading. It is, indeed, the individual who is placed at the
center of such plays as *Beyond the Horizon* (1918), *The
Emperor Jones* (1920), *The Hairy Ape* (1921) and *All God's
Chillun Got Wings* (1923); and the action of each play is
concentrated on the tragic fate of its protagonist. Each is a
work of art complete in itself; but, if regarded in the context
of all O'Neill's plays, they may be said to represent psychological studies on a grand scale, becoming significant stages in
the playwright's progress toward the form suitable for his
concept of modern tragedy.

In defining these plays as "psychological studies," I do
not mean in the least that they are devoid of social significance
or that they take no notice of the problems which contemporary life forced literature to confront. Quite to the contrary, smashing conventions of the commercial theatre, which
had a middle-class mentality, O'Neill boldly introduced into
American drama new aspects of social reality. The ruin of
farmers, racial and social inequality, distressing conditions
the working man was forced to accept—being doomed to
tedious, cheerless labor while others who produced nothing
enjoyed its fruit—these are the themes O'Neill has the honor
of bringing to the American stage and audiences for the first
time. But his historical achievement is not limited to this
pioneer role, to his discovery of themes and conflicts revealing
the true character of American society, although this alone
would have been enough to secure him a permanent place
in the annals of national drama. Of no less importance is his
profound artistic grasp of reality.

The depth and originality of O'Neill's insight are, in
fact, the result of his highly critical attitude toward American
society. Thus the protagonists of such plays as *The Emperor
Jones* or *All God's Chillun* are presented as victims of a
society where blacks must remain pariahs or outcasts forever.
The playwright denounces the fundamental injustice of the
social order that his characters confront and depicts it as the
main source of tragedy. But the tragedy of Jones or that of
Jim and Ella demands, implicitly, a change of social order;
for the plays assert racial equality as the *only* principle com-

patible with truly humane values and norms, although
O'Neill's disillusionment with America left him with little
hope about the possibilities of social progress.

What should be noted is that O'Neill, apparently, was
not satisfied with the assertion of the ideal through implication, that is, through the negation of what *was*. It is possible
to speak in certain cases about a direct presentation of the
ideal in his dramatic construction. Let us consider but two
examples. O'Neill chose to begin *All God's Chillun Got
Wings* with children on the stage, which puzzled directors;
the presence of children in an "adult" cast often proves to be
a great obstacle. Critics were also bewildered by "the untidy
and unnecessary first scene."[4] But O'Neill did not include it
as an unaccountable whimsy or as a result of some gross
error of judgment. Neither can one quite agree with R. B.
Heilman, who believes that elements of this kind appear in
dramatic compositions because modern drama betrays tendencies characteristic of the novel, striving to incorporate
inherent qualities of epic forms alien to drama.[5] The playwright seems to have had other reasons to include this scene
in the play; it embodies the ideal he contrasts with reality
and contains the moral statement he wished his audiences to
draw from the play. The scene presents black and white
children playing together. While their relations are far from
idyllic, it is the ideal, not the idyll that interests O'Neill. Like
any children, they quarrel, fight, and mock each other. Yet,
they are free from what spoils the relations of their elders
in similar situations. The scene takes place before their "fall,"
before they join a society governed by prejudices. They are
not aware yet of the ways with which one can humiliate the
other by insulting his racial pride. Thus, the contrast between the opening scene where human relations are drawn in
their natural state and other scenes of the play serves to emphasize the unnatural character of existing social norms, to
stress the corruption of values in society, on the one hand,
and to make the ideal graphically clear, on the other.

The final scene of the play confirms that the episode it
begins with may and must be taken as the expression of the
ideal. Here Ella is depicted as a woman who has been driven

insane by the racism of a ruthless society, and she instinctively goes back to the games of her childhood when her love for black Jim did not appear criminal to her playmates. But the natural relations open to children are beyond the characters' grasp when they grow up. Ella can return to them only through madness when she *imagines* herself as a little girl. But now their love becomes impossible—from now on it will always be an adult's concern for a hopelessly sick child.

A similar principle of presenting the ideal is used in *The Hairy Ape*, which opens with a scene in the firemen's forecastle. A visual image of the caged condition of the stokers, corresponding to the dramatic solution of the central conflict of the play, is given in the description of the setting ("the ceiling crushes down upon the men's heads," "imprisoned by white steel," "the steel framework of a cage"[6]). The emphasis is obviously on the stokers' humility, on the inhuman conditions they are forced to live in, their postures physically projecting their oppression by society.

During the quarrel between the stokers, three points are made that correspond to their different attitudes toward their position in society. They form the play's conceptual field of force. Long, a socialist, encourages his companions to fight against capitalists, explaining to them what evils are brought about by exploitation of workers, which is at the root of all the great commercial empires. Paddy, who used to be a sailor on a sailing ship, believes labor has lost its beauty and dignity on a streamer with its smoke and dirt; it degrades and humiliates man, for he has become a servant of the machine. Paddy speaks, in fact, about the social phenomenon described by Marx as the alienation of labor. Paddy sees it as a simple opposition of man and machine.

Both these views are rejected by the protagonist of the play, Yank, as an indication of cowardice: with Paddy, the weakling, it is the fear of the machine, which he, a man of olden times, cannot handle; with Long, it is the fear of capitalists, who, as Yank believes, are nothing more than "baggage" that one need not take into consideration. Yank is sure he and his fellow workers are better men than the first-class passengers. He thinks labor is the source of all the riches in the world and the basis of his superiority. The earth does not "belong" to those who possess ("dem boids don't amount to nothin' "[7]) but to those who work. The uselessness of the rich, whose presence is not even necessary to "run dis tub," is juxtaposed with the pride of a man whose hands will make the whole world move. It is expressed with utmost clarity in Yank's great speech in the opening scene of the play:

> Hell in de stokehole? Sure! It takes a man to work in hell. . . . It's me makes it move! . . . I'm at de bottom, get me! Dere ain't nothin' foither. I'm de end! I'm de start! I start somep'n and de woild moves! . . . I'm de ting in coal dat makes it boin; I'm steam and oil for de engines, . . . I'm de ting in gold dat makes it money! And I'm what makes iron into steel! . . . Slaves, hell! We run de whole woiks. All de rich guys dat tink day're somep'n, dey ain't nothin'! Dey don't belong. But us guys, we're in de move, we're at de bottom, de whole ting is us![8]

By the end of the soliloquy, the individual "self" of the protagonist is transformed into the collective self of working people. Yank turns into a figure acquiring monumental proportions, exhibiting a great affinity with both the cosmic "I" of Whitman's poetry and heroes of folk legends.

But this natural order—which Yank believes to be the only proper one, for it alone is in accord with what, for him, is the true state of things—is perverted in bourgeois society. To be "at de bottom" does not mean to be "de start" or a sort of demiurge; it means rather to be stuck at the base of the social ladder without any hope of ever rising in the world, to be trampled on, being fully aware of one's strength, and to possess nothing while creating all. When Yank hears what Mildred, a steel king's daughter, thinks of him and of his buddies, whom she regards as the scum of the human race, as creatures almost subhuman, when he sees her instinctive fear of them, he is stunned because he suddenly realizes that his idea of the world has nothing in common with the actual world, that in reality everything is turned upside down. The world is run by those who are "just baggage," whereas those who are "at de bottom" have to do nothing but play the pitiful part of machine slaves. The source of the tragedy, therefore, is a monstrous social injustice.

The nature of O'Neill's drama was perfectly understood by Alexander Taïrov, who was the first to make Soviet theatre acquainted with the work of the American playwright. His brilliant productions of such plays as *The Hairy Ape* (1926), *Desire Under the Elms* (1926), and *All God's Chillun Got Wings* (1929—it was entitled *The Negro* at the Kamerny Theatre), which O'Neill—who saw them in Paris—greatly admired, are still the best interpretations of O'Neill's drama on the Russian stage. It was, undoubtedly, the dramatist's concentration on the foremost issues of the day that attracted Taïrov in the first place. Both the playwright and the theatre strove to embody on the stage the world around them with its real dramas and tragedies; that is why the paths they followed crossed. They seemed to have had "this date with each other from the very beginning." Unaware of each other's existence, they were brought together by the course of their respective development. The theatre owed it to the playwright as much as he to the theatre that the convergence was a tremendous success.

Taïrov viewed his production of *Desire Under the Elms* as inevitable and said:

> . . . if the play did not exist it should have been invented, so fully is it in accord with the two factors on which we now build up our theatrical work. Firstly, we need plays on great and concrete problems. Secondly, we need such dramatic material which would allow us to establish on the stage the true fundamental principles of the new concrete realism. O'Neill answers these requirements splendidly in his *Desire Under the Elms*.[9]

Fortunately, the play did not have to be invented. O'Neill's dramas satisfied perfectly the innermost needs of Taïrov and his company, who were striving after reality. Based on contemporary life and depicting its most vital social conflicts, these plays helped the Kamerny Theatre to comprehend more profoundly and to establish on its stage what Taïrov called the principles "of a concentrated realism which alone can claim to become the true style of our epoch:"[10] (it is "a concentrated concrete realism" in another manuscript[11]). It is significant that in his attempt to master principles of realism, Taïrov regarded O'Neill as his ally and not as his opponent, whereas critics stressed mainly those aspects that allowed them to interpret the dramatist's work as being opposed to realism.

It was a difficult, even a crucial, period for the company. There was a great danger in its enthusiasm for the aesthetics of theatricality, which could make them lose touch with life and confine them to the fantastic world of the play. Acquaintance with O'Neill's drama had a beneficial effect on the company. O'Neill's dramatic world brought to the theatre a hot breath of nonfictitious passions and an awareness of the sufferings of man, ruthlessly crushed by the social mechanism of bourgeois society. The accuracy with which the social parameters of the dramatic action were projected ensured the great success of O'Neillean productions at the Kamerny Theatre in the first place. Following exactly the track of the dramatic material in *All God's Chillun*, Taïrov put "a severe malady of racial hatred and antagonism," "the tragedy of the white and black races"[12] at the center of his production. In discussing *Desire Under the Elms*, he said: "The principal accused one is, of course, the possessive instinct, the very institution of ownership which gives rise to abnormal relations between people."[13] The director's understanding of the conflict fully coincides with O'Neill's own interpretation of the play as "a tragedy of the possessive—the pitiful longing of man to build his own heaven here on earth by glutting his sense of power with ownership of land, people, money."[14] The affinity of their views of the conflict is especially important because Taïrov did not and could not know O'Neill's statement; his interpretation was based on a close reading of the work itself.

At the same time, while working on O'Neill's plays, Taïrov was quite aware of the fact that he did not deal with reality as such, but with reality transformed by the author's subjective vision. His concern was not merely the interpretation but also the forms and techniques used for its projection on the stage. Acknowledging the dramatist's right to be subjective, Taïrov's company reserved this privilege for itself, too. Taïrov believed, and with good reason, that the role of theatre cannot be restricted merely to a faithful reproduction on the stage of a play's "text" or a dramatist's conception (this would mean, for him, an utterly passive attitude). While he worked on the repertoire of O'Neill's plays, he felt it was necessary to juxtapose the author's vision with his own view of reality. This double perspective should, in his opinion, bring forth a distinctly new and original work of art—a stage production.

Certainly, this approach is not quite safe since an interpretation of a play can deviate so far from it that the director's conception may run counter to that of the author's. But, despite certain changes—the most radical one was Ella's death at the end of Taïrov's production of *All God's Chillun* (as far as we know, the playwright who saw it did not object to this liberty taken by the theatre)—one can say that, in this particular case, the theatre brought its vision in line with O'Neill's conception; it did not adjust the author to its own criteria.

Taïrov's analysis of methods and principles that he used in his work on O'Neill's plays is of great interest in this respect. He spoke of them in 1931 in his lectures on the Kamerny Theatre's methods when he touched, among other things, upon the impact of a phenomenon that can be witnessed in life and in its theatrical counterpart. Thus, he said in connection with *The Hairy Ape*:

> What we saw on the steamer is reality. What took place at the theatre is an image of reality which is the result of our subjective idea of this reality, and the latter has grown out of a number of perceptions of this reality. . . . but besides that there was also a subjective attitude toward this reality. This subjective attitude reflects the unbearableness of [forced] labor, the horror of this kind of labor, the social injustice that characterizes the condition of man . . . i.e. a number of factors which determined our subjective view of this reality, and *we expressed it in an image of this reality*

*which represented the essence of our idea. The image, in
effect, proved to be much more impressive than reality; the
organized image of reality proved to be more impressive,
precisely because it was organized, because we had taken the
essence of the phenomenon, the essence of reality;* moreover,
if you consider the cross-section of the whole setting of *The
Hairy Ape*, with the stokehole, the cages of the firemen's
forecastle having neither light, nor air, and the blue promenade deck with the blue expanse around it where the girl
and her aunt are, you will see that here our setting is already
transformed into an image of the environment that exists
in subjective reality, i.e. an image expressing our subjective
view of this reality which manifested itself in the dispro-
portion between the firemen's premises and the upper deck
[author's italics].[15]

It is easy to see that the director's interpretation, including his treatment of the stage space, corresponds to the
author's conception and develops in plastic images the
imagery built up by the playwright by means of drama
(action) as well as of the narrative (stage directions). It was
not, however, only the affinity of their views of reality that
brought the playwright and the company together. O'Neill
and the Kamerny Theatre also had much in common as far
as their specifically artistic aims were concerned; the goal
of both was to create modern tragedy.

As has been mentioned previously, O'Neill tried to
realize this objective first in his "cycle" of sea plays. In his
dramas of the first period following the "sea cycle" up to
Desire Under the Elms, it is in the sphere of individual consciousness that, in contrast to it, the tragic is embodied. In
these plays the tragic is the extent of deformation of consciousness under the pressure of the hostile environment. This
deformation is eventually the cause of the individual's destruction. The shift of the center of gravity to the individual's
consciousness changes the structure of O'Neill's drama. The
protagonist emerges out of the masses that represent man in
the "sea cycle." The tragedy loses its universal characteristics
and becomes the protagonist's own personal tragedy, al-

though, despite the individualization of his character, he exemplifies in the tragic conflict all the victims of social injustice.

The principal means of characterization in the plays of this period is the interior monologue. Of greatest interest, perhaps, is its structure in *The Emperor Jones*, for it provides an understanding of the main principles of this kind of monologue in O'Neill's drama—principles the playwright was to use in all his later works. As a matter of fact, the whole play—except the opening scene, which is an extensive exposition, and its final episode (an epilogue)—unfolds as a continuous interior monologue of the protagonist who declared himself the emperor of an island and later tried to escape the punishment that the islanders who rebelled had in store for him. Its consecutive episodes represent stages of disintegration of Jones's consciousness. Though the core of the play's action is precisely the attempt to escape it, his inner voice convinces Jones that the revenge for the cruelty with which he ruled over the island is inevitable. This arouses Jones's fear, enhanced by expectation of punishment for crimes he had committed earlier. The inner consciousness of his own guilt turns his escape into a race inside the vicious circle, at the end of which the day of reckoning awaits him.

O'Neill, however, does not characterize Jones only as a criminal who is condemned by his own conscience. Were it so, there would be no tragedy at all. Like Lear, he could say: "I am a man/More sinned against than sinning." The "sin" of others is, in O'Neill's interpretation, first and foremost, the social evil that condemned him, America's black son, to eternal torments by injustice and humiliation. The protagonist's consciousness mirrors the ambivalence of his position as a tyrant and usurper, as a criminal awaiting a just revenge for the wrong he had done, as well as a victim who is to be avenged in the name of supreme justice. To emphasize this, the playwright does not simply re-create the protagonist's past but expands his personal experience and personal history by connecting it with the history of American black people. For this he introduces elements of collective memory which bring to life scenes from the past that Jones did not and could not experience himself: the slave auction episode, the scene on board a ship carrying its live cargo of blacks to America. The crimes, committed by whites against his people and kept alive for him by the memory of his ancestors, have become that social and psychological reality which determines the protagonist's consciousness and behavior. In accordance with Jones's character, the playwright transforms the recollections into a number of visual images; if organized verbally these images would have violated the psychological authenticity of the character. Jones does not have the mental and verbal ability to express all the intricate associations, connecting his personal story with the history of his people. But he has a rich imagination; and visionary scenes, flashing through his inflamed mind, brilliantly convey both his mental processes and his psychic state. At the same time, they increase the dramatic tension emphasizing the protagonist's inability to control his thoughts; and this, in turn, drives Jones to his tragic end.

The ambivalence of the protagonist's position has other consequences as well. It is the cause of that split in his consciousness which, under the influence of fear, leads to the disintegration of his personality. Yet, fear is but a catalyst, not the cause of his deterioration. In conformity with his double role, Jones's consciousness is not integral or monolithic. It is presented in a state of dialogue, and the sides he takes are diametrically opposed to each other and even irreconcilable. The extremes between which his consciousness operates are viewed as absolutes; therefore, its integrity can never be restored. This accounts for the fierce never-ending struggle going on in Jones's heart, for his frantic rushes back and forth from one extreme to the other. Beginning with this, a similar mental rushing back and forth becomes the principal means of projecting psychological reality in O'Neill's plays.

O'Neill's tragic hero since *The Emperor Jones* is presented in a state of continuous dispute with himself. Taking both sides simultaneously, he contradicts himself, endlessly bringing forward new arguments and repudiating what he insisted on just a moment ago. The playwright does nothing to weaken these contrasts or to make the changes of the protagonist's mind and mood less sharp and sudden. Moreover, he deliberately stresses the impossibility of bringing into harmony the extremes of Jones's consciousness, torn by contradictory impulses, by the struggle between human aspirations and antihuman norms imposed by his environment. The contrasts are, in fact, made harsher, showing the increasing disintegration of the hero's personality, and this leaves no chance for crowning the play with a "happy ending."

The depiction of the protagonist's consciousness, maintaining a dialogue with itself, is obviously connected with the Doppelgänger theme in romantic literature. The influence of romantic traditions on O'Neill's works has been studied in detail. But at the same time, it is necessary to bear in mind that the multifariousness and changeability of the individual's personality, maintaining its identity in the very changes it undergoes, which correspond to the real contradictions in human nature, are one of the cornerstones of realism. Therefore, as far as psychological reality is concerned, O'Neill's dramatic world should be regarded not only from the standpoint of its connections with the aesthetics of romanticism, but with that of realism as well, and primarily so.

One more change may be observed in O'Neill's plays that is connected with the emergence of the protagonist: the appearance of the antagonist who has no counterpart in the sea plays. Yet it would be useless to look for him among the characters of the plays. O'Neill did not personify him, did not create the "villain" who is at the root of the tragic action. The antagonist is neither a personality nor even a person, and this shows once again the true originality of the playwright's dramatic vision. The antagonist is the environment, the hostile world, the reality of bourgeois society as the playwright saw it in twentieth-century America. This solution demonstrated a great audacity on the part of the author that enabled him to deal effectively with the most vital problems of his time, enlarging the range and scope of his artistic vision.

The characters who represent or belong to the hostile

environment, whoever or whatever they may be—"the steel king" Douglas and his daughter Mildred or the fashionable crowd on Fifth Avenue in *The Hairy Ape*; the prison guard, the auctioneer, and the southern planters at the slave market in *The Emperor Jones*; or the people who reside in black and white quarters, respectively, in *All God's Chillun*—are all insignificant, "secondary" figures without identities. That is why the blows, which Yank strikes right and left so brutally, hurt nobody. He comes to Fifth Avenue to have a fight with his enemy, but he does not understand that actually he is revolting against the present social order and not against the wealthy well-dressed ladies and gentlemen, who can ignore this riotous disturber of the peace as long as his actions are directed just against them personally.

In a sense, the antagonist may be regarded in these plays as the result of a certain split in the form of universal tragedy as it was represented in the sea plays. The protagonist is a personality in the first place, and everything about him is aimed at the utmost individualization of his character. In contrast, the antagonist is utterly impersonal; he is something aggregated, typical, stereotyped as opposed to the individual. They are juxtaposed in the conflict and, similarly, the methods of their characterization are entirely different. The protagonist's character is evolved by means of psychological analysis; the delineation of the environment, on the other hand, is emphatically devoid of psychological dimension. It is standardized in all its aspects or, in other words, regulated by society's ideological conventions fixed in the form of its written and unwritten laws.

Accordingly, the protagonist is a three-dimensional figure, whose evolution is essential for his portrayal; he is associated with movement through time. Movement through space is its visual stage equivalent, invariably symbolizing the passage of time, which produces fatal changes in the hero's consciousness, as is exemplified by Jones's wandering in the woods at night, Yank's traversing the city, or Jim and Ella's traveling between two continents. The hostile world is flat and static and admits no movement or change in principle. These are different worlds, in the true sense of the word; they have nothing in common, thus making the destruction of the protagonist, powerless before the omnipotent society and its mass attacks, inevitable.

Yet, the form of the individual's tragedy, which O'Neill developed successively in *Beyond the Horizon, The Emperor Jones, The Hairy Ape,* and *All God's Chillun,* did not quite satisfy him. *Desire Under the Elms* (1924) was his first attempt to synthesize the two forms of tragedy by combining the individual's tragedy with the universal tragedy. In this play, the protagonist's position is shared now by three characters, thus embracing, in effect, everybody involved, as did the sea plays. Old Cabot, Eben, and Abbie are each entitled to claim the part, although the prominence of the other two characters renders its attribution to any one of them impossible. Yet, unlike what we saw in the sea plays, their characters are projected from within. Delineation of changes, taking place in their hearts and minds through their involvement with the conflict, plays the most important part in the development of the dramatic action. The depth of psychological characteristics attained in *Desire Under the Elms* can be attributed to O'Neill's bold experiments in characterization in the individual's tragedy which preceded it. Although the playwright uses now a different dramatic structure, the technique of the interior monologue, conveying the individual's inner struggle, maintains its essential features, described previously with reference to *The Emperor Jones.*

The form of the universal tragedy required, in its turn, a different arrangement of characters in relation to the central conflict. As in the sea plays, it was impossible to bring the protagonist and antagonist face to face since the latter was not personified or objectified in any of the characters in *Desire Under the Elms.* This is what makes the play different from the individual's tragedy, where the antagonist is represented by a certain group of characters embodying the hostile environment. The other characters of the play are only a background. They are neither victims of the tragedy nor part of the antagonistic world. Uninvolved in the action of the conflict but by no means disinterested witnesses, they have not the slightest impact upon the course of events.

Once again the tragedy is a natural result of life itself, in whose treatment one can clearly distinguish contours of bourgeois society with its acquisitive mentality, which poisoned the protagonists' consciousness, making them thirst for possessions, and thus deprived them of the possibility of having genuinely human relations. This interpretation of "life" as the primary source of tragedy, more than anything else, is what brings O'Neill's tragedy close to the classical Greek tragedy (for instance, the use of elements of classical myth in the plot of *Mourning Becomes Electra*, 1931).

The fact that the action of *Desire Under the Elms* takes place in the middle of the nineteenth century is extremely important for understanding the further evolution of O'Neill's art. Trying to create modern tragedy, the playwright found he could synthesize the two forms, which he developed, only on the basis of historical material. The next phase was marked by his return to contemporary themes and subjects. The form of the individual's tragedy returned with them, too. But it did not simply return; it came back transformed, showing now traces of the influence of the universal tragedy and a certain tendency to synthesize the forms.

It is possible to describe this form as the individual's tragedy because the center of such plays as *The Great God Brown* (1925), *Strange Interlude* (1927), and *Dynamo* (1928) is still the tragic fate of the protagonist. Psychological analysis is again the principle means of developing individual characterizations, though the playwright uses different devices in each particular case. His ingenuity is truly amazing. Not confining himself to what he discovered in *The Emperor Jones* or *The Hairy Ape*, he now introduces masks in *The Great God Brown*. Symbolizing the split of the protagonist's consciousness, the mask is its outward manifestation that fixes his crisis of identity in a visual image. With the mask, different aspects and qualities of the personality become autonomous, showing that, in the hero's mind, the centrifugal forces prevailed. The same goal is achieved in *Strange Interlude* by means of the sharp contrast between the dialogue and the stream of consciousness. The personality is identical to itself in neither of these qualities and aspects, nor even in all of them taken together, for the sum is not equal to the harmonious whole. But the individual can never recover it, for what produced the disintegration lies outside him. Its root cause is social reality, over which the individual has no power.

At the same time—undoubtedly under the influence of the concept of universal tragedy—the antagonist disappears from the plays of this period never to return again. The environment is now presented as a background, which, though not quite indifferent to the protagonist's fate, cannot be regarded as a force driving him to destruction. If one tries to identify the conflict of any single play of this period with the collision between the protagonist and any other character, the tragedy will inevitably lose its scope, and the comprehensive vision of reality will be reduced to a fragmentary view of the given events.

It is *The Great God Brown* that is most likely to become the object of this kind of interpretation. The conflict of the play appears to be the one between Dion Anthony, the architect, a vulnerable man of artistic disposition, and Billy Brown, the businessman, who exploits Dion's talent. Yet the playwright's concept is much larger in scope. Although he uses the two types of consciousness to reproduce the central conflict—the nonconformist consciousness of the artist and the conformist middle-class mentality of the businessman— the dividing line does not pass between Billy and Dion. O'Neill created the tragedy of the artist in a spiritually sterile society, and the artist's antagonist is not the simple-minded, pitiful Billy, but the society itself. This is emphasized by Dion's use of the mask. He can take it off only when he is alone or with Cybel, which is, in essence, the same thing; for she is the symbol of Mother Earth. Nobody else accepts his true "self." In this treatment of the world around him there are traces of the interpretation of the environment as the antagonist as in *The Emperor Jones* or *All God's Chillun*. On the other hand, the use of masks by all the central characters (nobody can be what he or she really is) shows the play's connection with the forms of universal tragedy.

This tendency is especially clear in the characterization of Billy Brown, who, after Dion's death, assumes the protagonist's position in the second part of the play. This moment, whose interpretation presents a certain difficulty, can be regarded as the introduction of elements of universal tragedy into the individual's tragedy. The result is not the synthesis of the two forms that we have in *Desire Under the Elms* but a combination of certain elements that are not harmonized. From the point of view of the individual's tragedy, which already has the protagonist (Dion), Billy can be placed either in the group of characters who represent the hostile world as in the earlier plays or of those who form the background, as in *Desire Under the Elms*. From the point of view of universal tragedy, however, the loss of identity embodied in Billy who, under other conditions, could have otherwise realized his human potential, is also its legitimate object. Although the motive can be found in the first part of the play, where it is connected with the "Great Pan is dead"[16] variation on the "God is dead" theme, it is expressly brought to the fore in its latter part. O'Neill obviously tried to emphasize the universal theme of his play. It is made explicit and is, in fact, declared at the end of the play when the answer to the question about the identity of Billy Brown, shot by a policeman, is one word: "Man!" The point is made. Let the will of the artist be done; O'Neill wished his play to be regarded as the *tragedy of man*.

But the tragedy of man—*the universal human tragedy*—is by no means indifferent to the human material it uses as its basis. It is not, of course, the matter of Billy's social function only; O'Neill maintains persistently the tragic character of the loss of humanity that marks the worshipers of the god of Success. Of utmost importance for the play's structure is the fact that Billy, as a character, stays too long the embodiment of conformity. His consciousness, unlike that of Dion's, the true O'Neillean tragic hero, is not presented in the state of dialogue with itself until Act III, when he painfully realizes for the first time he is "not strong enough to perish—or blind enough to be content."[17] The shift of emphasis takes place too late in the development of the action, and neither the evolution of the character nor the course of dramatic events prepares one for this. Moreover, the turn of the plot by which Billy's transformation is executed—he steals Dion's mask when the latter dies—is not immediately comprehended. Having secretly appropriated—under the other's mask—the love of Dion's wife and children, his fame, and his creative power, Billy now lays a claim to something even greater—his part of the tragic hero. The legitimacy of his pretensions—and not at Dion's expense but *together* with him—becomes apparent only at the end of the play. This also makes the play's conception clearer; but the clarification cannot, in itself, remove the contradiction between the essence of Billy's character (as it is presented from the beginning) and the structural function it is required to fulfill.

The new attempt at synthesis, after O'Neill's experiments with the form of the individual's tragedy during the late 1920s, was his trilogy *Mourning Becomes Electra*. The result of O'Neill's experiments was, as earlier, not a mechanical combination of the discovered and approved but the creation of principally new forms—not merely equal to the sum of the ingredients that were found valid but rather the perfection of the forms that proved effective. For example, in comparison with *Desire Under the Elms*, the circle of protagonists in the trilogy is much wider, although it does not comprise yet all the characters. *Mourning Becomes Electra* has a greater resemblance to the form of universal tragedy than what was achieved earlier. At the same time, there is still a substantial difference in the delineation of the protagonists and the background figures. The playwright attempts to create complex effects in projecting the complex "egos" of his protagonists by a combination of several techniques (the use of masks, the stream of consciousness, etc.).

What is true of the whole structure is also true of specific devices; they are not applied mechanically to the new material but are reconsidered in accordance with it. The use of the mask can serve as a good example. The make-up mask replaces the sculptured one, and this alone is enough to produce a far greater subtlety in the treatment of it, which corresponds to a more intricate pattern of the interaction between the face and its disguise.

The tragic story of the Mannons, which follows, in general, the line of the fall of the house of Atridae, is unique among O'Neill's plays. It is the only instance when the protagonist triumphs at the end of O'Neill's tragedy, and the triumph is of such a nature that the limits of the genre as intended by the playwright are not violated. As in the classical tragic cycle, the roots of the events in O'Neill's trilogy go far back beyond the actual time of the action. The protagonists of the play, one after another, try to free themselves from the power of the past. They believe this can be achieved by a single act of the will—by the mere rejection of it. The result, however, is contrary to their expectations; they are even more entangled in a past that keeps them prisoners awaiting their death sentences.

In the end there is only Lavinia. As the one surviving heiress of the Mannons' family curse, she may have the opportunity to escape it. This is presented by O'Neill as a psychological motivation. She can marry Peter Niles and enjoy the bliss of love and family life. But Lavinia herself realizes how illusory is this hope: to do so would mean to follow in the footsteps of the dead Mannons and to bequeath the curse to the generations to come. By the playwright's wish, Lavinia decides otherwise. She parts with Peter forever and has the shutters of the house nailed; she will enter it never to go out again.

O'Neill reveals the light of truth to his heroine only in her last hour. For what else but a family vault can we call the mansion; what else but a living death is Lavinia's voluntary entombment in it? Her choice is determined by her acceptance of the power of the past, but there is not the slightest trace of submission to fate in Lavinia; it is a challenge, a combat with all the possibilities of flying from the battlefield rejected beforehand. Like other tragic heroes, Lavinia enters the contest fully realizing what her moral duty is, being aware that she will perish in it and, yet, prevail. Since she refuses to share her lot with that of another person, the family curse will die with her; this awareness gives her unfailing fortitude at the crucial moment.

The freedom that Lavinia thus achieves is an act of consciousness. But it is the consciousness of his contemporaries that the playwright appealed to before all else, for he believed the human consciousness to be the means of prevailing over hostile circumstances. Like Faulkner, O'Neill did not regard the transformation of the present world as something that could be realized quickly, by a deliberate effort coming from the outside. He felt that it could ripen but very slowly, little by little, in those depths that open up in the hearts of men. It is in this respect that both writers largely deviated from the mainstream of American thought in the 1930s. But in the depth of their historical analysis, they outdistanced everything that was done during this period. As in *Desire Under the Elms*, the synthesis achieved in *Electra* is based on historical, not contemporary, materials once again.

However, O'Neill did not give up his ambition to create modern tragedy in the full sense of the word. His desire was fulfilled in two of his last plays which were to crown his career—*Long Day's Journey into Night* (1940) and *The Iceman Cometh* (1939). He achieved in them—at last—a complete synthesis of the forms of universal tragedy and the individual's tragedy, producing an organic and harmonious whole, although it could be said that *The Iceman Cometh* is closer to the former and *Long Day's Journey* to the latter.

In accordance with the form of universal tragedy, the circle of the tragic heroes embraces all the characters of both plays. O'Neill found that the means best suited to present it was the human community, acting as a nucleus through which the main characteristics of society could be revealed. The collected group of characters is a family unit in one instance and, in the other, a company of "have-beens," the debris of the "great society," a monstrous, grotesque image of the social construction towering over them.

John Henry Raleigh has shown that *The Iceman Cometh* can virtually be regarded as a historical play.[18] There is, first of all, a thirty-years distance between the action of the play and the time of its creation. The action is concentrated entirely on the past because the characters live in their memory world and their recollections take them back ten or twenty years; the world they really inhabit is, in fact, that of the 1890s. Yet the historical context of the play is much wider. It is not by pure chance that the characters mention American historical figures from time to time, such as Jonathan Edwards or Washington and Jefferson, the heroes of the American Revolution. On one occasion Larry Slade cites sarcastically the American Constitution: "It is a great game, the pursuit of happiness."[19] Obviously, the playwright, in widening thus the historical background of his play, felt it imperative to view modern life in its connection with the sources of American civilization, referring to America's past as the source of the American tragedy.

The principal means O'Neill uses to characterize his protagonists in these plays, as in all his other work, is the individual's tragedies, the projection of his inner landscape, largely by the interior monologue, with the typical dual rendering of consciousness and abrupt changes of moods and attitudes.

For its beauty and subtlety of characterization, *Long Day's Journey* surpasses all other plays by O'Neill. Of course, the depths of precipices opened in the hearts of the tragic heroes of this play, "written in tears and blood,"[20] could not be achieved in *The Iceman Cometh* with its huge cast. Only one of its characters, Hickey, is portrayed with that psychological intensity which reminds us of the utter complexity of human nature. But this does not transform the other characters of the play into background figures. The playwright endows each of them with a certain feature or features that bring their ambivalence into relief. Then he unites them in a group portraiture. Because of the original structure of the play, the general formula of the essence of human existence given in it comprises each and every one of its characters.

To be exact, the formula itself, on which both the early and late plays are based, is actually pronounced in *Long Day's Journey*: "life has made him like that,"[21] Mary Tyrone says of her son. Later, she remarks to her husband: "James! We've loved each other! We always will! Let's remember only that, and not try to understand what we cannot understand, or help the things that cannot be helped—*the things life has done to us* we cannot excuse or explain" [author's italics].[22]

Behind this formula is American reality in all its manifestations, with its past and present, that was the source of O'Neill's profound pessimism. It is this reality, this "life," in whose grip the characters of *Long Day's Journey* are held as they trudge along toward complete fulfillment of their destiny. James Tyrone's fear of poverty leads him to prostitute his acting talent; and his greed, which he cannot stifle, makes him "economize" even on the health of his family. His wife, who was once treated by a "cheap quack" of a doctor, becomes a drug addict; his younger son will probably die of tuberculosis at the state sanitorium for the poor! The list of examples of the father's miserliness is too long to be given here in full. Thus, "life" is not included in the framework of O'Neill's drama as an abstract idea. It is socially meaningful, and the key to the meaning is provided by the fates of his characters.

The long journey of experiments brought O'Neill to the goal he cherished all his life. He did create in *Long Day's Journey into Night* his "one hundred percent American tragedy"—the true summit of his career.

NOTES

[1] Isadora Duncan, *My Life* (London, 1969), p. 255.

[2] Louis Sheaffer, *O'Neill: Son and Artist* (Boston, 1973), p. 441.

[3] Quoted in *O'Neill and His Plays*, edited by Oscar Cargill, N. Bryllion Fagin, William J. Fisher (New York, 1961), p. 331.

[4] Ibid., p. 274. (Francis Fergusson, "Melodramatist").

[5] R. B. Heilman, *The Iceman, the Arsonist, and the Troubled Agent* (Seattle, 1973), ch. IV.

[6] Eugene O'Neill, *The Hairy Ape* in his *Nine Plays* (New York, 1954), p. 39.

[7] Ibid., p. 44.

[8] Ibid., p. 48.

[9] Alexander Taïrov, *Zapisky regisseura* (Moskva, VTO, 1970), p. 302.

[10] Ibid., p. 303.

[11] Ibid., p. 549.

[12] Ibid., p. 318.

[13] Ibid., p. 306.

[14] Sheaffer, pp. 441–442.

[15] Taïrov, pp. 215–216.

[16] Eugene O'Neill, *The Great God Brown* in *Nine Plays*, p. 318.

[17] Ibid., p. 366.

[18] John Henry Raleigh, *The Plays of Eugene O'Neill* (Carbondale, 1965), pp. 66–75.

[19] Eugene O'Neill, *The Iceman Cometh* (New York, 1967), p. 14.

[20] Eugene O'Neill, *Long Day's Journey into Night* (New Haven, 1973), p. 7.

[21] Ibid., p. 61.

[22] Ibid., p. 85.

EUGENE O'NEILL AND
GEORG KAISER

Horst Frenz

Critics have occasionally commented on certain similarities in
the works of Eugene O'Neill and the German dramatist
Georg Kaiser.[1] Some have assumed or at least implied that
The Emperor Jones was influenced by *From Morn to Midnight (Von morgens bis mitternachts)*. Others simply accepted O'Neill's denial that he had known Kaiser's work
prior to the New York production of *From Morn to Midnight* in 1922 which he attended after he had already completed *The Emperor Jones* and *The Hairy Ape* ("a direct
descendant of *Jones*.")[2] O'Neill even maintained that *The
Emperor Jones* was written long before he had ever heard of
Expressionism. In this essay an attempt will be made to compare in some detail *The Emperor Jones* to the German play,
and to ascertain if and to what extent O'Neill could have
known Kaiser's work. There will be a brief closing comment
on the relationship between the three German plays, *From
Morn to Midnight, The Coral (Die Koralle)*, and *Gas I*, and
O'Neill's *The Hairy Ape* and *Dynamo*.

A brief summary of *The Emperor Jones* and *From Morn
to Midnight* reveals certain external similarities. In Kaiser's

Note: This paper is part of a larger project entitled *Eugene O'Neill—
World Dramatist*, supported by a research grant from the National Endow-
ment for the Humanities.

play a self-deluded cashier in a small German city absconds with a large sum of money and rushes off in a frantic search for a new life. In a state of wild insanity he throws off all inhibitions of civilized man; the distorted visions of his subconscious are projected on the stage. His attempt to find something of value for which to exchange his fortune and his life ends in suicide. In the American play, the black Brutus Jones, an ex-Pullman porter, murderer and escaped convict, exploits the superstitious natives on an island in the West Indies. He faces a rebellion and has to cross the island jungle to escape to safety. The steady drumbeat of his pursuers produces in his distraught mind various hallucinations, and his past appears before him in a series of dreamlike scenes. Unable to free himself from the power of these apparitions, he is finally killed by the natives who have been waiting for him.

In both plays otherwise ordinary human beings, a middle-aged cashier and a Pullman porter, become emperors, and each in his own way strives for self-fulfillment in an artificial exaltation. Both, however, have to come to terms with themselves when the outward glory fades: Jones as the visions of the past close in on him in the jungle; the Cashier as he makes his confession in the Salvation Army hall. Yet there is a difference. Jones is merely a victim who is hunted down by his past. In contrast, the Cashier remains the pursuer until the end.

Both plays begin with a kind of prelude, a look at the situation before the flight—Jones's talk with Smithers in the imperial hall, the Emperor's seat of power; the Cashier's behavior in the bank, with the usual everyday routine. Then the protagonists depart suddenly and, following the model of the "Stationendramen," move from station to station in a succession of loosely connected scenes. These stations serve as spiritual testing grounds for the two men. Each encounter ends in failure and necessitates the continuation of the flight. The number of the stations varies in the two plays, but the pattern of the flight is identical. Jones gets lost in the jungle and wanders around in a circle; a significant phrase in the

Cashier's last speech is "I run raging in a circle." The outcome of the two plays, both of which cover roughly the period from morning to midnight, is forecast by the silver bullet (*The Emperor Jones*) and the skeleton (*From Morn to Midnight*), two symbols of importance in the action of the two dramas.

The snow scene (Scene III) in Kaiser's play[3] and the first jungle scene (Scene II) of *The Emperor Jones* in particular show many similarities. Primarily, both protagonists attempt to adjust to the new situations and surroundings. They recognize their excitement.

THE CASHIER: "My appetite is whetted. My curiosity is hugely swollen."

JONES: "What you gettin' fidgety about?"

and must check their reaction:

THE CASHIER: "I'm drudging here in a snowdrift, fooling with two bits of dirty linen. These are the gestures which betray a man."

JONES: (lights a match, then puts it out)—"Is you lightin' matches to show dem whar you is?"

Both are occasionally thinking about their past,

THE CASHIER: "This morning I was still a trusted employee. . . . At noon I'm a cunning scoundrel."

JONES: "Dat soft Emperor job ain't no trainin' fo' a long hike ovah dat plain in de brilin' sun."

but know that there is no turning back. They try to convince themselves that they can make it:

THE CASHIER: "I'm on the march—there's no turning back, no falling out. . . . I'm playing too high to lose."

JONES: "You is still in the pink—on'y a little mite feverish. Cool yo'self. Remember

you done got a long journey yit befo'
you."

The Cashier talks of man as a mechanism and Jones speaks
to his feet as if they were independent mechanical agents:

THE CASHIER: "The mechanism runs silently in his
              joints. Suddenly the faculties are
              touched and transformed into a gesture.
              What gave animation to these hands of
              mine?"

JONES: "Feet, you is holdin' up yo' end fine an'
              I sutinly hopes you ain't blisterin' none.
              . . . You is still in de pink—on'y a little
              mite feverish."

Not Jones and the cashier are escaping, but their limbs seem
to assume a life of their own; they become almost personified.
This device serves as a means of showing man's self-discovery.
The Cashier who looks at himself for the first time discovers with surprise and delight what a wonderful mechanism he is: "Now my wits begin to work again. I see with
infallible clearness" (Scene III). When Jones, in his attempt
to escape, talks to himself, he does so in order to keep up his
personality as Emperor. The "I" reveals more and more the
helpless creature going to pieces; the "you" is the desperate
attempt to put a stop to his disintegration: "Nigger, is you
gone crazy mad? . . . .Fo' Lawd's sake, use yo' haid. Gorry,
I'se got to be careful" (Scene II).

It should be noted that the Salvation Army scene provides a close parallel to the series of jungle episodes. Here the
Cashier is made to account for himself after his brief career
as "Emperor." The various sinners that appear re-enact the
stages of his own life, just as the visions re-enact the crimes
of Jones's life. The build-up of tension in each play is equally
effective. The first sinners tell the story of the Cashier's
escape: these things that are new and recognized as false by
the Cashier do not touch him closely. But when the sinners
move back to his earlier life, their confessions strike home.
Whereas the scenes in Kaiser's play move more closely to-

wards the center of the Cashier's life, in O'Neill's play the visions go beyond Jones's own experiences and show how he becomes more and more identified with the racial past from which he tries to escape.

In both works, monologues and soliloquies play an important part. A stylized language is used and a staccato effect is achieved by short sentences and elliptic constructions. Kaiser's play is filled with sounds which remind one of the use of the tom-tom in *The Emperor Jones*. For instance, at the beginning of the play, the Cashier is repeatedly rapping the window ledge. In the scene in the Salvation Army hall, flourishes of kettle drums and trumpets abound and at the end of his confession the Cashier picks up the drum sticks himself and accentuates his words with drum beats, ending in a prolonged roll breaking off abruptly. In the final monologue, the Cashier blows the trumpet repeatedly until the last sound fades away. Of course, the tom-tom in O'Neill is a continuous sound effect, which increases in intensity and leads to an overpowering emotional experience, while in Kaiser the sounds are interrupted and varied. The noises at the bicycle race[4] are a kind of tom-tom, for they are an expression of the mass psyche. However, here again is an interesting difference. While Jones shies away from the tom-tom, the Cashier revels in the outbursts of the crowd, for to him they signify the release of pent-up emotions. Nevertheless, both the beating of the drums and the various outbursts of the masses, the sound of the bands, the playing of the trumpets achieve the same effect—all these noises convey the state of the protagonists' emotion: heightened excitement, lack of control, and predominance of violence.

Automatons or masked figures are found in both plays; "little formless fears," convicts, slaves in O'Neill's work; judges and bicycle racers in the sports arena, masked guests in the ballroom scene, the Cashier's family in the German play. Nature appears to both playwrights as an evil force; for instance, jungle and snow represent a vast, threatening world through which the two protagonists must wander in pursuit of their goals. O'Neill's "Great Forest" with its "little formless fears" laughing mockingly reminds one of Kaiser's stage direction, "Snowflakes, shaken from the branches, stick in the tree-top and form a skeleton with grinning jaws."[5] With the help of nature certain messages are conveyed, aiding or foreshadowing the fate of the two characters, who are determined to assert themselves. However, the degree of their assertion is differentiated by Jones's fear and the Cashier's resignation.

In both plays the confrontation between the individual and the masses creates a major conflict. In *The Emperor Jones* the primitive natives are set against the "enlightened" individual, but the contrast turns out to be an illusion. In the course of the play Jones becomes part of the masses, participates in their rites, loses his identity as Emperor, and ends up as the victim of a mass ritual. When he finally fires the silver bullet which has been protecting his identity, his disintegration is complete. In Kaiser's play, on the other hand, the Cashier is intoxicated by the psyche of the masses. He wishes to release their pent-up energy, to eliminate social barriers, and to create a new wellspring of humanity: "There we have it. The pinnacle. The summit. The climbing hope fulfilled. The roar of a Spring gale. The breaking wave of a human tide. All bonds are burst. Up with the veils—down with the shams! Humanity—free humanity, high and low, untroubled by class, unfettered by manners. Unclean, but free. That's a reward for my imprudence" (Scene V). However, a union with the crowd proves impossible, and at the end the Cashier stands alone, isolated from the masses.

Both men rely on the power of money to provide their future well-being; in both plays first the importance and then the uselessness of money are stressed. While Jones brags about the wealth he has accumulated, it later becomes evident that the hidden money is of little use to him. Likewise, the Cashier concludes in the confession scene that "You can buy nothing worth having, even with all the money of all the banks in the world."

Each character progresses from being "civilized" to a recognition of a primitive aspect of the self which had previously been repressed, and it is interesting to see how each playwright applies these ideas in his play. The scene moves from a comfortable life in Jones's palace to the flight through the jungle; from routine activities in the bank to the hoped for adventure with the lady from Florence and to the excitement of city. In both instances this "civilized" world, which had at first been found acceptable, is recognized as either temporary or inadequate or both. Jones tells Smithers he knows that his present situation as Emperor cannot last and Kaiser expresses the Cashier's feelings in the family scene this way: "Warm and cosy, this nest of yours; I won't deny its good points; but it doesn't stand the final test." Each man is indifferent to the fate of those who fall by the wayside in their attempt to get their money's worth. Jones has, prior to the beginning of the play, exploited the "ign'rent" natives, while the Cashier dismisses without much concern or compassion the dead bicycle racers, the waiter in the ballroom, even his own family.

Each protagonist is concerned with his identity, but we have to keep in mind that we see the two figures at two different stages. At the beginning of the play, Jones's identity has been established, even if only temporarily, and we see him lose it. The Cashier has not yet achieved his new identity; in the course of the play we watch him groping for it. It is probably this ending which prompted O'Neill to say that he did not think much of Kaiser's play, that it was "too easy" and therefore "would not have influenced" him.[6]

Ashley Dukes translated *From Morn to Midnight* for the Incorporated Stage Society of London, with which Dukes was associated in an advisory capacity. The play was first performed in March of 1920, according to brief reviews in the *London Times* of March 30 and April 15 of that year. A notice appeared on April 8 in the *London Times Literary Supplement* mentioning Dukes's translation of Kaiser's play published by Hendersons. However, according to the *English Catalogue of Books*, the official publication date for Dukes's translation was May, 1920. The notice in the *London Times Literary Supplement* mentioned the recent performance of the German play in Berlin under the direction of Max Reinhardt (first performance at the Deutsches Theater on

January 31, 1919), and Kaiser is characterized as a pioneer of "Expressionism," relying heavily on graphic gestures, with an economy of spoken words. Finally, Dukes's translation of Kaiser's play was published in the autumn issue of the Boston magazine *Poet Lore.* Thus all through 1919 and into the fall of 1920, the playwright Georg Kaiser, his *From Morn to Midnight,* Max Reinhardt's interest in it, and Dukes's translated version made international theatre news.

O'Neill began writing *The Emperor Jones* in the middle of September and completed it on October 2, 1920. It is conceivable that O'Neill, prior to the writing of that play, might have had access to Dukes's translation of *From Morn to Midnight.* The German edition of the play had appeared four years earlier (1916), but there is little evidence that the American playwright knew enough German to read the original. It is more probable that he heard a great deal about the German dramatist and his work in his frequent gatherings with fellow artists, for the striking stage innovations and new plays of post-war Germany were much discussed by the circle of friends around O'Neill.[7]

Louis Sheaffer cites various sources for O'Neill's play—among them the anecdote about a onetime president of Haiti and the silver bullet, his idea of "a deposed ruler in flight through the jungle," his reading about "religious feasts in the Congo" and the use of drums, O'Neill's own experiences during "the bottomless black nights in the Honduran forests," Gordon Craig's imaginative ideas on such dramatic arts as dance, masks, and pantomime, and such literary sources as Conrad's *Heart of Darkness* and Ibsen's *Peer Gynt.*[8] My comparison of *The Emperor Jones* with Kaiser's play goes beyond parallels which might be explained by the common use of expressionistic techniques. The similarities and the interest the German playwright had aroused on the international theatre scene suggest that O'Neill was familiar, at least indirectly, with some aspects of *From Morn to Midnight.* Kaiser's name may thus be added to the list of possible sources for O'Neill's *The Emperor Jones.*

O'Neill admitted that he had read Kaiser's *From Morn to Midnight* before writing *The Hairy Ape* and added "but not before the idea for it was planned,"[9] obviously in order to disclaim any impact of the German play on his own. By then, Kenneth Macgowan's discussion of *From Morn to Midnight* in *The Theatre of Tomorrow*[10] would have been known to O'Neill, for the latter received a copy of the book as a Christmas gift and wrote to Macgowan on December 24, 1921, that he was looking forward to reading it "as a whole,"[11] which implies that he had been reading portions of the book before. Louis Sheaffer quite rightly sees a basic resemblance of *The Hairy Ape* to Kaiser's work: "In both the lowly protagonist is jolted out of his rut by encountering a 'lady' and at last finds peace, after a series of bewildering experiences, in death."[12]

There are striking parallels in Kaiser's *The Coral (Die Koralle)* and O'Neill's *The Hairy Ape*, except that there is so far no evidence that the American playwright had any knowledge of *The Coral*, the first play of the *Gas* trilogy. Here the son who has just boarded his father's yacht insists that a stoker who collapsed from heat stroke be brought on deck and be treated like a human being. The contrast between the luxury on deck and the hard labor and the miserable conditions in the engine room is common to both *The Hairy Ape* and *The Coral*. In Kaiser's play the stoker is brought on deck, while Mildred Douglas in *The Hairy Ape* actually visits the stokeroom; a major change is that Mildred faints, while the daughter of the Billionaire is converted to social consciousness at the sight of the stoker. The Billionaire's description of the ship, ironically called "Meeresfreiheit" (*Freedom of the Sea*), on the deck of which well-dressed passengers are loafing while below men are suffering from the burning flames in the fiery stokeholes, could apply easily enough to the situation in *The Hairy Ape*. The symbolism of the color white, which underlines the contrast between the blackness of the stokers and Mildred's white dress in *The Hairy Ape* (Scene III), is to be found also in *The Coral* (Act II), where white clothing and white furniture predominate. Yank's statement that after an unhappy childhood he had found some kind of peace and some sense of power in the stokehole (Scene V) reminds one of the Billionaire's remarks (Act I):

YANK:	"I runned away when me old lady croaked with the tremens. I helped at truckin' and in de market. Den I shipped in de stokehole. Sure. Dat belongs. De rest was nothin'."
THE BILLIONAIRE:	"The factory, with its machines— with its people set between me and the horror—that was the first I ever knew of rest."

Yank, the central character of O'Neill's play, wants to "belong"; he thinks he belongs to the engines and builds his philosophy on them. The Secretary's statement that "Our gas feeds the industry of the entire world!" in Kaiser's *Gas I* (Act I) and the Engineer's exhortation later in the play (Act IV), "It is *your* work which creates these miracles in steel. Power, infinite power, throbs in the machines which you set going—Gas!" sound an echo in Yank's pride to be able to use his own hands to make the ship move. However, the visit of Mildred Douglas in her white dress shatters his view of the world, and he searches for another which he does not find until his death in the gorilla's cage. The fact that Yank is a stoker and that his life is determined by the machines is subordinate. Yank is "man" rather than "worker."

This idea becomes even clearer in *Dynamo*. By the time O'Neill wrote that play, *Gas I* was available in translation,[10] productions had been staged in the United States,[14] and essays had been written about Kaiser's trilogy.[15] In O'Neill's vision, the dynamo does not affect the life of a community, but is simply a significant experience in the life of a young man who becomes an atheist and looks about for something to believe in. Young Reuben is as superstitious as his father; instead of fearing lightning he worships the machine. It is not the dynamo that dominates and determines the plot. Reuben is not a victim of the machine; he is a victim of his own superstition. In the *Gas* trilogy, on the other hand,

Kaiser attempts to give a systematic account of how the machine affects mankind in its various forms—the workers, the industrialists, the politicians, and the engineers. All classes are at the mercy of the machine; they cannot live without it. Gas dominates the action in the trilogy; all the complications arise from the presence of an industrial society. The voice of humanity represented by the son of the billionaire cannot assert itself; so the only logical end is the self-destruction of a society that has willingly made itself the victim of the machine.

Kaiser is not so much interested in the situation of the individual, as in that of the industrial society, of the masses. He is primarily a reformer; O'Neill, on the other hand, makes use of the industrial society only to illustrate individual problems which could exist in any society. He is vitally and more often than not pessimistically concerned with individual human lives, their fears, their frustrations, and frequently, their final defeat. Kaiser is more the activist, concerned with the creation of a better society and the liberation of man from social and political evils; O'Neill is more the mystic, concerned with the liberation of man's soul.

In spite of considerable differences I have been trying to touch upon in the five plays by Kaiser and O'Neill, there remain enough similarities to reach the conclusion that Kaiser's impact on the American playwright was greater than O'Neill was willing to admit. At the time the American playwright was occupied with his "Expressionistic" plays, he seems to have been concerned that his critics might throw some doubt on his originality. He voiced his differences with the German Expressionists on the matter of characterization; he believed that dramatic characters had to have some individual identity and their action should at least partially be explained in terms of this identity. Yet it is difficult to find much characterization in the stokers or the figures on Fifth Avenue or even in Yank himself. Brutus Jones and Reuben Light are symbols rather than men; Mildred Douglas in *The Hairy Ape*, the cockney trader Smithers in *The Emperor Jones*, and the minor roles in *Dynamo* are types rather than fully developed characters. Another reason for O'Neill's reluctance to acknowledge Kaiser's importance for his work may well have been his admiration for the Swedish playwright August Strindberg, whose writings he praised frequently and publically and whose "supranaturalism" he appreciated highly.

The American playwright stood so much in the center of the various movements of the European drama and felt so close to his European predecessors that he was unaware of the exact nature of their impact on him. After all, he was an artist, not a critic. Expressionism furnished O'Neill with the inspiration for a significant experimental interlude in his writing career. During this period, Georg Kaiser was surely no stranger to him.

NOTES

[1] For instance, Clara Blackburn, "Continental Influences on Eugene O'Neill's Expressionistic Dramas," *American Literature*, 13 (May 1941), 109–133; Ann Gertrude Coleman, "Expressionism—40 Years Later," *CEA Critic*, 27 (February 1965), 1, 7–8; and two publications by Mardi Valgemae: *Accelerated Grimace: Expressionism in American Drama of the 1920's* (Carbondale: Southern Illinois University Press, 1972) and "Expressionism in the American Theater," in *Expressionism as an International Literary Phenomenon*, ed. Ulrich Weisstein (Paris and Budapest: Didier; Akadémiai Kiadó, 1973), pp. 193–203.

[2] Cf. Barrett H. Clark, *Eugene O'Neill* (New York: McBride, 1929), p. 125.

[3] Since Ashley Dukes's translation of *From Morn to Midnight*, which was published in *Poet Lore*, 31 (Autumn 1920), 317–363, may have been available to O'Neill and certainly was read by him at a somewhat later date, the following quotations will be taken from that version.

[4] It is an interesting coincidence that Kaiser has written a scene filled with the excitement and the noise of a six-day bicycle race and O'Neill, in *The Hairy Ape*, refers in the stage direction to the "chanting formula of the gallery gods at the six-day bike race" (Scene III). It must be added that O'Neill attended and enjoyed such races.

⁵ In these settings, Jones loses his Panama hat, and the Cashier's hat is blown off. The hat is often used as a symbol of middleclass values in German Expressionism.

⁶ Clark, p. 125.

⁷ Among them, scene designers such as Robert Edmond Jones and Cleon Throckmorton, the critics George Jean Nathan and Kenneth Macgowan, and the would-be editor Saxe Commins. Cf. Kenneth Macgowan, *The Theatre of Tomorrow* (New York: Boni and Liveright, 1921) and Edmond Jones and Kenneth Macgowan, *Continental Stagecraft* (New York: Benjamin Blom, 1922).

⁸ Louis Sheaffer, *O'Neill Son and Artist* (Boston: Little, Brown, 1973), pp. 27–29.

⁹ Here O'Neill is obviously thinking of the short story "The Hairy Ape," which he supposedly wrote in 1917.

¹⁰ The discussion on pages 256 to 263 ends with this statement: "We will accept an imaginative treatment of human beings in unaccustomed *locale* while we would ban it if the place were Main Street or Harlem." This is a remarkable prediction for the events surrounding the first production of *All God's Chillun Got Wings* in New York in 1924.

¹¹ I am grateful to Professor Travis Bogard for providing me with this information from his forthcoming edition of the O'Neill-Macgowan correspondence.

¹² Sheaffer, p. 76. As Mardi Vargemae has pointed out, in Kaiser's *The Coral* the Billionaire and his Secretary "have identical physical features; the only distinguishing characteristic is a small piece of red coral worn by the Secretary on his watch chain." In the course of the play, "the Billionaire murders the Secretary, assumes the dead man's identity in an effort to obtain the victim's peace of mind, is mistaken for his murdered subordinate and is executed for having murdered himself, as it were." This is similar to the events in *The Great God Brown* except that "ONeill handles the change in personality with the skillful use of masks." (*Accelerated Grimace*, p. 38).

¹³ *Gas I* was translated by Herman G. Scheffauer and published in Boston (Small, Maynard and Co.) and London (Chapman and Dodd) in 1924. *Gas I, Gas II,* and *The Coral* were republished by Frederick Ungar Publishing Co., New York, in 1963 with an introduction by Victor Lange.

¹⁴ See the notes on the (first American) "constructivist" production of Georg Kaiser's *Gas* at the Goodman Theatre, Chicago,

on January 27, 1926, by Samuel Putnam, "For an Etymologic Theatre," *The Drama*, 16 (February 1926), 164; 169–170.

[15] For example, Herman George Scheffauer, "The Dynamic Dramatist; Georg Kaiser and his New Dramatic Forms," *Shadowland* (1922), pp. 27, 59–60, 63.

PART 2

An American Perspective

INTRODUCTION

Virginia Floyd

Whether it was his tragedy or the source of his inspiration, O'Neill lived haunted by the curse of the misbegotten, creating in his work a world of characters similarly afflicted. Believing he had been ill-conceived and borne, he searched gropingly throughout his life, rootless from beginning to end, longing to belong to something not only here in this world but to what he calls a "behind-life"[1] force greater than himself. His characters reflect the inner need of their creator; depicting the universal plight of modern man, they are a combination of an abstract Everyman and the concrete figure seeking roots in place and time in America, yet never quite belonging.

The early Puritans had merely to face the rigors of an alien land; later waves of immigrants encountered not only the hostile land but the stoic rejection of its possessors. Newcomers found that they had to forfeit a portion of their Old World birthright—their hereditary traits, customs, values—to become even partially assimilated. The rejection of the Irish by Yankee New Englanders that O'Neill portrays was personally experienced by him and his family when they attempted to find acceptance by native New Londoners. Ruth Newcomb, member of an old Yankee New London family with a summer home located near the O'Neill home, told me: "We didn't fraternize with the O'Neill's and Irish stock. They didn't have heritage or background. We had a clique and the Irish weren't in it. They had no money or prestige." Shortly before her death, Beatrice Ashe Maher, one of the few "nice" New London girls in the playwright's early life, told me that his father and brother "didn't even try to be accepted, but the men were distressed about New Londoners' rejection of the family because of the pain it caused Ella O'Neill."

The key factor that determined O'Neill as a man and influenced him as a playwright was his Irishness. As he himself stated: "The one thing that explains more than anything about me is the fact that I'm Irish and strangely enough it is something writers who have attempted to explain me and my work have overlooked."[2] The essays of the second part of this collection focus on four aspects of the dramatist: his Irish Catholicism, New England Puritanism, humanism, and mysticism. While these aspects may seem unrelated, they do have a common denominator: each is rooted in the playwright's Irishness. Taken together, they will "explain" not only his native quality but his universality, the microcosm reflecting the macrocosm. A dominant theme in the canon is to belong; and O'Neill, the son of an immigrant, becomes our national Everyman. He, in himself, best exemplifies the dichotomy of the American character because of his Old World Irish Catholic heritage and "new" world Puritan environment. In his life, as in his plays, these two cultures inevitably must clash. Retaining one's faith and ideals in a Puritan cultural milieu seemed an impossibility. The compromise was made: outwardly, O'Neill rejected Catholicism. At the age of fifteen, he ceased to practice his religion. But the damage had been done; he was left with only an adolescent concept of faith and was simply not able to interpret it. What he had unconsciously absorbed were the rigid, harsh tenets of Catholicism gleaned from childhood, heavily tainted with a persistent strain of Puritanism with its emphasis on sin and predestination. Perhaps he can best be described by the term "Irish Puritan," or the label he attaches to Mike Hogan in *A Moon for the Misbegotten*, "a New England Irish Catholic Puritan Grade B."[3]

Irish Puritanism, that mixture of Jansenism and Calvinism imposed on the Irish Catholic Church by a set of historical factors, was, in turn, forced upon the Irish people by the Church as one of the means of survival during the centuries of English domination. In the seventeenth and eighteenth centuries, emigrants of England, Scotland, and France brought respectively Puritanism, Calvinism, and Jansenism to Ireland. A great number of Puritans settled in County Tyrone, home of O'Neill's ancestors; and in time the Irish Catholics absorbed some of the tenets and moral attitudes of these immigrants. In the seventeenth century the Irish were prohibited from having Catholic seminaries, and many of the young men, who were sent to France to study, attended the Jansenist-dominated University of Paris and the Irish College Des Lombards. Generations later, French priests emigrated to Ireland during the French Revolution; and Ireland experienced another influx of Jansenism, which is similar to Puritanism in that both contain Calvinistic elements.

While the early nineteenth-century Irish Catholic Church, which formed and determined the religious and moral attitudes of O'Neill's grandparents, was orthodox Roman Catholic in theory, it did, then, contain Jansenistic-Puritan elements. The playwright's father brought this particular type of Irish Catholicism to America and into his home. Irish Catholicism and surviving New England Puritanism have obvious similarities: the Calvinistic Old Testament fear of an avenging God, a moral restraint that produced a sense of repression and too often led to sexual excesses, the incapacity to associate love with honest sexuality, a historical heritage of isolation that was the result of persecution and living in a closed society.

What ironic hand of fate ordained that English and Irish Puritans converge in New England where the rigors of climate and environment could only serve to reinforce the harshness of their religion? The Yankee Puritan and Irish Catholic characters, as O'Neill portrays them in his New England plays, have similar religious, social, and familial attitudes. The theme of isolation is found in all these plays. Geographically and sociologically, New England provided the type of closed society most congenial to the paradoxical nature of the Yankees and the Irish alike. The Cabots in *Desire Under the Elms* are literally imprisoned, trapped, in one way or another, on their rocky, impoverished New England farm. Living in the illusionary world of her garden summer house, the Yankee Deborah Harford endures even greater alienation than the Cabots. While at times the Irish are indefatigably gregarious, John Henry Raleigh observes that they are also "capable, especially in an alien environment, of great isolation and loneliness as *Long Day's Journey* evidences. The Tyrones, like their ancient ancestors, are, to a man, non-communal."[4] In a futile attempt to be accepted by Yankee society, Con Melody experiences intolerable loneliness when he cuts himself off from those he considers "shanty Irish." After the death of his mother, Jim Tyrone finds himself alone in an unloved and unloving world.

The renegade Irish Catholic characters bear the scars of spiritual as well as psychological isolation. They go through the long journey of life resisting any kind of moral awakening. The fathers, like Con Melody and Phil Hogan, mock the Catholic Church and its clergy; the daughters, Sara and Josie, emulate the irreverent and irreligious attitude of their fathers. The sons, Edmund and Jamie, are atheistic and blasphemous in words and deeds. Only the Irish mothers, Nora and Mary, lament their lost faith. Mary's belief is as strong as Nora's, but, being a century removed from immigrant status, she does not have her vitality. Nora stands on the threshold and at least contemplates making a definite move to regain her lost faith; Mary can only bemoan its loss.

In O'Neill's plays, neither the Irish nor the Puritan Yankees can avoid a mutual fate: a nearly perpetual state of unhappiness. The restrictions of their racial and religious heritage lead to a repression of virtually all normal love and affection and to an expression of abnormal lusts and vices. Unable to reconcile themselves with God and man, the characters seek various ways to escape from life. As in so many of the plays, alcohol provides the best route to oblivion. The sons in both *Desire Under the Elms* and *Long Day's Journey* begin drinking early in the day, and the fathers in

both plays become inebriated. Along with alcohol, the pro-
verbial "heart-of-gold-tart" lurks somewhere in the background: Min in *Desire Under the Elms,* the whores Con had
known before he married Nora, Fat Violet in *Long Day's
Journey,* the "blonde pig" in *A Moon for the Misbegotten,*
the prostitute-wife Sara in *More Stately Mansions,* the would-
be whores, Abbie, Deborah, and Josie.

For the Irish male, consorting with whores and resorting
to alcohol could only serve to increase the sense of guilt in a
conscience already burdened by an act of apostasy. In the
context of Catholicism, sin scars or kills the soul. The lapsed
Irish Catholics of *Long Day's Journey* and *A Moon for the
Misbegotten* show some symptoms of sickness, the outward
manifestation of the scarred soul. Josie calls Jim Tyrone a
"sick child" (p. 396), "a dead man walking behind his own
coffin" (p. 322). Tyrone says he usually wakes in the morning
feeling "damned sick remorse" (p. 405). In discussing the
disastrous effects he has had on prostitutes, he states: "When
I poison them, they stay poisoned" (p. 386). In *Long Day's
Journey* the visit to the doctor confirms Edmund's fear that
he has tuberculosis; O'Neill describes him as "sick right now,"
"plainly in bad health; his eyes appear feverish and his
cheeks are sunken."[5] While James Tyrone at the outset of the
play has "never been really sick in his life" (p. 13), by the
end of it even he has become "sick and sober" (p. 172), for
him a crucifying combination. Mary Tyrone is, of course,
most afflicted. Disoriented by excessive drug dosage, she
manifests visible signs of illness. Her face "does not match
her healthy figure"; "her eyes are accentuated by her pallor";
"her hands have an ugly, crippled look and she cannot control the nervousness which draws attention to them" (p. 12).
Even the New England environment shows signs of being
infected; the foghorn is described as a sick whale in the back
yard. Through this imagery O'Neill makes a literary statement that expresses a personal conviction: sickness pervades
the American society and soul. O'Neill believed a "playwright must dig at the roots of the sickness of today as he
feels it—the death of the old God and the failure of science
and materialism to give any satisfying new one."[6] In *Long*

Day's Journey the sickness of America taints even the mother figure who had previously been almost immune—depicted as the lone surviving custodian of cherished ideals in the family unit.

Through no fault of her own, Mary is surely the destroyer, the Strindbergian "Pelican," swallowing its young, holding a double-edged sword: the ability to sow the seeds of destructive gnawing guilt; the threat to self-destruct, to sever the frail and drug-blurred tie with this life. Both sons angrily lash out at the mother in the play, expressing feelings of frustration and guilt. They resent the mother for abandoning them mentally as she slips away, as she had so many times in the past, into a drugged world; they blame her for the aborted suicide attempt. The four Tyrones, as the natural descendants of the Irish Melodys, bear in their soul the ravages of a century's assimilation. The idealistic but real-life poet stance of Con Melody has been replaced by the cheap, artificial stage pose of James Tyrone; he is a captive Edmond Dantes frittering his life away in muddled alcoholic regrets. While her husband escapes painful reality in acting and drink, Mary Tyrone takes the morphine route, wallowing in self-pity for the failure of her life. She blames her husband and sons for what she has become—a "dope fiend," but concludes: "None of us can help the things life has done to us" (p. 61).

Perhaps no other character portrays more effectively than Mary Tyrone the cruel consequences of the migration of the Irish to America. Very simply, why did she have such difficulty adjusting to the role of wife of an apparently loving husband who happened to be a successful stage actor? Were her failure as wife and mother and her retreat into an illusionary world forms of revenge? Like Con Melody, she desperately wants the acceptance and approval of native New Englanders. The Harfords, the Chatfields, the ghosts of Puritans past, "stand for something." They belong. The Irish never had, never would. Mary's constant lamentation for a home demonstrates the essential rootlessness of the Irish. She is locked in a lonely, meaningless "now," nostalgic for a dimly remembered but more meaningful past. Who can forget her

anguished cry at the end of the play when she wanders, dazed
by drugs, into the world of alcoholic men: "What is it I'm
looking for? I know it's something I lost. . . . Something I
miss terribly. It can't be altogether lost" (p. 173). A dazed
Con Melody, stunned by the blows of the superior Yankees
because he dared to pose as a "gentleman," staggers into the
final scene of *A Touch of the Poet*. As Tom Olsson points
out, "the tattered uniform and the trailed wedding gown
serve the same purpose." They are pitiful reminders of a lost
past: for him, the safe, certain old world when he was an
officer and his life had meaning; for her, the hour of con-
secration when the church blessed her declaration to bind
her life to another's in meaningful love. And the spouses of
these casualties of life? Nora holds and folds the torn jacket,
agonizes over the shattered soul. Tyrone helplessly holds
"the wedding gown in his arms with an unconscious clumsy,
protective gentleness" (p. 172). What Mary Tyrone has
actually lost is her religious faith and with it the inner core
of her existence. O'Neill goes to great length to define her
spiritual nature: "Her most appealing quality is the simple,
unaffected charm of a shy convent-girl youthfulness she has
never lost—an innate unworldly innocence" (p. 13). As the
dramatist depicts her, this sensitive spirit could not survive
the harsh realities of life—the hostile New England atmosphere, the wake of lonely one-night stands of theatrical tours.

Like the Melodys, their literary ancestors, the Tyrones
are renegade Irish Catholics; their loss of faith can bring only
anguish and unhappiness. During the seven hundred years
the English occupied and exploited Ireland, they robbed
the Irish of everything but their Catholicism. The Irish had
fought so desperately to retain their faith during the centuries of domination that the loss of it is the equivalent to
the forfeiture of the meaning of life. The long day's journey
ends in the dark night of the soul. The Tyrones' and, by
autobiographical implication, the O'Neills' rejection of
Catholicism, and their Yankee neighbors' rejection of them,
alienate these Irish from God, New Londoners and, in the
end, from each other. The inner conflict of the Tyrone-
O'Neill family—spiritual vacuity and blind attempts to fill

the void with drugs, drink, and sex—reveals the important role Catholicism plays in the lives of the Irish. The Tyrones are haunted not only by what was lost but by what replaced it: those subconscious layers of guilt. If their illness of body reflects an inner sickness of soul, only one possible remedy can effect a cure: confession. O'Neill obviously implies that there is, at least, the hope of salvation, that these shattered souls can be healed. He once stated: "In all my plays sin is punished and redemption takes place."[7]

John Henry Raleigh shows how profoundly O'Neill's early Catholic indoctrination affected his most autobiographical work—the late plays. The emphasis on sin and redemption in Catholicism arouses in the flawed psyche strong guilt feelings and the need to confess and be forgiven. Was it merely a coincidence that the "sin" of Don Parritt and Jim Tyrone involved, in some way, a betrayal by and of the mother? Neither can find peace in this life nor go to his death without confessing his sin: Parritt to the father figure, Larry Slade; Tyrone to the mother figure, Josie Hogan. While the penance seems to be the same for both men—suicide—there is a difference in the degree of severity and urgency in the punishment. Jim Tyrone's self-imposed retribution is his slow, agonizing embrace with dissolution; Parritt's will be quick. decisive—a sudden "hop off the fire escape." The father figure is harsher in the exacting of penance: "Go! Get the hell out of life, God damn you, before I choke it out of you! . . . Go, for the love of Christ, you mad tortured bastard, for your own sake."[8]

One can only wonder how efficacious O'Neill thought Parritt's private and Hickey's public auricular confessions were. (And was there any surrogate priest in the dramatist's own final days had he felt the need to confess?) While confession to a layman is effective if it is reported subsequently to a priest, given the circumstances of possibility, a major heresy is involved here: a layman cannot impose penance; he can only urge to "Perfect Contrition." Slade's imposition of suicide on Parritt for what he had done is totally outside the church's acceptance.[9] Clifford Leech maintains "the penance imposed in the early church could be severe, and

Cyprian, who was extreme, argues that only one such offense could be tolerated—i.e., the sinner would be expelled from the church if he/she did it again."[10] The timing of the absolution differs in the two plays: after death in *The Iceman Cometh*—Slade mumbles "God rest his soul in peace" (p. 258); before death in *A Moon for the Misbegotten*—Josie says at the end of the play, "May you rest forever in forgiveness and peace" (p. 409).

There is in the two plays the usual woman dichotomy: the mother versus the whore. Woman for O'Neill, as for Strindberg, symbolizes the split soul in the dual role of mother-mistress she plays—man's potential savior and destroyer. The dual longings in the male illustrate the American dilemma: his obsession for the mother and the ideals she represents demonstrating his nobler side on a personal and national level; his desire for the whore and the materialistic American Dream which, like the prostitute, can be bought, manifesting his physical nature. At the end of the two plays, however, the purely physical is rejected: Parritt says, "I'm through with whores" (p. 221), and Tyrone angrily rejects Josie when she plays the whore, saying, "Nix on the raw stuff" (p. 370). The mothers in the two plays are unable to provide the means to attain social and personal ideals. Rosa Parritt tries to promote The Movement with people "who were cheating suckers with a phony pipe dream" (p. 220). After the death of his mother, Tyrone finds his life a shambles: "I knew I was lost, without any hope left—that all I could do would be to drink myself to death" (p. 392). Maternal indifference, the ultimate betrayal, caused either by social or personal pressures and weakness, is the unpardonable sin. The acts of revenge, however, meted out to the mothers, become a source of greater punishment to the sons who must live with guilt for their "sins."

While *A Moon for the Misbegotten* is, as Raleigh maintains, the "purest example of the confessional mold" because it is devoted to the absolution of "the most guilt-ridden sinner O'Neill had known—his brother Jamie," it is also the dramatist's most Irish play because it reflects the patriotic pride and loyalty of his father if the James Tyrone character in *Long Day's Journey into Night* is an accurate autobiographical representation. Although Phil Hogan is supposedly a portrait of John "Dirty" Dolan, an Irish pig farmer, and O'Neill calls this the "Dolan Play" in his early drafts, Raleigh is correct when he asserts that "parts of James O'Neill's character and some of his habits have been incorporated into Phil Hogan." When Edmund tells the Shaughnessy-Hogan pigs-in-the-pond story in *Long Day's Journey,* James Tyrone's first reaction of glee at the defeat of the Yankee Harker*—"Admiringly before he thinks. 'The damned old scoundrel! By God, you can't beat him!'" (p. 25)—approximates that of Phil Hogan in *A Moon for the Misbegotten.* There is a line in O'Neill's notes for the play, which he omitted, that reveals Hogan's delight in the Irish victory over the Yankee Harder,* his sense of humor, and his vindictiveness. At the end of the play, Hogan tells Josie they should make certain Harder's fence is still down to give the pigs access to the pond and adds: "When I think of that jackass in jockey's pants, it's a terrible sorrow to me we don't own a herd of elephants."

Strangely enough, it was the pond incident that gave O'Neill his first conception of the play. In an entry in the Work Diary dated October 28, 1941, he writes: "S. play idea, based on story told by E. in 1st Act of 'L.D.J.I.N.'—except here Jamie principal character & story of play otherwise entirely imaginary except for J's revelation of self." There is a speech in *Long Day's Journey* that perhaps inspired O'Neill to draw his brother into the plot of *A Moon for the Misbegotten.* When Jamie laughs heartily at Edmund's story, his father "turns on his older son and says: 'and you're worse than he is, encouraging him. I suppose you're regretting you weren't there to prompt Shaughnessy with a few nastier insults. You've a fine talent for that if for nothing else'" (p. 26).

---

* The prototypes for the rich pro-British Standard Oil man Harder in *A Moon for the Misbegotten* and Harker in *Long Day's Journey* are the multimillionaire Edward S. Harkness and the wealthy Edward C. Hammond, whose estates were located a short distance from the O'Neill family home in New London.

While Jamie's laughter is again heard in *A Moon for the Misbegotten,* so also is the cry of his heart's sorrow—and the confession of guilt to the mother-figure Josie Hogan. Raleigh maintains that, "the major impulse behind *A Moon for the Misbegotten* was an urge to pronounce a benediction on Jamie O'Neill." In a first draft (October 1941), O'Neill makes no reference to the confessional aspects of the play; the main theme centers on the relationship between Tyrone and Josie. O'Neill's early title, "The Moon Bore Twins," reflects this as does Josie's speech in Act IV: "This is the night when the moon bore twins, me and my brother here and it's the night when I, a virgin, bore a child who died at birth."

From the very start, O'Neill envisioned Josie as a virgin. She becomes the twin also of the mythological bride of Cuchulain, the virginal Emer to whom Raleigh compares her. He states O'Neill "added his own component" to the myth "by making his Gaelic warrior-virgin a confessor as well." O'Neill injects Irish atavism into much of *A Moon for the Misbegotten,* but he Christianizes the Celtic mythological aspects. It is, in the end, an Irish Catholic world O'Neill creates for his characters, for they must suffer: Tyrone and Josie part—never to see each other again—and Phil Hogan sorrowfully tries to bring solace to his daughter. As Raleigh notes: "In O'Neill's imagination suffering is a secular equivalent to the notion of Original Sin."

Indoctrination to Irish Catholicism instilled in the dramatist a moral code that viewed sin as bringing a kind of spiritual death to the soul. Living in a New England environment gave him an awareness of the deadly effects of Puritanism which, like Irish Catholicism, preaches the doctrine that sin annihilates the soul, robbing it of life in this world and the next. O'Neill was aware of Puritan decadence, of the financial and sexual exploits of members of old Yankee New England families like the Plants, Chappells, and Gardiners. His rebellion against the harsh Calvinistic spirit that blighted the lives of the early twentieth-century New London Yankee descendants of the Puritans is reflected in many of his New England plays. He stated in his last interview with the press in 1946 that "the battle of moral forces in the New England scene is what I feel closest to as an artist."[11] Frederick Wilkins observes that it is not the ideals of early seventeenth-century Puritans that O'Neill attacks in his plays, but "the distorted moral and social dictates that replaced those ideals when Puritan theology was abandoned and was reduced to the hypocritical curses of stony patriarchs like Ephraim Cabot." In time, Yankees became, in a sense, Puritan renegades. Like their Irish contemporaries, they, too, were beset by guilt and felt their souls tainted by sin. According to Wilkins, *Dynamo*, which O'Neill called "a study of the sickness of today," illustrates that "much of the sickness is the result of Puritanism having reached a dead end."

Although they were as obsessed with sin as Irish Catholics, the Puritans lacked the consolation that confession provided—the peace that issued from here-and-now forgiveness. O'Neill uses appropriate imagery to describe the hopelessness of the "death-in-life" condition of his Yankee characters. Death becomes the Mannons. Wilkins notes: "The Mannons are bound—that key word in Shenandoah—bound as if in the hands of an angry God whose covenant with their ancestors had been perverted." The word "bound" here is interpreted as "cabined, cribbed, confined." But there are also other meanings for this word: "to leap forward or upward," or "headed for." In this sense, "bound" implies, as Clifford Leech suggests, "I am on my way, at last, so hurray, even though it may be the way of my death, and perhaps all the better for that: the ultimate vision is what matters."[12]

"Bound" is not only the key word in Shenandoah, but, with its dual implications, it is also the key to a better understanding of O'Neill's conception of a "behind-life" force. The first interpretation of the word implies the Mannons are irrevocably tied by that angry Puritan God to place—their New England ancestral home. When Lavinia walks into the Mannon tomb at the end of the play, accepting this living death to expiate the sins of her family, she is acknowledging the inevitable dictates of fate. In his notes for this play, O'Neill states: "Fate from within the family is the modern approximation of the Greek conception of fate from without, from the supernatural." The playwright shared with Lavinia the concept of family as a fatal determinant and identified with her—"I'm the last Mannon [O'Neill]. I've got to punish myself." In a Catholic theological context, Lavinia is performing a penance for the Mannon dynasty—this death-in-life.

In contrast, the second interpretation of "bound"—"to leap forward or upward, to be headed for"—holds the promise of life-in-death. Here one strives for the "ultimate vision." O'Neill believed there was something within man that would not allow him to succumb to defeat, to his harsh fate, as the late plays demonstrate. In these plays characters are depicted as survivors, clinging to life, sustained very often only by a "hopeless hope," a pipe dream that a better life is possible. All five major characters in *Mourning Becomes Electra*—the four Mannons and Adam Brant—express an ardent desire to escape the family past and curse and travel far away to the Blessed Isles. Living as they are in seaport town, the Mannons, land-locked by their fate, are constantly reminded of the freedom and happiness that such an escape holds. The sea becomes the symbol that would allow them to "leap forward or upward." O'Neill's Celtic temperament led him to think in symbols, and throughout the canon the sea takes on a mystical quality; it enables man to achieve a kind of harmony that the land can never provide; it holds the promise of the ultimate vision.

Albert Bermel maintains Edmund Tyrone found this kind of harmony at sea: "I belonged, without past or future, within something greater than my own life, or the life of Man, to Life itself! To God, if you want to put it that way." Alone, dreaming, watching the coming of dawn at sea, he experienced "the moment of ecstatic freedom. The peace, the end of the quest, the last harbor, the joy of belonging to a fulfillment beyond men's lousy, pitiful, greedy fears and hopes and dreams!" (p. 153). The last harbor—some blessed isle—lies *beyond* the sea, but for him here on land—again New London—there is only discord within and among men.

The four Tyrones are not land-locked, as are the Mannons, by a New England Puritan heritage; but they are

victims nonetheless. Fate, the historical past of the Irish in
this play, seems to have shipwrecked the Tyrones and thrown
them up from the sea upon an unknown, alien land where
they would never quite belong. It is the sea that separates
them from their native land just as it splits the Old World
from the New World, the idealistic way of life from the
materialistic one. Appropriately, Bermel compares the summer house in *Long Day's Journey into Night* to a fog-bound
ship and finds the Tyrones drifting "on the surface waters of
this night and the undertow of all their yesterdays. They are
at the mercy of their collective fate which lies many fathoms
deep in the remote past." The love of the sea that characterizes Edmund, O'Neill's self-portrait, reflects the longing of
the mystical Irish to return to the past, to recapture that
which was lost in the great transatlantic migration. What was
lost, of course, was a faith that would put meaning into life.
And so they drift, sinking deeper and deeper into degrading
drug and alcohol addiction. Each longs to recapture what was
lost, but only Edmund actually voices the desire to soar "beyond and forward."

O'Neill once remarked that he wanted to see the "trans-
figuring nobility of tragedy in seemingly the most ignoble,
debased lives. And just here is where I am a most confirmed
mystic, too, for I am always trying to interpret Life in terms
of lives, never just in terms of character. I'm always acutely
conscious of the Force behind—Fate, God, our biological
past creating our present, whatever one calls It—Mystery
certainly."[13] As Bermel remarks, the "biological past" of characters like Yank and the Tyrones in early and late plays leaves
them dislocated and fills them with a longing for "a mystical
union; for a oneness with whatever lies beyond the self." He
observes that after a long, futile search, Yank "can belong
only by being dead," and that the retreat of the four Tyrones
to a world of "hard liquor and drugs" is a "quest for mystical
unity" and the "next best thing to a mystical experience."

Are these then the only two alternatives O'Neill offers
modern man to satisfy his yearning to belong to something
outside himself: the finality of death or that other slow kill-
ing of the mind—the escape through alcohol, drugs, pipe

dreams to the world of illusion? Like his characters, those isolated outcasts gathered in Harry Hope's saloon contemplating a hop off the fire escape or clinging to the final dream down at the bottom of a bottle, O'Neill was haunted by what was lost and yearned for something to give life meaning. Clifford Leech, the English critic, disagrees with Bermel—and even the playwright himself.

> We saw him, not as a mystic, but as a man hankering after mysticism, after anything to replace the Roman Catholicism he had lost. We saw him as a man haunted by those chaps and girls on the Mayflower and their descendants. But all of that didn't matter much. What did matter was his sense of how human beings behaved in relation to their ancestry, to each other, and to their immediate environment.

Awareness grows from the vantage point of Harry Hope's "Bottom of the Sea Rathskeller," "the End of the Line Cafe"; a substitute is needed for the elusive "hopeless hope" of Old World faith. Esther M. Jackson maintains that "O'Neill was, throughout his life, engaged in a search for a way of verifying the existence of an eternal principle in human experience. His approach to the problem had significant correspondences to those of modern humanists, both religious and secular." There is something in William James's extended definition of religion—"man's total reaction upon life"—which she provides that resembles O'Neill's concept of a "behind-life" force. "James observes that these total reactions differ from casual responses, for to get at them, 'we must go behind the foreground of existence and reach down to that curious sense of the whole residual cosmos as an everlasting presence.'" Jackson claims that O'Neill's "treatment of religious themes remained unorthodox" . . . mirroring "his anguish at his own inability to confirm or deny the existence of God."

Because of the need for a certitude appropriate to his interpretation of the search for meaning in modern American life, O'Neill's humanism, as she points out, differs from that of European playwrights of the nineteenth and twentieth centuries in the "extent of the moral freedom he attributes to man." In the early plays—which focus on the nature of responsibility—personal morality, in itself, provides no meaningful solutions to the problems of the world O'Neill creates for his characters. In his discussion of *The Hairy Ape*, O'Neill reveals his awareness that man is either unwilling or unable to assume responsibility for his fellow man, to make his own life or the lives of others more meaningful. The dramatist points out that the work is timely "because I think we are all sick of answers that don't answer. *The Hairy Ape* at least faces the simple truth that, being what we are, and with any significant spiritual change for the better in us probably 10,000 years away, there just is no answer."[14] Jackson asserts O'Neill came "to the conclusion that the appropriate exercise of moral freedom in a democratic society requires a pattern of shared belief" and that he "engaged upon the creation of a new iconography—a system of signs, images, and symbols expressive of the relationship between man and the universe in the New World." While the late plays expose the "failures of their protagonists to achieve humanistic goals," she sees in their response to the tragic fact of this limitation an indication not only of "man's nobility but also of his humanity."

While death is frequently the only escape from the pain of reality in the early plays—*The Emperor Jones, The Hairy Ape, The Great God Brown*—it is only contemplated as an alternative in the late works. The characters might be sorely tempted to plunge into that final abyss, but they refuse, to use Dylan Thomas's words, to "go gentle into that good night." They are indeed "grave men, near death, who see with blinding sight," but they will not accept defeat. They struggle, rage, endure. Only Parritt, with the curse-blessing— "Get the hell out of life"—of the father-figure upon him, goes. "And you, my father, there on the sad height,/ Curse, bless, me now with your fierce tears, I pray."

O'Neill himself is very much present in the late plays, locked with his characters in their hell of existence—waiting for the release of death. He is Edmund in *Long Day's Journey into Night*—always a little in love with death; and—not so obviously—the Night Clerk in *Hughie*, stifling any desire to enter into the game of life, listening distractedly to the tales of the Jamie O'Neill-like character, Erie Smith. But he is, I believe, very obviously portrayed in the old Irish "foolosopher" Larry Slade in *The Iceman Cometh*.[15] In *Long Day's Journey into Night* Edmund confesses he once tried to kill himself—and in that very place where Larry sits, longing, as he says, to die. As in *Hughie*, another character—Parritt—interrupts his reveries, tries to force him to get involved in the life of another. O'Neill makes some very important statements in *Iceman* that are carried over into *Hughie*, for he is, as Kenneth Macgowan claims, "a kind of chain-stitch playwright."[16] Larry finally does "listen" to Parritt and acts, revealing that man must assume responsibility for his fellow man. While the other characters strive desperately throughout the play to achieve some kind of harmony with each other, Larry is the only one who finally does. Even the pipe dream that he nourishes "may be a Black Irishman's name for Faith."[17] At the end of the play when Larry hears the thud of Parritt's body striking the ground, "a long-forgotten faith returns to him for a moment" (p. 258), and he is filled with pity. The others, completely oblivious to the human tragedy being enacted in their midst, burst into song, but "each starts the chorus of his or her choice" (p. 259).

While *The Iceman Cometh* ends with a death, *Hughie* begins shortly after one has occurred. Carrying a torch for the dead Hughie, Erie tries desperately to form a friendship with the detached Night Clerk, who, like Larry, is eventually "kicked out of his dream." Erie succeeds in touching the depths of a similarly lonely other, of establishing a communion of souls: "Beatific vision swoons on the empty pools of the Night Clerk's eyes. He resembles a holy saint, recently elected to Paradise."[18] In these last plays, O'Neill seems to be saying that in view of the uncertainty of any other-world paradise, man has the capacity—though he often lacks the will—to create a heaven-on-earth state for his fellow man. Above all, the one clear message is that man should adjust to the sense of loss that accompanies religious uncertainty and not succumb to the lure of "easy" death; he must struggle to survive and give this one life he has some semblance of meaning—even if he must fortify himself with illusions.

J. Dennis Rich examines the struggle that the isolated exiles inhabiting the desolate world of O'Neill's last plays wage to cope with loss, to give their existence meaning. He points out that O'Neill in his late work "ceases his earlier search for transcendence or salvation, and the human effort becomes a search for a means of survival." Haunted always by the thought of what life once was in the past or could be in the future, the characters are, nonetheless, conscious of ever-present reality. Because of the contrast between "ideal images of life and reality," Rich claims the "problem of existence is encountered in the climate of the absurd." He states that O'Neill explores the possibility of existing in such a climate "by examining his own life experience in a family setting" in *Long Day's Journey into Night* and "in less personal terms" in *The Iceman Cometh*. The question to be asked is "whether life is or is not worth living." In view of O'Neill's concept of man and/in the universe, the answer is affirmative and leads to a further inquiry concerning the quality of existence in a world devoid of absolutes.

While in *Long Day's Journey* each of the characters confronts the "terror of existence" from his own individual cell of isolation, there are familial ties—bonds of love and hate—that unite them. In contrast, in *The Iceman Cometh*, as Rich asserts, "none is married; they have no families; in fact, they have no identity save the 'lie of the pipe dream.'" Their world is "so dark and silent that only conjured illusion gives it substance." As always, there is that alternative to illusion—death—but eventually even Larry admits his dream of death is a lie—that he drinks so he will not hear himself praying: "Beloved Christ, let me live a little while longer at any price." Larry is, as Rich claims, "one of the few O'Neill characters to stare into the abyss of emptiness and survive." Brustein states the play reveals "the impossibility of salvation in a world without God." The only saving grace comes, as Rich notes in his discussion of *Hughie*, when the characters "come together in a kind of communion of souls, a giving of the self to another. . . . The two men make contact; they recognize one another's humanity and help each other to survive."

The bleak world that O'Neill depicts in the last plays does not represent his final statement on the human condition, on what is truly necessary for man to survive. This would have come in his, until now unknown, final play, *The Last Conquest*, which would have been his most religious drama. Its message is that man can expect little help from his fellow man and must turn to his Redeemer God—not the golden graven image that man in the two thousand years of Christianity has molded to his own materialistic likeness, but the bleeding crucified Christ. Lack of faith has ushered in an Orwellian world. In a letter dated December 16, 1942 to Dudley Nichols, O'Neill says it is about the "World-Dictator fantasy of a possible future, and the attempted last campaign of Evil to stamp out even the unconscious memory of God in man's spirit."[19]

Man's obsession with material things has left him spiritually dead. Again the Biblical question is asked in the play: "What would it profit a man to gain the whole world and lose his own soul?" In this uncompleted last play, O'Neill repeats again a concept that has dominated his work: the greed and materialism of the American character and the disregard of the spiritual. Even though the majority of the people have lost even the vaguest memory of God, there are, as there will always be, a few who will cling to their faith. When a character is asked if he remembers Christ, he replies that he does not. He thinks for a time and says, "I remember grandfather kept a Bible hidden under his mattress. I told the police and they came and took him away. And then they hung grandfather and grandfather laughed"—just as Lazarus laughed—with the laughter which is Life, with the certainty of eternal life.

At no other time in the history of modern man has the need for such a message been greater. But would O'Neill's countrymen have heeded it had the play been completed— or even listened? Would they not, as they have in the past, again reject their native modern-day Lazarus? It is incomprehensible to the Europeans represented in the first part of this collection why O'Neill has not received the recognition and acclaim in this country that he deserves, why he is considered, as Timo Tiusanen says, "an embarrassment" to Americans. Like a man who refuses to accept the reflection he sees in the mirror as his own, Americans continue to reject the dramatist and his vision of life and the need for a "behind-life" force.

O'Neill was Irish and claimed that this "explained" him. He was more than that, however, being an *American* Irishman. How different he would have been had his father and mother's parents never come to this country, and had he been born in Ireland: Catholicism untainted by American materialism (and possibly not rejected); family unscathed by the struggle with the Yankees—descendants of those English foes of the Irish—to belong in New England. Yet without the tensions and conflicts that life in the United States created in him and his family, without exposure to democratic idealism, would he have ever become a playwright? He was so typically American in the things he liked: fast cars (and women); ragtime; and sports—baseball, boxing, horse racing. But he was *not* a nationalist. He decried the evils and weaknesses he saw in his country and its people and determined to expose and right them. Deploring the cultural wasteland of his own country in the early twentieth century, he crossed the borders of the mind, took on a world view— turning to Europeans for theatrical, literary, and philosophical inspiration: to Strindberg, Ibsen, Chekhov, Hauptmann, Kaiser, and Toller; to Conrad and Zola; to Nietzsche, Freud, Schopenhauer, and Marx. Fundamentally, however, it was to the ancient Greek dramatists he turned for his tragic vision of man, victim of his flawed inner self and fated by some outer force. In doing so, he demonstrated his universality, his power and ability to transcend national boundaries and his own cultural heritage to become a prime force in world literature.

In life, the dramatist experienced both personal and theatrical rejection; he was a dislocated Irish American, a playwright in search of a theatre. Possibly the thoughts reflected in this book may hasten the day of his acceptance, understanding, and recognition. It may be that in the coming years Americans will embrace the "world view" presented here, and O'Neill will finally belong—live onstage in the American theatre.

NOTES

[1] Playbill for the Provincetown production of Strindberg's *The Spook Sonata*, January 3, 1924.

[2] Croswell Bowen, "The Black Irishman," in *O'Neill and His Plays*, ed. by Cargill, Fagin, and Fisher (New York, 1961), p. 65.

[3] Eugene O'Neill, *A Moon for the Misbegotten* in *The Later Plays of Eugene O'Neill*, edited and introduced by Travis Bogard (New York, 1967), p. 302. Future references to this play are from this edition and appear in parentheses in the text.

[4] John Henry Raleigh, "O'Neill's *Long Day's Journey into Night* and New England Irish-Catholicism," *Partisan Review*, XXVI (Fall 1959), p. 588.

[5] Eugene O'Neill, *Long Day's Journey into Night* (New Haven, 1956), p. 20. Future references to this play are from this edition and appear in parentheses in the text.

[6] Quoted by Joseph Wood Krutch in his introduction to *Nine Plays* (New York, 1941), p. xvii.

[7] Croswell Bowen, "*Rehearsing The Iceman Cometh*," in *O'Neill and His Plays*, Cargill et al., p. 460.

[8] Eugene O'Neill, *The Iceman Cometh* (New York, 1957), p. 278. Future references to this play are from this edition and appear in parentheses in the text.

[9] Letter from Clifford Leech, June 4, 1977, one of many in a treasured collection from a man who was a true dedicated scholar and a warm, compassionate human being. Even though he was a Renaissance specialist, he was deeply interested these past two decades in O'Neill scholarship and planning, even on the day prior to his sudden death, to participate in an O'Neill session I chaired at the 1977 Modern Language Association Convention. Like O'Neill, he was a former practicing Catholic and did considerable research on the confessional aspects of *The Iceman Cometh* and *A Moon for the Misbegotten* in response to questions raised in our discussion of these plays. After consulting Catholic theologians, he states: "Confession can be made to a layman if a priest is not available (as I suppose one would not be

available to Don Parritt or to James Tyrone, for psychological reasons). He [Father Lawrence Shook] was a bit shocked by what I told him of Josie's last words in *A Moon*. He also gave the, to me, astonishing news that (i) auricular confession was not the practice of the early church, (ii) it was introduced by the Irish missionaries to the European continent. So—but surely O'Neill didn't know this? Hickey in his public confession was reverting to an early practice of the church. As, I suppose, Raskolnikov was, though I have never enquired about the Russian Orthodox practice of confession."

[10] Leech, Letter of May 28, 1977.

[11] Croswell Bowen, *The Curse of the Misbegotten* (New York, 1959), p. 314.

[12] Leech, Letter of May 28, 1977.

[13] Eugene O'Neill, "A Letter to Arthur Hobson Quinn," in *O'Neill and His Plays*, Cargill et al., p. 125.

[14] O'Neill's letter, April 3, 1939, to Theresa Helburn of the Theatre Guild suggesting the possibility of a musical adaptation of *The Hairy Ape*. (Eugene O'Neill Collection, Yale)

[15] In 1943 when the tremor of O'Neill's hand prevented him from writing his plays in longhand, part of him yearned, like Larry Slade, for death; yet the dramatist clung tenaciously to life for another decade. In a futile effort to encourage O'Neill to dictate his plays, Lawrence Langner sent him a Sound Scriber. Discussing experiments with the machine in a letter to Langner dated May 13, 1944, O'Neill states:

> I read into the mike of the Sound Scriber a favorite bit of mine from "The Iceman Cometh"—Act Three, the brief passage between Hickey and Larry when Larry is forced to admit, while refusing to admit, that his saving dream that he is finished with life and sick of it and will welcome the long sleep of death is just a pipe dream. When I played the record back and listened to the voice that was my voice and yet not my voice saying: "I'm afraid to live, am I?—and even more afraid to die! So I sit here, my pride drowned on the bottom of a bottle, keeping drunk so I won't see myself shaking in my britches with fright, or hear myself whining and praying, 'O Blessed Christ, let me live a little longer *at any price*! If it's only for a few days more, or a few hours even, let me still clutch greedily to my yellow heart this sweet treasure, this jewel beyond price, the dirty, stinking bit of flesh which is my beautiful life!' "—well, it sure did some-

thing to me. It wasn't Larry, it was my ghost talking to me, or I to my ghost— . . . It really was a moment of strange drama.

(Eugene O'Neill Collection, Yale)

[16] Kenneth Macgowan, "The O'Neill Soliloquy," in *O'Neill and His Plays*, Cargill et al., p. 449.

[17] Bowen, "The Black Irishman," p. 65.

[18] Eugene O'Neill, *Hughie, The Later Plays*, p. 287–88.

[19] One of the many letters written to Nichols by the dramatist (dating from April 20, 1932 to March 20, 1949). By late 1942 O'Neill had finished the first draft of *A Moon for the Misbegotten*, but he was unable to rewrite it. Discussing *The Last Conquest*, he states:

. . . again in this play, I soon feel my creative impulse blocked by the hopeless certainty that it could not be understood now, or its possibilities admitted—more than that, a feeling in myself that, until this war, which must be won, is won, people should concentrate on the grim surface and not admit the still grimmer, soul-disturbing depths. I censor myself, so to speak, and with this shackle added to recurring spells of illness and mental depression—In short, "The Last Conquest" remains for the most part in scenario, although it constantly haunts me.

(Eugene O'Neill Collection, Yale)

THE LAST CONFESSION
O'Neill and the Catholic Confessional

John Henry Raleigh

I

The mode of private or auricular confession, with absolution granted by the priest who also decrees a private penance, appears to have stemmed from the doctrines and practices of the Celtic Church of the fifth and sixth centuries. The Penitentials, vast compendiums of sins, with designated penances, were also developed most extensively by the Celtic monks. In those same fifth and sixth centuries Colambanus and other Celtic missionaries to Britain and to Europe imported the Celtic confessional system to these other lands where it finally won out over the Roman system of the confessional: confession of sin to a bishop or priest; a public exmologesis, that is, a penance, often terribly harsh, that entailed public humiliation; and a public reconciliation or absolution, which had to be effected by a bishop. In the Celtic system the penance and the reconciliation were private, and a priest, rather than a bishop, was the minister of reconciliation. Furthermore confession, and what it entailed, under the Roman system, was, like Baptism, a once in a life-time experience, with no second chance although deathbed reconciliations, if not with the Church at least with God, were thought to be possible. The Celtic Church, on the other hand, enjoined frequent and recurrent confessions. By the middle of the twelfth century penances, once harsh, were beginning to be softened or mitigated. The Lateran Council of 1215 made obligatory the practice of recurring confession for all Christian people in the Latin Church. In the sixteenth century during the Counter-Reformation the confessional box was introduced, especially designed for the confessing of women whose confessions often led to matters other than absolution and penance, and the Council of Trent established the principal doctrines and practices, including the confessional, that guided and animated the Catholic Church until the second half of the twentieth century. Thus the modern Catholic confessional, stemming principally from the Celtic Church, was essentially, except for the confession box, in place by the thirteenth century.[1]

I proffer this capsule history, and it is only the barest schema for an extremely complex, and sometimes debated, subject, to underline a fine historical resonance or irony, namely, that it was in the first part of the twentieth century (whose second half was to see the transformation or even, in some respects, the disappearance of that Church formalized by the Council of Trent) that two "Celts," both Catholic apostates, one a native Irishman, the other an Irish American, gave the most powerful literary representations of the practice, and the psychology, of the Catholic auricular confession, the one, James Joyce, in an explicit manner, the other Eugene O'Neill, in an implicit, even unconscious, manner.

For if the auricular confession of the Latin Church was extraordinarily important for millions of people for many centuries of Western civilization,[2] it would be difficult to realize this on the evidence of the bulk of Western literature, precisely the medium where one would expect the Confessional, with its unique moral and psychological configurations and implications, to appear. There was nothing quite like it in the ancient world, and there is nothing quite like it in the modern world, except for those Catholics who still go to confess although, so I am told, the institution itself has changed or is changing, like so many other aspects of the Old Church. Modern psychoanalysis, or any other kind of modern psychological "cure," bears little resemblance: No God, no

Biblical sanction, no "keeper of the keys," no Church, no
Heaven or Hell or "sin" or "absolution" or "penance" or
"prayer"; in short, nothing of the essential apparatus that
made the confessional work" (and it was free, too).

But it turns up very seldom in serious literature until
comparatively modern times. I use the word "serious" because stories, often scandalous, and characteristically involving a lecherous priest, about the confessional do appear in
medieval *fabliaux* and folk-tales. Henry Osborne Taylor, in
The Medieval Mind, mentions several in order to emphasize
the singular habits of mind that the confessional engendered,
as surely it must have.[3]

I shall confine my remarks about the appearance of the
confessional in literature to literature written in English
although I have the general impression that it does not surface with great frequency in either the literature of the Latin
Catholic cultures, Spain, France, and Italy, or in the literature of the countries of the Orthodox Church.[4]

The confessional is, of course, mentioned in medieval
English literature. Sir Gawain goes to confession. Its misuses
are mentioned in *Piers Plowman*. But even in the works of
Chaucer, the greatest English Catholic poet, the confessional
does not loom large, even though we are told that the Friar
is an easy confessor and the Pardoner is a fraud, as *Piers
Plowman* also testifies and as was no less than the historical
truth about so many members of this "profession." Since
Shakespeare's father, and even Shakespeare himself, have
been claimed by some to have been Catholic and since so
many of Shakespeare's plays take place in an historical past
and since Shakespeare's England was so close to Catholic
England, one might expect the confessional to appear with
some frequency in the plays, especially the English history
plays or the ones that take place in Italy. But such is not the
case.

"Shrift" plays a role in *Romeo and Juliet* (this word,
according to *The Harvard Concordance to Shakespeare*, occurs only nine times in all of Shakespeare's works, five of
them being in *Romeo and Juliet*). In *Measure for Measure*,
the Duke, disguised as a friar, confesses Juliet. In *Hamlet*,

Hamlet sends Rosencrantz and Guildenstern to Hell. Of equal significance is the infrequency with which the great, and once resonating, words connected with the confessional appear in Shakespeare: "contrition" never appears: "absolution" turns up once; "absolv'd" three times; "penance" nineteen times, often in a purely secular sense; the word "sin" appears only one hundred and seventy-nine times (out of a total of 884,647 words, 29,066 of them being different words); "confession" itself shows up only seventeen times, often in a secular sense. And all the variations of the word "confess" appear very infrequently and often, once more, are secular in their meaning. The same tends to be true of Elizabethan drama as a whole. Only in Ford's *'Tis Pity She's a Whore* does a confessing Friar play a prominent, and ambiguous, role. From Shakespeare's time on, of course, English literature is mainly written by Protestants, and the confessional might not be expected to appear, as it does not. Milton's Adam and Eve, for example, are Protestants and therefore confess their sins, with tears, contrition, and sorrow, directly to the Deity, in this case the son of God (*Paradise Lost*, X, 11. 1097–1104). But neither is the auricular confessional important in the works of English Catholic poets, from Crashaw to Thompson and Hopkins.

Thus one of the great moral and psychological components of human life for millions of people over centuries of time appears very seldom in serious literature. Why this should be so I do not know. Perhaps its very secrecy—only the sinner, the priest and God were involved—"the seal of the confessional"—kept it in the dark. In any event, the Celts seem to have had the first and last word on the subject.

The confessional first surfaces in a detailed and explicit way in the nineteenth century in the work of an American novelist, himself a Protestant of a New England heritage. I refer, of course, to Hawthorne's *The Marble Faun* and the three chapters (38, 39, 40) in which at St. Peters in Rome the guilt-ridden Protestant woman, Hilda, actually kneels at the confessional box and unburdens herself of her guilt to a wise old priest. She (or Hawthorne) cannot bring herself actually to join the Church, as the priest wishes her to do, nor can she believe that the priest has actually absolved her (only God can do that), but, nonetheless, she feels "beatitude" after her confession and concludes that the Popish faith is "a miracle of fitness" for "all human occasions"—if only its priests were free from error or that there were angels to work the system. Historically, this sequence in *The Marble Faun* would represent the vestigial remains of the once powerful New England Puritan tradition paying a belated tribute to what it thinks was the moral and psychological wisdom of the Old Church.

It is in twentieth century literature that the confessional appears more generally: in the novels of Graham Greene and Mauriac, for example. But it appears most prominently, as I have said, in the works of apostate Irish Catholics, pre-eminently, in an explicit way, in Joyce and, in an implicit way, in O'Neill. Paralleling these major treatments are two classic short stories (once more by an Irishman and an American Irishman) about the effect of the confessional on young boys: its possibilities for wild humor in Frank O'Connor's "First Confession," and its possibilities for sheer terror in F. Scott Fitzgerald's "Absolution." To which should be added the rather more grim confessional humor of O'Connor's "News for the Church." The most detailed and powerful treatment of the confessional in high or serious literature appears in Joyce's *Portrait of the Artist as a Young Man.* This same institution is analyzed from a secular point of view in *Ulysses* by Shrewd Mr. Bloom (*Ulysses,* 82–83), and Gerty McDowell describes for the reader her confession to Father Conroy (358), as does Molly Bloom hers to Father Corrigan (741). The word "confession" is woven into *Finnegans Wake* in a variety of clever ways: for example, "daily comfreshenall" (F.W., 619.15). Indeed it is not fanciful to see *Finnegans Wake* as a vast, secular Penitential and Joyce himself as a secular reincarnation of that same Colambanus whose name he had invoked several times in *Ulysses.* By all odds the work of Joyce provides the largest visible memorial to the ancient and venerable institution of the confessional. Its largest invisible memorial, so I shall argue, is in the plays of Eugene O'Neill, especially his last plays.

II

The chief detritus of Catholicism left to the Apostate O'Neill was the psychology and, to a certain degree, the form of the confessional, which, like almost every other deeply-felt experience in his earlier life, was to surface most markedly and powerfully in his late plays, specifically in *The Iceman Cometh, Long Day's Journey into Night* and *Moon For the Misbegotten*.

Before proceeding to a demonstration of this proposition I wish first to set forth the manner in which in his youth O'Neill was indoctrinated with the Catholic faith and especially with the elaborate and solemn rite of the confessional. From about the age of seven to about the age of fourteen O'Neill was in Catholic schools. Of these years three things should be remarked: first, he was an altar boy and thus participated in the rites and rituals of the Mass; second, beginning at the age of eight, he began to ingest, with great fervor, the Catholic Catechism (ten years later, at eighteen, he was to adopt *Thus Spake Zarathustra* as his mature catechism); and third, in his twelfth year, and with similar devotional zeal, he received his first communion being in that process confirmed and participating in the sacrament of the Holy Eucharist.

The first thing to be underscored is how meaningful the Confirmation ceremony must have been to a youthful believer in the light of the assertions and injunctions of the Catechism which, with its question-and-answer insistency, would by now have been drummed into the consciousness of the acolyte. O'Neill was confirmed on Ascension Thursday, May 24, 1900. This means that the night before he would have confessed to a priest both his venial and mortal sins. If he had been sincere, and there is no reason to believe he was not, he would, according to the injunctions of the Catechism, have gone through the following four experiences: first, a sense of contrition which was interior, supernatural, sovereign, and universal; second, and spoken to the priest, a confession which was entire, humble, sincere, and short; third, he would have felt satisfaction; fourth and finally he would have been granted absolution by the priest, the keeper of the keys to the kingdom, who would also stipulate a penance. The next morning, having fasted from midnight on and being in a state of grace, he would have undergone the sacrament of the Eucharist, receiving, in the form of bread, the body of Christ, while the priest on the altar would be receiving both the body and the blood (wine) of Christ. Having been Confirmed, he would have had bestowed upon him the seven gifts of the Holy Ghost: Wisdom, Understanding, Counsel, Fortitude, Knowledge, Piety, and Fear of the Lord.

I go into such detail in an attempt to give a sense of how awesome, portentous, solemn, and final this elaborate ceremony for the remission of sins must have appeared to a youthful, sensitive, and sincere believer and how important to him thereafter would be the problem of the remission of sins, irrespective of the mechanism used, but with the significant difference that the mature O'Neill replaced the word "sin," which appears very rarely in his work, with the word "guilt," which is omnipresent: the transition, so to speak, from Christ to Freud. The corollary positive term is the word "forgive," which also occurs with great frequency in O'Neill's own plays.[5] In fact, the basic moral dialectic in his plays is that between "guilt" and "forgiveness."

In his darkest mood, not infrequent, O'Neill thought that nobody, not even God, could ever be forgiven. In *All God's Chillun Got Wings* he has Jim say of the Deity: "Maybe He can forgive what you've done to me; and maybe He can forgive what I've done to you; but I don't see how He's going to forgive—Himself." (II, 3) Similarly, in his single most guilt-ridden play, if only for the fact that it is the longest, *Mourning Becomes Electra*, his chief characters reiterate that there can be no forgiveness and that guilt is an infinite regress into which one sinks and sinks.

At the same time there is an insistent and equally powerful urge among these assorted sinners to confess, as they often do, and sometimes at great length. Especially as they get older do the O'Neillian characters wish to "confess," and not always to wrong-doing but simply to tell the truth about themselves although they may also feel that in the last analysis they are confessing their own special "truth" only to the empty air. Thus Tiberius in Scene I of Act IV of *Lazarus Laughed*:

> I know it is folly to speak—but—one gets old, one becomes talkative, one wishes to confess, to say the thing one has always kept hidden, to reveal one's unique truth—and there is so little time left—and one is done! Therefore the old-like children talk to themselves, for they have reached that hopeless wisdom of experience which knows that though one were to cry it in the streets to multitudes, or whisper it in the kiss to one's beloved, the only ears that ever hear ones secret are ones own!

However, they also may occasionally confess a specific transgression to another person and gain a kind of secular absolution. Thus when in Act Eight of *Strange Interlude* Nina confesses her guilty secret of the real paternity of her son Gordon to Charlie Marsden, he assures her that he understands all that she has suffered and concludes, "— and I forgive you." She in turn then forgives her deceased father, who, she believes, had caused all the trouble in the first place.

But it is in the last plays that a secular version of the confessional—contrition, confession, a hoped-for absolution —appears more clearly and pervasively.

The most complex of these secular equivalents to the Catholic confessional occurs in the last act of *The Iceman Cometh*, for here there are two, simultaneous contrapuntal confessions going on, Hickey's and Parritt's, the one public and the other private. In an unexpected way these two confessions encompass, in a very rough fashion, a history of the development of the Confessional itself, although I have no reason to believe that O'Neill was aware of this. Hickey's confession is full of archaic echoes, with its public admission of guilt and its public self-condemnation. One of the reasons for public confessions and penances in the early Church was the notion that the sin of one member infects the whole social body and that therefore society itself must deal with the transgressor and his transgressions both because of pity for the sinner and for the sake of its own purity. And in a

weird, ironical, upside-down way one could say that Hickey's
public confession disinfects the congregation of Harry Hope's
saloon, which he himself had infected in Act I of the play.
Second, Hickey deals with two of the three sins that the early
Church thought so abominable that it would not grant absolution for them: adultery and murder, the third being
idolatry (later replaced by heresy). It did not, however, rule
out of the question that God Himself could absolve the
sinner. Third, Hickey's confession is inordinately long and
detailed, seemingly interminable to its reluctant auditors,
and is thus a reminder that historically a true Catholic confession must not be a generalized account of sin but a specific
account, "one by one." In the Middle Ages learned "doctors"
expended enormous ingenuity in devising manuals of inquiry
by which the penitent would be questioned minutely.

The Lateran canon of 1216 enjoined that sinners be
interrogated on the Decalogue, the seven Deadly Sins, the
abuses of the five senses, the thoughts and lusts of the heart,
and so on. Sacerdotal insatiability for details, sometimes quite
explicit, even brutal (O'Connor's priest in "News for the
Church" pursues this line of questioning), had been considerably curbed in more modern times, with the Jesuits,
come to be known as the most skillful confessors, having
exercised a moderating force. There was an allied and
reciprocal tendency for particularly anxious sinners to "over-
confess." In the *Waning of the Middle Ages* Huizinga describes one such person, whom he read of in Froissart, a man
who near the end of his life was shriven twice a day and would
not allow his confessor to leave his side. As might be expected, *Finnegans Wake* describes this phenomenon too:

> he confessed to it on Hillel and down Dalen and in the
> places which the lepers inhabit in the places of stones and in
> pontofert jusfaggading amoret now he come to think of it
> (*F.W.* 350.3–5).

For all these reasons O'Neill's Catechism told him a confession should be short (a habit which he, like most over-
confessors, could never acquire). But a confession must also
(one's mind boggles at the subtlety of distinctions that the

Church Fathers had to make) be full and circumstantial. Above all it must not be vague: "Wee, confused the Gripes limply . . ." (*F.W.* 156.31). Thus when in *Ulysses* Miss Marion Tweedy remembers confessing, before her marriage, to Father Corrigan that a man (one Leopold Bloom) had touched her person, Father Corrigan immediately wishes to know just where on her person she was touched (it was on her "bottom"). So in *The Iceman Cometh* Hickey must tell it all, down to the last unsavory detail.

Finally, Hickey's confession embodies the three principal meanings that the word "Confession" has historically encompassed. First, it is a confession in a legal sense, that is, an admission of a crime, and with two policemen listening to it. As Rocky says to Detective Moran, "And if yuh want a confession all yuh got to do is listen." Second, it is a Confession in the more philosophical sense of that word, à la St. Augustine or Rousseau, that is, a profession of a belief of some kind, albeit that in Hickey's case the "belief" is a series of negatives: the fallacy of pipe dreams, the inability of humans to endure endless guilt, and finally, and most terribly, his sudden revelation to himself, at the end of his confession, that he really hated his wife, with the grim reminder that in the "foul rag and boneshop of the heart" love and hate are difficult to disentangle. Thus his is a recital not only of what he did but a dissertation on the ambiguities of the human psyche. Third, it is a confession in the moral or Catholic sense, detailing the wrongs over a great number of years he had done to his wife, all his mortal sins served up in a rush and capped by a homicide.

Counterpointing this is Parritt's brief auricular confession to Slade, who, we know, will observe the "seal of confession" and never reveal to anyone else what Parritt has told him, namely, that like Hickey, his supposed love—for his mother—was only a mask for hatred. Further, he demands of his secular confessor an appropriate penance, equal or worse than that of Hickey, who is going to the Electric Chair. And Slade finally awards him the most terrible sentence of all: suicide. After the faint sound of the dull thud of Parritt's fallen body penetrates the "No Chance Saloon," Slade, who was based on Terry Carlin, a friend of O'Neill in his early days and like O'Neill an apostate Catholic, whispers to himself: "Poor dèvil! (*A long-forgotten faith returns to him for a moment and he mumbles*) God rest his soul in peace." But he quickly reneges on this hoary banality, citing Hickey, and remembering that God is dead, "Ah, the damned pity—the wrong kind, as Hickey said." There is even a curious ancient reverberation in this grim demise of Parritt, for in the early centuries of public penance, the penances were sometimes so severe that the penitents committed suicide to escape these exactions.

Long Day's Journey was O'Neill's own confession and act of forgiveness. Carlotta O'Neill said that his memories of his family haunted and "bedeviled" him and that he had to "forgive" whatever it was that caused the tragedy between himself and his father and mother. In *Long Day* there is one ardent Catholic, Mary Tyrone, one conventional believer, James, one sceptic, Edmund, and one nihilist, Jamie. The psychology of the confessional appears only at the extremes of the spectrum, in the believer and the nihilist, for the mutual autobiographical outpourings of James and Edmund Tyrone in Act IV of the play are not so much confessions of sins, although some are admitted, as they are justificatory apologia, each explaining to the other why he is what he is and why he has done what he has done. The only confession is delivered by Jamie in Act IV when he tells his brother of his secret and lethal desire to make his brother a failure like himself, after which he mumbles: "That's all. Feel better now. Gone to confession. Know you absolve me, don't you, Kid? You understand."

Mary Tyrone's dilemma is the classic one of the true believer: like Claudius in *Hamlet* she cannot make a perfect Act of Contrition because she knows it would be a lie:

> If I could only find the faith I lost, so I could pray again!
> *She pauses—then begins to recite the Hail Mary in a flat, empty tone*
> "Hail Mary, full of grace! The Lord is with thee;
> blessed art Thou among women."
> *Sneeringly*

You expect the Blessed Virgin to be fooled by a lying dope
fiend reciting words! You can't hide from her! (Act III)

This is only one of several references to the Virgin Mary by
Mary Tyrone, who never prays to God or says the Lord's
prayer and whose remembrance of her girlhood prayers is
always to the Blessed Virgin. The reasons for this are various:
that she had been educated by nuns in a convent school
named St. Mary's; that the Virgin represented purity; that
her own name was Mary; and so on. But the chief reason is,
as the Catechism explains in Lesson XXIII—"On the Lord's
Prayer and Hail Mary"—that Mary, of all the saints, had the
greatest intercessory power with the Lord:

Q. And why do you always say the Hail Mary after the
Lord's Prayer?

A. That by intercession we may more easily obtain what
we ask for in the Lord's prayer.

Moreover, in the aura with which the Virgin Mary is
encompassed, on one side of her, in her cult, motherly, sweet,
compassionate, once a sorrowing mother herself, one can see
how the Mary Tyrones of this world would turn to her. There
is in particular a prayer to the Virgin Mary in the Catechism
which perfectly mirrors the mood, its desires and its despair,
of Mary Tyrone on the day and night of the long day's
journey. Whether O'Neill had it in mind I don't know, but
he had certainly read it as a boy, as had his mother in her
convent school days. Both had heard it many times, for this
is the prayer said by the priest and the congregation at the
end of the Low Mass, after the "Hail Mary" had been recited
three times:

Hail, holy Queen, Mother of Mercy, hail, our life, our sweet-
ness, and our hope. To thee do we cry, poor banished children of Eve. To thee do we send up our sighs, mourning
and weeping in this valley of tears. Turn, then most gracious
advocate, thine eyes of mercy toward us; and after this, our
exile, show unto us the blessed fruit of thy womb, Jesus. O
clement, O loving, O sweet Virgin Mary.

By a strange and happy irony, so rare in the world of the
O'Neills, the mythical Virgin Mary did finally intercede for

the real Mary Ellen O'Neill, who did in fact finally overcome her morphine addiction by a self-imposed sojourn in
a convent.

The simplest and purest example of the confessional
mode among O'Neill's plays is, appropriately, his last, *A
Moon for the Misbegotten,* which is devoted to a vicarious
absolution of a dead person who was the greatest, as well as
the most guilt-ridden, sinner O'Neill had known, his brother
Jamie. Moreover, the central action of the play constitutes a
lay confession, which would have been accorded some sanction by the Church itself. And once more, as in *The Iceman
Cometh,* age-old reverberations of the Catholic faith can be
detected.

One of the most explicit of the apostolic commands for
confession in the Bible is St. James' injunction (V.16): "Confess your faults one to an other, and pray for one another,
that ye may be healed." In other words, confession of sins is
to be mutual and open, and there is no mention of priests.
And even after the twelfth century, when the priestly class
was firmly established as the keeper of the keys and the sole
dispenser of absolution, the question of the efficacy of lay
confession still remained debated and debatable. For example,
in an emergency, such as a ship-wreck, lay confession was
deemed efficacious. It was even maintained by some learned
doctors of the church that confession to a "righteous person"
was valid. St. Thomas Aquinas' opinion was: confession to a
layman can be made in the absence of one's own parish
priest; the act itself is more important than the person to
whom it is made; and though a layman cannot absolve, this
defect can be supplied by God. What this meant is that although the sinner in a lay confession might be reconciled to
God, he could not be reconciled to the Church. In other
words, even St. Thomas could not solve completely this
dilemma. However, according to the logic of this situation,
the penitent, although he or she would finally go to Heaven,
would have to spend a longer time in Purgatory by virtue of
the fact that he or she was not reconciled to the Church. In
the sixteenth century the Council of Trent, which determined the evolution of the modern Catholic Church, left

the question open although, of course, it maintained that only priests could absolve.

In *A Moon for the Misbegotten* the confessional is the front steps, elevated like an altar, of Phil Hogan's shanty in Connecticut, the "priest," or "priestess" is Josie Hogan; the penitential sinner is James Tyrone. Josie herself is, preeminently, a righteous person. In Tyrone's words: "You're real and healthy and clean and fine and warm and strong and kind" (I've not done an empirical study of the matter, but I doubt that in all of O'Neill's plays any other character has attributed to him or her such a series of positive attributes). It is thus to this great Earth-Mother, upon whose ample breasts he lays his sodden head, that Jamie Tyrone in the dark watches of a moonlit night confesses his deepest guilts: his drunken behavior at his mother's death bed and during the four-day train ride bearing the corpse from California to New York for a funeral he never attended. In the morning both the priestess and the penitent feel that a genuine confession has been effected. Josie: "I understand now, Jim Darling, and I'm proud you came to me as one in the world you know loves you enough to understand and forgive—and I do forgive!" To her father she gives a darker and more explicitly theological version of this miracle in the night: "it was a damned soul coming to me in the moonlight, to confess and be forgiven and find peace for a night." And Tyrone, on his part, feels that sense of "satisfaction" that the Catechism says is an integral part of a true confession: a "nice, dreamy peaceful hangover for once—as if I'd had a sound sleep without nightmares." Further he feels, as there is every reason to believe the real Jamie O'Neill never felt: "Sort of at peace with myself—as if all my sins had been forgiven." In this constellation of words and phrases: "forgive," "damned soul." "Confess," "as if my sins had been forgiven," one can hear the echoes of the Catholic confessional and beyond that, more faintly, the scriptural injunctions from James, Matthew, and John, principally, upon which that institution was based.

Such a confession as that of Jamie Tyrone to Josie Hogan could not be considered the equivalent to a churchly one. According to Father O'Neill of the Jesuit Theological Center at Berkeley, Jamie's confession would have to be considered "devotional" rather than "sacramental," i.e., involving absolution. But then if Aquinas was correct, God Himself could have intervened and granted absolution, finally, to the most turbulent of the turbulent O'Neills, to the one who must have been the most unquiet in his grave but who, because of his brother's act of forgiveness, would now stir no more.

NOTES

[1] For my remarks on the confessional I have, in part, relied on my memories of a Catholic childhood and a rereading of the Catholic Catechism. For its history I have consulted several books and articles: Oscar D. Watkins, *A History of Penance* (London, 1920); R. C. Mortimer, *The Origins of Private Penance in the Western Church* (London, 1939). Mortimer's book was written precisely to contradict the thesis of Galtier's *L'Eglise et la Remission des Peches* (Paris, 1921), namely that private or auricular confession developed out of the Roman or Continental Church rather than the Celtic Church, as the majority of scholars in the field believe to be the case, as does Watkins. John Bossy's *The English Catholic Community, 1570–1850* (London, 1976) was helpful, as was his "The Social History of Confession In the Age of The Reformation," *Transactions of the Royal Historical Society* (Read March 8, 1974) pp. 21–38. Also Thomas N. Tentler, "The Summa for Confessors as an Instrument of Social Control," *The Pursuit of Holiness in Late Medieval and Renaissance Religion*, ed. Charles Trinkhaus and Heiko A. Oberman.

The great work in English on the Confessional is the massive—three volumes—and magisterial compilation of Henry C. Lea, *A History of Auricular Confession and Indulgences in the Latin Church* (N.Y., 1968—orig. pub. in Philadelphia in 1895). The fact that Lea is a hostile witness to the institution he is describing in no way detracts from his authority. As Lea says in his Preface, he consulted no Protestant writers; only original sources, that is, Catholic authorities across the ages and popular works of devotion. Bossy in his "The Social History of Confession," cited above, calls Lea's work a "neglected masterpiece."

And Lea is named as an authority on "Penance" in *The Catholic Encyclopedia* itself.

² Lea is especially emphatic about the historical importance of the confessional. "The history of mankind," he says, "may be vainly searched for another institution which has established a spiritual autocracy such as that of the Latin Church, or which has exercized so vast an influence on human destinies, . . ." I, p.v; ". . . its vast and majestic omnipotence, profoundly affecting the course of European history and moulding in no small degree the conception of the duties which man owes to his fellows and to God." Ibid. p.vi. "Through the instrumentality of the confession, the sodality, and the indulgence (the Holy See's) matchless organization Is thus enabled to concentrate in the Vatican a power greater than has ever before been wielded by human hands." Ibid. Again in Volume I of his *History* in rehearsing the arguments by which the priests and prelates of the early Church had annointed themselves as the lineal descendents of Christ's apostles, Lea remarked:

"The transmission of the power from the apostles to those who were assumed to be their successors is the most audacious *non sequitur* in history and the success of the attempt can scarce be overestimated as a factor in the development of religion and civilization." Ibid. p. 109.

These portentous sentiments were uttered in America in 1895 when in fact the Roman Catholic Church was a much more powerful and controlling force in Western civilization than it is today. Furthermore, they were written by a Protestant who was, as I have remarked, a hostile witness to the historical phenomenon he was describing and who, like most hostile witnesses, exaggerated the power of the institution he disliked. Nevertheless, Lea was immensely learned and accurate on his subject and no remarks of his are to be taken lightly.

³ For example, no matter how many times the folk were told that a confession was never valid unless true penitence was sincerely experienced, in the popular mind the act of confession itself came to represent the whole fact. There had also come into being the idea that the Virgin Mary was a peculiarly efficacious intercessor for sinners. Thus Taylor tells the Medieval story of a widow who had committed incest with her son. The devil, in disguise, plotted to bring her before a secular tribunal for punishment. But she went to confession and prayed night and day to the Virgin. Came the trial and the Virgin drove away

the devil. Again, a person was possessed (*obsessus*) of a devil within him; this devil could make known the *unconfessed* sins of anyone brought before him although he could not recognize or remember confessed sins. A knight, suspecting, correctly, that a priest had seduced his wife, planned to bring the priest before the *obsessus*. But on the way the priest managed to escape for a few moments from the knight, darted into a barn, and confessed his sin to a layman there. Thus when he was brought before the *obsessus*, he escaped scot-free. Henry Osborn Taylor, *The Medieval Mind* (London, 1911) Vol. I, pp. 505–9.

[4] There are, of course, some instances of which I am aware. In *The Charterhouse of Parma* while preparing himself for confession Fabrizio thinks of the peculiar psychology that the confession had developed in his own mind.

That religion [Fabrizio had been educated by Jesuits] *deprives one of the courage to think of unfamiliar things*, and especially forbids *personal examination*, as the most enormous of sins; it is a step toward Protestantism. To find out of what sins one is guilty, one must question one's priest or read the list of sins, as it is to be found printed in the books entitled, *Preparation for the Sacrament of Penance*. Fabrizio knew by heart the list of sins, rendered into the Latin tongue which he had learned at the Ecclesiastical Academy of Naples. Stendhal, *The Charterhouse of Parma*, trans. C. K. Scott Moncrieff (New York, 1956), p. 211.

Since *War and Peace* contains virtually everything, the confession turns up several times. Natasha makes a "good" confession to an Orthodox priest (IX, xvii, Maude translation), and Hélène makes a "bad" confession to a Jesuit (XI, vi). Finally, Pierre Bezukhov, about to become a Freemason, thinks of the sense of "awe and veneration" he had experienced as a boy at confession (V, ii).

[5] J. Russell Reaver, *An O'Neill Concordance* (Detroit, 1969). For example, the word "sin" appears only forty-four times, while "guilt" (and its variants, "guilty," "guiltier," etc.) appears 275 times. "Forgive," and its variants, appear 229 times. But "contrition" turns up only seven times; and "absolve" only twice.

THE IRISH ATAVISM OF
A MOON FOR THE MISBEGOTTEN

John Henry Raleigh

If autobiographical memory is at the root of *Long Day's Journey* and *A Moon for the Misbegotten* and is the source of much of their power, then, I wish to suggest that a kind of racial or cultural memory is also at work in *A Moon for the Misbegotten*, making O'Neill's last play one of the most Irish, if not the most Irish, of all his plays. Only *A Touch of the Poet* is comparable. He was very much aware of this himself. "Are you Irish? What percent?" asked O'Neill of Mary Welch, the first Josie Hogan, for the 1947 production of the play. "I want as many people as possible connected with my play to be Irish." Since both of Miss Welch's parents had come from Cork and she was able to slip into a brogue for O'Neill's benefit, she passed muster.[1] And although the 1947 production proved to be a disaster, at least one reviewer, Russell McLaughlin of the *Detroit News* recognized what an atavistically Irish play it was:

> . . . he [O'Neill] is an Irish poet . . . His present characters . . . are actually dark, eerie, Celtic symbol-folk, probably contemporaries of Cuchulain [Cuhoolin] or Ossian, who beat their breasts at the agony of living, battle titanically and drink like Nordic gods, but are finally seen to wear the garb of sainthood and die for love. . . . Don't forget, whatever they say, that it's all a love lament played on ancient pipes.[2]

This shrewd intuition is correct, I believe, and gets immediately to the heart of the matter for *A Moon for the Misbegotten*. But I would elaborate further. I think the play's Irishness is both historical and mythical, as McLaughlin says, and that this aspect is most powerfully dramatized in the character of Josie and at the same time is sociological and contemporary, these aspects being concentrated in Phil Hogan and his family as a whole, including in-laws, and in their relationship to the world they inhabit.

Hogan and his family represent a miniature dramatization—O'Neill's version—of the Irish diaspora, principally by immigration to America, of the nineteenth and twentieth centuries. In fact, what O'Neill did was to transfer a plot of land, a shack, some pigs and potatoes, and a redoubtable peasant, a widower with four children, from Ireland to the state of Connecticut near New London. As in Ireland, the peasant does not own his land and as in Ireland the threat of eviction, one of the most powerful and pervasive forces in the terrible history of the Irish peasant, is always present; in *A Moon for the Misbegotten* the threat of eviction, or the imagined threat of eviction, is the main-spring of the plot (such as it is). As in Ireland, the living on this land is difficult, although for New England reasons—rocks, ticks, poison ivy, snakes, skunks. What the Hogans actually do on their farm, besides feeding the pigs, is somewhat of a mystery although the use of a pitchfork is mentioned. They also grow potatoes since Hogan mentions potato bugs as one of his afflictions and sings about them: "Oh the praties they grow small/ Over here, over here." As in Ireland, the family is in the proces of disintegration, as the sons leave the land and immigrate to "foreign" cities where they become either cops, as Thomas Hogan does in Bridgeport, or bar-keeps, as John Hogan is in Meriden. The daughters stay at home, and if they do not marry, remain virgins and finally become old maids, either companions or termagents or both to their aging parent(s). By the end of *A Moon* Josie, age 28, has passed over into this role.

But if the peasant has a difficult time scratching out a living on his barren barony with the threat of eviction over

his head and continuous border skirmishes with a wealthy
Anglo landowner whose estate abuts his own shabby patch
of land, he has at the same time great weapons in his armory:
he is a man of infinite peasant cunning, so crafty that he does
not just concoct schemes; he always has another and deeper
scheme behind or within the more apparent scheme. Second,
he is possessed of the ultimate Irish weapon, "the terrible
tongue" by the exercise of which he can reduce any inarticulate Anglo foe first to silence and second to flight. Third, he
is very powerful physically and when to his might is added
the even greater might of his Amazonian daughter, he then
becomes impervious to any physical threat. Finally, he has a
solace that is endless and never-failing: whiskey.

In short, O'Neill, as an Irish patriot, concluding his
career as a playwright with the setting of an Irish shanty, the
kind of place in which his father could have been born, made
his peasant not cringing and submissive but cunning, crafty,
and powerful. Above all, he is a free spirit, uninhibited, above
ordinary conventions, full of *joie de vivre*, a consumate actor,
switching his own roles easily and rapidly. Even when he has
been drinking, his role-playing never ceases and only he
knows how clear or unclear he is in the head (we finally learn
that he is always clear-headed, no matter how much alcohol
he has ingested).

As the character of Hogan unfolds—and he is not fully
revealed until the end of the play—the spectator begins to
realize that although O'Neill was using a historical archetype,
the Irish peasant using his age-old cunning in a new situation,
he departed more and more from the archetype as the play
unfolds and Hogan's character complicates. On his Irish
peasant side he is one of O'Neill's great comic creations.
But, it is finally revealed, he has a great soul too and fully
participates in that "love lament played on ancient pipes."
He constitutes as well a kind of final tribute to James O'Neill,
as will be explained.

In the creation of Hogan and his family, O'Neill devised
his own Irish myth: there are two kinds of Irishmen, and this
bifurcation is explained by the usual O'Neillean genetic
configurations. Hogan, a red-blooded Irishman, had married

into a family of anemic Irishmen. Fortunately, his wife was a genetic exception in her family, and out of the union of her physical power and untrammeled spirit with the similar attributes of Hogan emerged the incomparable Josie. Unfortunately, the genes of the wife's family were dominant in the creation of the rest of the Hogan progeny, Thomas, John, and Mike, who are Irish Catholic Puritans, Grade B—self-righteous, church-going, abstemious, prayer-saying. These are the types who are easily and quickly assimilated into the working and lower-middle classes of America. But the real Irish, tough and full of spirit, like Josie and Phil, are intransigent and unassimilable and remain, so to speak, in Ireland, in the shack on the land with the pigs and the potatoes, from which they rout the greatest force that the United States can pit against them, a multi-millionaire.

One can almost see the ghost of James O'Neill applauding this final act of Irish patriotism by his son. And in fact O'Neill Senior is a presence in the play itself, in two respects. First, he is remembered and referred to by the three chief characters, with affection by the Hogans and detestation by his oldest son. But the hostility of the son, such a force in *Long Day's Journey*, is finally annulled by the fact that Josie Hogan, probably the most admirable character that her creator ever conceived, is given the final benediction on James Tyrone-O'Neill: "He was one of the finest, kindest gentlemen who ever lived."

And O'Neill-Tyrone actually appears on the living stage since, as is so often the case with fathers in O'Neill's plays, parts of James O'Neill's character and some of his habits have been incorporated into Phil Hogan; the sheer human vitality, the virtually indestructible survival powers, the role-playing, the rapidly changing styles of rhetoric, the epic ingestion of whiskey all point to James O'Neill who had been described in *Long Day* as an Irish peasant. When to the picture is added the fact that Hogan, under all his bluster and talk, is unashamedly loving and sentimental about his dead wife and his living daughter, then the identification to James O'Neill becomes even more explicit. If the major impulse behind *A Moon* was an urge to pronounce a benediction on Jamie O'Neill, then certainly another impulse on O'Neill's part was to further the absolution of his father, which had been begun in Act IV of *Long Day's Journey*, and also to conclude his career with a burst, half comic, half serious, of his father's Irish nationalism.

In the O'Neillean family symbology, the mother had stood for Catholicism and the father for Irish nationalism. *Long Day*, because of the centrality of Mary Tyrone, is then the concluding Catholic play, while *A Moon* is the concluding Irish play, whose un-Catholic or anti-catholic bias is underlined by the fact that neither of the authentic Irish, Phil and Josie Hogan, attends Church or says prayers or worries about sin, except insofar as, in Josie's case, she can help to absolve the sins of another.

But I think O'Neill's Irish nationalism was much more atavistic than his father's and that this aspect of *A Moon* is chiefly embodied in Josie Hogan. Josie is one of O'Neill's most interesting and original characters. Her sources, in O'Neill's life, and her archetypes, in his plays, have often been noted, and I shall not review them here. Furthermore, I do not think any of them really account for Josie who is *sui generis* and has that startling originality of so many of O'Neill's mature creations. I do think, however, that the Irish atavism of *A Moon*, noted by Russell McLaughlin, goes further toward putting her into her proper frame of reference than almost any other explanation. The key episode in the play for this approach occurs in Act One when Hogan, furious that Josie has stolen six dollars from his little green bag to give to her run-away brother Mike, threatens physical violence to Josie, whereupon she stands up, broom handle in hand, and confronts him. He blusters some more, but soon gives up:

> (*Suddenly his eyes twinkle and he grins admiringly.*) Be God, look at you standing there with the club! If you ain't the damnedest daughter in Connecticut, who is? (*He chuckles and sits on the boulder again.*)

Granted that no actress can probably ever be found who combines both the physical requirements and the acting abilities to play the role of Josie, one can visualize in one's imagination what O'Neill had in mind here: powerful, barrel-like, squat Phil Hogan, laying down his arms in physical helplessness, and in admiration, before the Amazon who confronts him, club in hand, five inches taller than he, a perfectly proportioned 180 pounds, with "long smooth arms, immensely strong." What this image of Josie calls up is the fabled warrior women of the Celtic race. In their book on Irish mythology, *The Celtic Realms*, Myles Dillon and Nora Chadwick cite Ammianus Marcellinus, fourth century A.D., for his "unforgettable" picture of Gaulish women warriors:

> A whole troop of foreigners would not be able to withstand a single Gaul if he called his wife to his assistance, who is usually very strong, and with blue eyes [which Josie has], especially when, swelling her neck, gnashing her teeth, and brandishing her sallow arms of enormous size, she begins to strike blows mingled with kicks, as if they were so many missiles sent from a string of a catapult.[3]

Lady warriors people Irish folktales as well. Lady Gregory's rendering of "The Courting of Emer" mentions Aoife [Eefa], calling her the greatest woman warrior in the world. In "The Conception of Conchobar," a woman Ni-Assa ("Not Easy"), seeking revenge for the slaughter of her twelve fosterfathers, went throughout the land harrying people and providing irresistible in her fury and her weapons. Not only were these Irish women warriors, they were also the teachers of skill at arms for the men, as well as being teachers of wisdom, too.

One is reminded that in the exposition of Act One of *A Moon* it is related that once in the past Hogan was getting the worst of it in a fight with the Crowley brothers, whom he had cheated, until, as Josie reminds him, "I ran out and knocked one of them tail over tin cup against the pigpen."

Warriors, teachers of wisdom and feats of arms, eminent in their society, women in one phase of Irish mythology were assigned an especially significant role in the cult of rebirth: it was the woman, not the man, who is the spiritual vehicle who conveys the soul of the dead to rebirth in a later generation. I need hardly point out that in the "little Ireland" of Hogan's farm Josie fills all these roles, including the last, as she tries, in vain as it turns out, to bring to rebirth the soul of the "dead" Jamie Tyrone.

But Josie is not only an Irish warrior queen; she is also, in Jamie's phrase, "my Virgin Queen of Ireland,"—that is, a monumental embodiment of female chastity, one of the most powerful taboos or prohibitions in Irish legend, and, for that matter, in a good deal of Irish history. For example, Lady Gregory's Emer, whom Cuchulain [Cuhoolin] courts and marries (he is, by the way, much taken by her breasts, as Jamie is by Josie's) is said to have had the six gifts: beauty, voice, sweet speech, needlework, wisdom, and chastity. Leaving aside the needlework and the times when Josie is acting and speaking like an "old cow," one can see that Josie herself has five of the six gifts.

But O'Neill, as usual, added his own component by making his Gaelic warrior-virgin a confessor as well. In this respect *A Moon* has a symbiotic relationship to *Long Day*, as it does in so many other ways. In *Long Day* the Virgin Mary, symbol of purity and the most potent of intercessors for sinners seeking absolution from the Lord, had been, through the tortured mind, of Mary Tyrone, a tutelary presence. But in that play the Virgin is only a mystique and her intercessory powers cannot be truly invoked by the guilt-ridden Mrs. Tyrone. In *A Moon*, however, the Virgin is of the earth earthy, grossly palpable, and her intercessory powers are so potent as to allay, for a time anyway, the immense guilts of Jamie Tyrone-O'Neill.

Finally, to the warrior-virgin-confessor O'Neill added such a constellation of prime human virtues—"healthy," "clean," "fine," "warm," "strong," "beautiful,"—as to create, for the first and thus the last and thus the only time in his career and on a large scale, in every sense of that phrase, a fully good and wholly admirable central character. The ironies of this pass all estimation or enumeration: that the dramatist of human weakness, sin and guilt, over a career spanning some thirty years, should finally in his last play have conjured up a kind of female Gulliver amidst the Lilliputians—a gigantic goddess of goodness, whose stature and character also reverberate with ancient Irish themes.

But, of course, even she cannot escape the primal curse that O'Neill had laid on his entire imaginary world: she must suffer. In O'Neill's imagination suffering is a secular equivalent to the notion of Original Sin, the inescapable outcome of the human condition. And in no other play did he assert his primary theme so poignantly as in *A Moon*: that underneath Hogan's bluster, Tyrone's drunken cynicism, and Josie's bravado there is a suffering human soul, in the phrases of T.S. Eliot's "Preludes:"

> The notion of some infinitely gentle
> Infinitely suffering thing.

NOTES

[1] Louis Sheaffer, *O'Neill, Son and Artist* (Boston, 1973), pp. 592–3.

[2] Ibid., p. 596.

[3] Myles Dillon and Nora Chadwick, *The Celtic Realms* (London, 1967), p. 154.

THE PRESSURE OF PURITANISM IN EUGENE O'NEILL'S NEW ENGLAND PLAYS

Frederick Wilkins

Eugene O'Neill's New England plays demonstrate the effects of the decline of the original ideals of seventeenth-century Massachusetts Bay colonists. They are indeed "history plays," and perhaps no American writer, not even Hawthorne, has captured so vividly the disintegration of the once-vibrant faith of American Puritanism and the effects of that disintegration on New Englanders of the nineteenth and twentieth centuries. This study will not review the tenets of Calvinism. But that is no loss, since O'Neill's quarrel with Puritanism isn't as theological as it is personal. Nor will it consider the specific motivations for this obsession of O'Neill's such as the mistreatment of Irish Catholics by the Anglo-Protestant leaders of New London, a snobbery and ostracism that O'Neill felt very deeply. It was this New England environment that contributed to the paradox, detected by a number of writers, that there was abundant Puritanism in the very fiber of O'Neill himself. If it is there, then the anti-puritan arrows of the New England plays may well be, in part, self-directed. Like Eben Cabot and Reuben Light, he was probably a very puritanical anti-puritan!

Prior to the arrival of the Arabella in Massachusetts Bay in 1630, Governor John Winthrop, in his sermon, "A Model of Christian Charity," stressed the Puritans' covenant with God and their very positive sense of mission: to establish, in

that "city upon a hill," a New Israel, a community founded
on love, humility, cooperation, and absolute fidelity and
devotion to God above self. However, despite the tone of
positiveness in most of the sermon, Winthrop added a
prophetic warning:

> If we shall fall to embrace this present world and prosecute
> our carnal intentions, seeking great things for ourselves and
> our posterity, the Lord will surely break out in wrath against
> us, be revenged of such a perjured people, and make us
> know the price of the breach of such a covenant.

This warning was echoed repeatedly by others during the
next three decades, suggesting how fearful the Colony's
leaders were of descent into the forbidden lust for physical
pleasures and material rewards. In 1668 William Stoughton,
who would later preside at the Salem witchcraft trials, issued
the following advice, using stone imagery that anticipates
O'Neill's:

> If we should so frustrate and deceive the Lord's expecta-
> tions, that his covenant interest in us, and the workings of
> his salvation be made to cease, then All were lost indeed;
> Ruine upon Ruine, Destruction upon Destruction would
> come, until one stone were not left upon another.

Six years before Stoughton's words, a severe drought
plagued Massachusetts Bay and God's providence was naturally inferred, as it is in Michael Wigglesworth's poem on
the subject, emphatically prophetic of the one seemingly
traced in *Mourning Becomes Electra*. In the poem, the deity
himself corroborates the earlier fears of Winthrop. Are these
the men, he asks, who forsook their land and homes and
inheritances to walk with God and "serve and worship him
with all their might?"

> If these be they, how is it that I find
> Instead of Holiness, Carnality,
> Instead of heavenly frames an Earthly mind
> For burning zeal, luke-warm indifferency,
> For flaming love, key-cold Dead-heartedness,
> For temperance (in meat, and drinke, and clothes) excess?
> Whence cometh it, that Pride, and Luxurie

> Debate, Deceit, Contention, and Strife,
> False-dealing, Covetousness, Hypocrisie
> (With such like crimes) amongst them are so rife,
> That one of them doth overreach another
> And that an honest man can hardly trust his brother?

That such a denunciation is not just the effusion of one sick mind is evidenced in the published conclusions of a synod of clergy and lay elders, led by Increase Mather, in Boston in 1679. Entitled *The Necessity of Reformation*, the document provides, as did God in Wigglesworth's poem, an amazingly extensive list of iniquities in that "city on a hill," less than a half-century after its founding: ungodliness, heresy, parental abdication of responsibility, social contentiousness, business immorality, and the sins of sex and drunkenness. "The eyes of the world are upon us," as every Puritan leader had said since Peter Bulkley in the 1620s. And what those eyes see is a terrible decline from our original intent and ideals.

One could take the lists provided by Wigglesworth and Mather and find evidences of each and every iniquity somewhere in O'Neill's New England plays—especially in *Ile*, *Diff'rent*, *Desire Under the Elms*, *Dynamo*, the *Electra* trilogy and *More Stately Mansions*.

The early history of Massachusetts is, as Alan Simpson says in *Puritanism in Old and New England*, "the story of men who shared an ideal, left the old world to realize it in the new, only to discover when the work of planting was done that the spirit had evaporated." And so had love, as O'Neill was most emphatic in showing. In contrast, of course, matter accumulated: witness the wealth of the Harford and Mannon dynasties. And as materialism grew, and spirit evaporated, the latter was replaced by a rigid, cold code of standardized, repressive behavior—which may have been exaggerated *since* then, but the actuality was there. Each of the ideals of Winthrop's sermon had, in later days, been stood on its head, and each of these reversals is vividly captured somewhere in O'Neill's New England plays. For example, humility had turned to pride (Captain Keeney in *Ile*); love had turned to hate or lust (Ephraim Cabot in *Desire Under the Elms*);

selfless fidelity had turned to fevered, selfish acquisitiveness (the Harford enterprise in *More Stately Mansions*); cooperation had turned to contentiousness (the family dissolution of the Mannons in *Mourning Becomes Electra*); and piety had turned to a morality which was really a prudery stultifying to life and feeling and sensibility (Emma Crosby in *Diff'rent*).

Considering such a descent from the terms and ideals of the Covenant, a Puritan God would quite rightly have a "controversy with New England." And O'Neill did too. Not that he necessarily opposed the theoretical tenets of Calvinism or the ideals of 1630. O'Neill's major controversy was with the distortions of those ideals after the backsliding of the seventeenth century, the ascetic and narrow emphases of the eighteenth century, and the evolution of materialism and a cold, business mentality in the eighteenth and nineteenth centuries, when men like Franklin turned the Protestant ethic of work away from its original goal, of glorifying God, to a new goal, of increasing man's material prosperity.

Sophus Keith Winther's statement, that a constant theme in O'Neill is "the deadly effects of the Puritan ideal," needs qualification. It is not the 1630 ideals of love, humility, cocoperation, and selflessness that he is attacking directly; it is, rather, the distorted moral and social dictates that replaced those ideals when Puritan theology was largely abandoned— except for the emotional outburst of the Great Awakening— and was reduced to the hypocritical curses of stony patriarchs like Ephraim Cabot. O'Neill's real enemy was with small *p* puritanism: all the anti-Dionysian elements that were there *in posse* from the start, but that later grew obsessively large. And his plays provide many illustrations of this decline of New England Puritanism.

Diff'rent is not a great play, but it is an interesting one in terms of O'Neill's attitude toward the small *p* remnants of a moribund Puritanism. Kenneth Macgowan considered the play "a vigorous and healthful attack upon the puritanism that eats away so much of the creative happiness of life." But certainly that argument would be stronger if it were understood why Emma Crosby is so obsessed with having what her uncle Jack calls "a Sunday-go-to-meetin'-Saint" for a husband. However, even if her obsession isn't motivated theologically—by some desire to wed one of the "elect"— nevertheless, her obvious loathing of sex, and the resultant rejection of Caleb Williams do seem to arise from a puritanical aversion, a fear of life—what O'Neill, in his working notes for *Electra*, calls "the Puritan sense of guilt turning love to lust." Unfortunately, Caleb can never convince her that they are both human, which is something that O'Neill's seafaring New Englanders seem to know better than those locked to the land. (Caleb has been to the South Seas, after all; a trip interestingly anticipatory of Orin and Lavinia Mannon's in *Mourning Becomes Electra*.)

Emma Crosby's case is not unique. New England Puritanism, as O'Neill treats it, seems to breed obsession and fanaticism. Think of Captain Keeney's monomaniacal drive in *Ile*, which is not motivated by greed but which certainly is symptomatic of a lack of humility. Think also of Reuben Light, Ephraim Cabot, and Deborah Harford—a few of the many whom the Puritan heritage seems to lead up to, or over, the brink of madness.

If *Dynamo* was, as O'Neill said it was, a study of "the sickness of today," then it seems that much of that sickness results from Puritanism's having reached a dead end. Reverend Light's harsh, Calvinist fundamentalism has not only failed to offer any positive, life-enhancing values to his son, Reuben; it is something that he himself can no longer fully believe in. For all his dogmatic assertiveness, Light is an interesting study of latter-day Puritans' decline of assurance in the faith of their fathers. (How ironic the Reverend's surname is!) And yet, as with Ephraim Cabot, the rant goes on. His voice, O'Neill says, "is the bullying one of a sermonizer who is the victim of an inner uncertainty that compensates itself by being boomingly overassertive." Like Cabot, Light is a tyrant, less sure of his faith than he thinks he is, who wants to shackle his son to the family calling and lifestyle. About a choice of career for Reuben, he says: "I have decided. He shall follow in my footsteps—mine, and those of my father before me, and his father before him. It is God's manifest will!" Reverend Light, appropriately frightened of lightning, fits the Puritan mold: he resents his wife's desire for "Comforts of life" and "the sinful sloth of the flesh." By Act Two, in O'Neill's description, his "whole face is a mask of stricken loneliness"—a picture that combines prophetic touches of the death masks of the Mannons and the "lonesomeness" of Ephraim Cabot.

The next-door atheist, Mr. Fyfe, is no better than his "Bible-punching" enemy. He is just as bigoted and life-denying. And Reuben, rejecting his father's creed, is left with no viable alternative, until he worships the Dynamo in a destructive and self-destructive madness at the end. Of course Reuben, like Eben Cabot, cannot really slough off all the Puritan conditioning he has lived through in the Light home. For instance, he tells Ada of his having almost prayed at his mother's grave: "It just goes to show you what a hold that bunk gets on you when you've had it crammed down your throat from the time you were born." He is "held" in much the same way that the Mannons are "bound"; his prayer to the Dynamo, even when addressed to a feminine deity, sounds distinctly Calvinistic.

Like *Diff'rent, Dynamo* is far from great theatre. But it is important in that Reverend Light (who projects a god in his own hard image) and Reuben (who outgrows his father's fundamentalism and searches, though unsuccessfully, for a substitute) offer a parallel to a fuller treatment of the same stone-father-versus-rebellious-son antagonism in a far greater play, *Desire Under the Elms*. This play and *Mourning Becomes Electra* have received abundant critical attention and perhaps need less coverage now. But they are *the two* documents for an understanding of O'Neill's attitudes toward the Puritan heritage in New England—a dying, love-denying, hard and icy heritage.

Consider the Mannon dynasty of the trilogy: rich, exclusive scions of Anglo-Protestant ascendancy. Death "becomes" the Mannons because their faith is love- and therefore life-denying, as is epitomized by the skeleton in the family closet: Abe Mannon's expulsion of his brother David for David's affair with an inferior, Marie Brantome; and his subsequent burning of the Mannon home and building, in

its place, the present structure, whose "pagan temple front"—
in Christine's description—"is stuck like a mask on Puritan
gray ugliness." Gray because it is stone; ugly because it is
founded on the metaphoric rocks of greed and hate, not
love. (The sin begins to compound when Abe's son Ezra later
refuses aid to Marie.) The Mannons are "bound" (that key
word in "Shenandoah")—bound as if in the hands of an
angry God whose covenant with their ancestors had been
perverted. Whether God be angry or not is really irrelevant
to O'Neill's purpose, which was clearly more psychological
than theological. The seeds of their destruction are in the
people themselves, though they have festered so long that
it is truly a "family curse." We can feel sorry for the last of
the Mannons—Lavinia and Orin—but Lavinia sheds her
Puritan inhibitions too late, and both seem compelled to act
out again the "sins of the fathers"—and mothers! The
Mannons, no longer capable of love, are death-obsessed.
Death "becomes" them because they represent, in John
Henry Raleigh's phrase, "the Puritan aristocracy willing its
own destruction."

Ephraim Cabot, patriarch of another doomed Puritan
family, claims to have grown hard in the service of a hard
God who "hain't easy." But actually he has projected his
own hardness onto his conception of the deity. His hypocrisy,
which is so clear to his sons, is the result of a willed (but unsuccessful) denial of the very potent life-force within himself—part of the pagan substratum that these New England
plays reveal. He is not a God-fearing Calvinist: he is a
lecher, and a miser, with a biblical footnote to defend his
every misdeed. He lacks love, humility, understanding, self-
awareness: all the ideals listed by Winthrop in his sermon
on the Arabella. The rocky New England soil has bred a rocky
man who created a rocky God and life. "Stone atop o' stone,"
says his son Eben, "makin' walls till yer heart's a stone ye
heft up out o' the way o' growth onto a stone wall t' wall
in yer heart."

There are, of course, two uses for stones: to build (a
church upon a rock, or a farm wall, or a stone mansion like
the Mannons'), and to crush. The tragedy of Puritanism in

America, as O'Neill portrays it, was the fact that the first use was replaced by the second. While the first Massachusetts Bay Puritans took the stones of the wilderness to build God's model community, their puritanic descendants used a stony, constricting morality to crush the natural instincts in themselves and their successors.

Not that the picture at the end of *Desire Under the Elms* is totally bleak. One cannot overlook the exultant element in the last scene, when Abbie and Eben, the doomed victims of puritanical repressions, free themselves from their sordid surroundings and from the Puritan conception of "sin." The lust of each (hers, for him and for the farm; his, for her and for vengeance) has turned to love, and the ghost of Eben's mother can rest. Whereas Ephraim, though we pity him (and doubtless respect his stolidity), is left, lonesomer than ever, in his life of solitariness and sterility, unaware to the end of the great guilt that is his. As in every O'Neill play in which Puritanism is dominant, the only hope seems to lie in rejecting it. And that hope is dim indeed.

O'Neill said in 1946 that "the battle of moral forces in the New England scene is what I feel closest to as an artist." And the plays set in that region show that one of the fiercest battles was between puritanical negativism—a death-force—and the life-force embedded in nature and in those characters able to avoid or escape stultification. Michael Wigglesworth's poem sought the reasons for the great drought of 1662. O'Neill, in his New England plays, is also concerned with drought—but of soul rather than of soil. He records the drought of spirit that followed the erosion of the ideals that John Winthrop had listed as the human conditions of the Puritan covenant with God: ideals like love, humility, cooperation, and service to God above service to self.

George Wilson Pierson spoke of the "moral stoniness' of New England Puritanism. Eugene O'Neill in his plays has provided as vivid a series of illustrations of that fact as one could ever dream of.

POETRY AND MYSTICISM
IN O'NEILL

Albert Bermel

A consideration of two kinds of nonverbal, tangential poetry in *Long Day's Journey into Night* may counter the hidebound, stupefying realism that seems to clog the play whenever it reaches the stage. The first type of poetry is the longing of the characters, singly and together, for a mystical union of sorts. The second is the influence on the characters (and on the audience) of the setting.

Mystical yearnings appear more obtrusively in certain earlier O'Neill plays, such as *The Hairy Ape*, and most obviously in the plays that are often considered inferior and critically dismissed, such as *The Moon of the Caribbees, Welded, The First Man, The Fountain, Lazarus Laughed,* and *Days Without End,* but they also show up in that popular work, *Ah, Wilderness!*, most noticeably in the beach scene (IV, ii), during Richard's musings.[1] Anybody who knows much about mystical consciousness or mystical experience— who is familiar with the writings of the celebrated mystics— will find these comments an oversimplification. With that apology delivered, I quote briefly from a student of mysticism, Walter T. Stace, who writes: "The most important, the central characteristic in which all *fully developed* mystical experiences agree, and which serves to mark them off from other kinds of experiences, is that they involve the apprehension of *an ultimate nonsensuous unity in all things,* a oneness

245

or One to which neither the senses nor the reason can penetrate. In other words, it entirely transcends our sensory-intellectual consciousness" (Stace's own italics).[2]

Broadly speaking there are two kinds of mystical unity or oneness. The first comes out of perceiving everything, the universe, matter and non-matter, as a great unification; the second comes out of meditating on the self and finding there the core of the mystical sensation. That is, the self can be macrocosm or microcosm. On the part of each one of the characters in *Long Day's Journey* there is such a yearning for a mystical union, for a oneness with whatever lies beyond the self. Years earlier, Yank in *The Hairy Ape* tried in his inarticulate fashion to define this yearning when he sensed that, in some indefinable way, he did not "belong." At first he felt that he was part of the machine that fed the ship, and part of the machine that was the city; but gradually he came to see himself as an outcast, scorned by Mildred, by the passersby on Fifth Avenue, by the I.W.W., his fellow workers, and even, finally, by the animal kingdom. O'Neill's last line in that "comedy of ancient and modern life" is one of the most bitter he ever wrote. After Yank collapses and dies in the gorilla's cage, and the monkeys set up a wailing noise, an inhuman mourning, the stage direction reads: "And, perhaps, the Hairy Ape at last belongs."[3] He can "belong" only by being dead.

For the four members of the Tyrone family, the apertures through to that great mystical unity are the two traditional American mind-freezers, hard liquor and drugs. The Tyrone men each crave for a state of animated suspension, a helpless marination that blots out the pain of living and is the next best thing to a mystical levitation as Baudelaire sums it up in his poem *Enivrez-Vous!*, which Edmund recites passionately to his father.[4]

To begin with Mary: Her yearning is nostalgic. It will take her back into a past that never quite was, when she had the love of her parents (or, at least, her father's), a sheltering home, the convent, and her music—one might say, the harmony of her music. She says she wants a home in which she will "belong," as opposed to this temporary one where she is only a summer visitor, but she sees no prospect of attaining that *heimkehren* while she is undrugged. Morphine helps. It extinguishes not only the anguish of the present, but the present tense itself. It makes her one with her girlhood when, her memory deceptively tells her, all was serene. So dramatic is this lapse in her normal consciousness toward the end of the play—the drug is working more effectively than ever before—that when she starts to speak of Mother Elizabeth and the convent, O'Neill marks the moment by mentioning that the three men *"slowly lower their drinks to the table, forgetting them."*[5] This is an otherwise unimaginable movement for these three souses. It demonstrates how powerfully they are affected by being wiped out of her life. But I stress that her nostalgic retreat is a mere substitute for a mystical experience. When Mary comes out of it, she will know, not the mystic's exaltation, but a terrible psychic hangover.

Next, Edmund: It seems that he, too, enjoys no exaltation when he emerges from a drunken jag. But he does occasionally soar into a condition of oneness with the Creation when he is at sea, as he describes in his long speech to his father.[6] Here we are reminded of the mystical proclivities of certain characters of Ibsen, a dramatist O'Neill fervently admired and (as in *Ah, Wilderness!*) quoted: Ellida Wangel's in *The Lady from the Sea* or the sense of "belonging" in the deep talked about in Act III of *The Wild Duck* by Hedwig and, fleetingly, by Gregers Werle. Unlike the religious mystics, Edmund recounts his visions in images of nature—the waves, the spray, the sky, the gulls—whereas the mystics speak of a wholeness in emptiness, a fulfillment in the void, a totally abstract realization. Edmund may have run off to sea *seeking* such a oneness. Back in Connecticut he had a similar experience while walking in the fog.

James Tyrone: He drinks in order to escape and he escapes (from Mary and the house) in order to drink. But he speaks little about his other mystical adventures—as an actor. For him the theatre proved a refuge from penury. In it, playing great heroes, whether in Shakespeare or a version of Dumas' *The Count of Monte Cristo*, he became one with his audience, as all great actors do—and such a sensation is

equally recognized, on rare occasions, by great spectators.
Tyrone is two of O'Neill's favorite character types blended:
the artist and the businessman. The theatre enabled him to
insulate himself doubly from the past: he became a rich
actor. But he still looks for some replacement for that early
unity he knew in his first family, and so far has been unable
to find it—except in the theatre. The demands of touring
broke up this family, his second. Away from the theatre, he,
too, like his wife, feels an irrevocable loss.

Finally, Jamie: He has no refuge on the order of his
parents' and brother's. He drinks to obliterate his consciousness of himself as a child murderer and a worthless,
hopeless human being. He rises, if he is lucky and gets
thoroughly pickled, into the stratosphere of other men's
poetry, Swinburne's, Dowson's, Wilde's, the music of late
nineteenth-century artistic rebellion, as a defense of his own
unhappiness and pessimism. He feels trapped, like the in-
habitants of the saloon in *The Iceman Cometh*.

In Act IV we watch the three men in the family tending
toward peace of a sort, even a union, as they come to terms
with one another. Mutual understanding, honesty, and forgiveness bring them almost into a family reconciliation. The
main point of contention between them still is Mary; her
movements upstairs, which they cannot help listening out
for, keep them slightly on edge. Then O'Neill walks right
away from anything like a conventional ending by destroying
the truce, let alone the hope of sleep or a drunken, oblivious
mutuality, when he brings her down among them and
plunges them into despair.

The other main poetic element in the play is the
setting. Poetic? All we have is an ordinary living room filled
with ordinary furniture and looking out through ordinary
windows on the harbor. During the action, this room will be
altered only by the incidence of light from without and
within, by the gradual darkening outside and then the
encroachment of the fog. The fog supervenes outside because they are next to the coastline. Fog also sometimes
drifts in through cracks in doors and forms little indoor
clouds. I can recall sitting at a concert in London's Festival

Hall when fog drifted in from the River Thames and blotted out the sight of the orchestra; we could hear the musicians perfectly, but all we could see was the bulk of gray that shielded them. I am not suggesting that a designer puff up some convincing gray smoke between the floorboards, or dangle some swatches of gray fabric from the flies and whisk them about a little. That would be literal, the stalest kind of realism, and, as I have suggested, O'Neill's plays already suffer enough on stage from limited imaginations. Rather, we can recall that a fog turns the land into something like a seascape. The summer house in New London becomes a stage image of a fogbound ship. Talking there, the Tyrones drift on the surface waters of this night and the undertow of all their yesterdays. Like a ship, the summer house is temporary quarters. In much the same way, the foghorn is not merely a sound effect that adds local color; it is a warning: Collisions ahead! The fog on land, a continuation of the sea, flows up to the windows of the house, or the "gunwales" of the "ship," which floats ungovernably through time, through the long journey of the night. The Tyrones, unavailing passengers, are at the mercy of their collective fate which lies many fathoms deep in the remote past.

How might the poetic sense of the play be caught and fixed by stage imagery? When we think of a household as a ship, we think of the setting Bernard Shaw invokes for *Heartbreak House,* that metaphor for Europe drifting rudderless into World War I, the captain rum-soaked and away from the helm, dreaming of the seventh degree of concentration while the bickering crew looks on helplessly. That is one kind of stage image. A second might be drifting in the sky, through a cloudscape; or trapped in an unreal drawing room as in Sartre's *No Exit* or in a dungeon as at the end of *Henry IV.* A further image suggests four people who, from time to time, drift into their private mystical reveries; they are separated —by lighting or by barriers of darkness; they try to form a group, but their preoccupations keep them apart from one another. Then there is the image of sickness, of a "magic mountain" at sea level where spiritual invalids cannot give one another guidance or sustenance but only aggravate everybody's ills. Or an image that yields us intimations of four larger figures: Mary the Mother, God the Father, Christ the Son, and Judas the unfortunate. Or come to that: Adam, Eve, Abel, and Cain or—why not?—Zeus, Hera, Apollo, and Dionysus.

The setting and atmosphere could be assisted by masks and other devices, depending on the courage—or recklessness —of the director. For instance, I believe that two sets of four masks or make-up designs, one based on Mary's features, the other on Tyrone's, much like the make-up decreed for *Mourning Becomes Electra*, would provoke a series of fresh responses from the audience. So would *un*natural dreamlike —or trancelike—gestures and motions, which tell of the alternating impulses of attraction and repulsion between the four characters.

We associate mysticism rather with the Noh theatre than with O'Neill's[8] and theatrical poetry with Cocteau, Artaud, Meyerhold, affectation, and incompetence. Is cross-fertilization of theatrical styles more feasible than it was in the past? And would any of it be applicable to O'Neill? How could we translate some of the images adduced here into the language of our stage without betraying the play? All I can say is that at this point the task of the critic shades off into the tasks of the director, the designer, the performers, and those expectant people in the auditorium who will keep their minds and emotions open if they receive the right sort of encouragement.

NOTES

[1] *The Plays of Eugene O'Neill*, Vol. I (New York, 1955), p. 277.

[2] Walter T. Stace, *The Teachings of the Mystics* (New York, 1960), pp. 14–15.

[3] *The Plays of Eugene O'Neill*, op. cit., Vol. II, p. 254.

[4] *Long Day's Journey into Night* (New Haven, 1956), p. 132.

[5] Ibid., p. 175.

[6] Ibid., p. 153.

[7] Ibid., p. 131.

[8] After I had written this paper, a friend, Elinor Finkel-stein, drew my attention to Henry F. Pommer's article, "The Mysticism of Eugene O'Neill," in *Modern Drama*, May 1966, pp. 26–39, which I recommend to readers as an earlier approach to O'Neill's drama as a whole that overlaps my own but does not coincide with it.

O'NEILL THE HUMANIST

Esther M. Jackson

It was the American philosopher William James who described religion as a "man's total reaction upon life." Such total reactions, he observed, differ from casual responses, for to get at them, "we must go behind the foreground of existence and reach down to that curious sense of the whole residual cosmos as an everlasting presence." Thus, James wrote, religion is the completest of all answers to the question: "What is the character of this universe in which we dwell?" James's definition is particularly useful in efforts to define the nature of the religious motive in the dramas of Eugene O'Neill. For O'Neill's dramas, from early plays such as *Thirst* (1913–14)* to late works such as *The Iceman Cometh* (1939), and *Long Day's Journey into Night* (1940–41) record stages in the evolution of the playwright's vision of the theological universe in which modern man lives.

O'Neill acknowledged this religious motive as the organizing theme of his work, observing that while other modern playwrights appeared to be absorbed in the relationship between man and man, he was interested only in the relationship between man and God. But if the primary motive of O'Neill's career as a dramatist was indeed theological in nature, the playwright's treatment of religious themes remained un-

---

* Dates given indicate approximate time of writing.

orthodox. This unorthodoxy, which Robert Brustein styles "revolt," seems not so much to have signified O'Neill's rejection of religion as it mirrored his anguish at his own inability to confirm or deny the existence of God. Actually, it can be claimed that O'Neill was, throughout his life, engaged in a search for a way of verifying the existence of an eternal principle in human experience. His approach to the problem had significant correspondences to those of modern humanists, both religious and secular. Like the "New Humanists" of his time, the playwright saw the rise of faith in science as a challenge, not only to traditional systems of value, but to the very humanity of man.

Plays such as *Strange Interlude* treat what New Humanists such as Irving Babbitt and Paul Elmer More interpreted as the essential dilemma of modern man—a crisis of faith. Others of O'Neill's dramas explore the range of New Humanist themes. The affirmation of man's humanity as the primary motive in history is a theme in both *The Fountain* and *Marco Millions*. *The Hairy Ape* examines the role of nature in the determination of human identity; while *Dynamo* is concerned with the need to humanize science and technology, *Ah, Wilderness!* celebrates an enlightened rationalism as the primary instrument of decision in a humane society; while the "cycle plays" are concerned with the individual American's responsibility to make ethical use of his political, social, and moral freedom. At least two plays treat major variations in the attitudes of the New Humanists toward religion. *Days Without End* reflects a rather conventional view of salvation, while *Lazarus Laughed* translates what the New Humanists regarded as man's constant yearning for the assurance of eternal life into a secular symbolism.

While there is no evidence that O'Neill was influenced directly by the writings of the New Humanists, it is clear that he shared many of their primary concerns. Moreover, he reflected, on occasion, differences of perspectives within their circle. Thus, it is that *Days Without End* (1931–34) interprets a humanism which is Christian in tone. Its resolution conforms to the notion of "true humanism" espoused by Americans such as Paul Elmer More and Europeans such as

Jacques Maritain. John-Loving finds his humanity in willing submission to God.

On other occasions, O'Neill's perspective paralleled those of rationalistic humanists. Like Irving Babbitt, he attempted to translate essentially religious concepts into a secular language. If *Mourning Becomes Electra* uses Freudian language to symbolize the concept of transgression, *Dynamo* attempts to translate the notion of temptation into a technological symbolism; while the late work *A Moon for the Misbegotten* offers a secular variation on the theme of *divine grace*.

Like the New Humanists, O'Neill appears to have regarded American democracy as the expression of a new theological situation, one which requires not only a reconsideration of the nature of man's responsibility for man but also a reappraisal of the role of God in human affairs. Perhaps the principal factor distinguishing the brand of humanism which emerged in his dramas from those varieties which had appeared in the works of European playwrights of the nineteenth and twentieth centuries is the extent of the moral freedom he attributed to man. O'Neill conceived such freedom in terms which were virtually absolute. Moreover, he attributed this freedom to men and women of differing races, classes, ages, regions, and occupations.

But O'Neill was concerned with more than the mere fact of freedom. Like humanists such as Babbitt, he was to ask a second question: What is the nature of moral responsibility in a universe where man is indeed free? He appears to have begun by interpreting the problem in personal terms. Personal responsibility is a theme in the early play *Thirst* (1913–14), where a gentleman, a dancer, and a West Indian sailor contemplate the implications of moral freedom, as they drift on a raft surrounded by sharks. In the same way, his treatment of responsibility in others of his early plays, including *Bound East for Cardiff* (1914), *The Hairy Ape* (1917), and *Beyond the Horizon* (1917–18), seems personal in tone.

Gradually, the challenge of freedom in the universe of O'Neill's description seems to have developed beyond the possibility of solution by means of personal morality. Rather, the playwright seems to have come to the conclusion that the appropriate exercise of moral freedom in a democratic society requires a pattern of shared belief. In his search for a basis for a community of belief, O'Neill again reflected a major preoccupation of American humanists of the nineteenth and twentieth centuries. Walt Whitman, recognizing the need for such a sense of community in a multicultural society, had in the nineteenth century called for the formulation of an ecumenical faith, accessible, open, and usable by all members of the society. Whitman wrote of this "democratic religion" in his Preface of 1872:

> As there can be, in my opinion, no sane and complete Personality—nor any grand and electric Nationality, without the stock element of Religion imbuing all the other elements. . . . The people, especially the young men and women of America, must begin to learn that Religion, (like Poetry,) is something far, far different from what they supposed. It is, indeed, too important to the power and perpetuity of the New World to be consigned any longer to the churches, old or new, Catholic or Protestant—Saint this, or Saint that. . . . It must be consigned henceforth to Democracy *en masse*, and to Literature. It must enter into the Poems of the Nation. It must make the Nation.

One way of interpreting O'Neill's experimental works is as an attempt to follow Whitman's mandate to let religion enter into a "new literature." In plays such as *Marco Millions* (1923–25), *All God's Chillun Got Wings* (1923), *Strange Interlude* (1926–27), and *Dynamo* (1928), he engaged upon the creation of a new iconography—a system of signs, images, and symbols expressive of the relationship between man and God in the New World. These works are, however, more than linguistic in their interests. For in them O'Neill attempted both to reveal the theological challenge embodied in modern American life and to formulate a tentative mode of response. There emerges in plays such as *Lazarus Laughed* (1925–26) a secularized theology, which synthesizes perspectives drawn not only from Greek, Judaic, and Christian religions, but also from tenets of belief codified by sciences and social sciences. *Lazarus Laughed* remains the most evident of his theatrical failures. Unfortunately, neither O'Neill's skill as a writer nor his sophistication as a thinker was equal to the task of rendering his humanistic theology in dramatic form. However, his notion of an ecumenical faith, supportive of the ideals of democracy, was not to be lost in theatrical history. It was to re-emerge in American theology in the fifties, sixties, and seventies.

If *Ah, Wilderness!* marks the high point of O'Neill's optimism about the potential for the achievement of humanistic goals in modern American experience, *The Iceman Cometh* appears to represent the depth of his pessimism. This work, like *Long Day's Journey into Night,* is an American interpretation of what critics such as Joseph Wood Krutch have described as a "tragic humanism." Although these late plays did succeed in revealing the contour of the universe in which modern man lives, they also exposed the failures of their protagonists to achieve humanistic goals. Through Hickey, Larry, and Parritt of *The Iceman Cometh* and the tragic Tyrones of *Long Day's Journey into Night,* O'Neill interpreted what he was finally to concede as humanism's limitations as a religion. They do not, however, seem to indicate his total rejection of a humanism as a social philosophy. Rather, these late plays suggest O'Neill's final acceptance of a tragic view of experience.

O'Neill's "tragic humanism" reaffirms the classical proposition that man's condition precludes forever the full realization of his ideals. It is, however, the individual's response to the tragic fact of his limitation that remains not only the measure of man's nobility but also of his humanity.

EXILE WITHOUT REMEDY
The Late Plays of Eugene O'Neill

J. Dennis Rich

I

Camus writes that neither man nor the universe is the singular cause of the absurd condition. "Absurdity springs from a comparison. . . . The absurd is essentially a divorce. It lies in neither of the elements compared; it is born of their confrontation. . . . The absurd is not in man (if such a metaphor could have a meaning) nor in the world, but in their presence together."[1] In the final plays of Eugene O'Neill the vision of the absurd described by Camus is dramatized. The playwright ceases his earlier search for transcendence or salvation, and the human effort becomes a search for a means of survival. In *The Iceman Cometh* (1939),* *Long Day's Journey into Night* (1940), and *Hughie* (1941), O'Neill arrives at the fundamental question of the absurd, whether or not life is worth living. The problem of man is "how to find himself in a world in which the ultimate reality is a return to nothingness."[2]

II

In *Long Day's Journey into Night,* O'Neill depicts the difficulty of living when the contours of reality are not easily identified, when truth is deceptive and evanescent. Within an

* Dates given indicate time of writing.

elusive reality, "the four haunted Tyrones"[3] aspire to happiness. But their aspirations are tragic. Deprived of an understanding of the world and divided within themselves, no such fulfillment seems possible.

The story of *Long Day's Journey into Night* describes the history of the Tyrone family, whose collective past is characterized by conflict and suffering. Central to their suffering are the morphine addiction of Mary Tyrone; the inability of either Jamie or Edmund Tyrone to find a place in life; and the intolerance and miserliness of the senior Tyrone, James. All of the Tyrones suffer from a lack of compassion. The drama unfolds in less than twenty-four hours, beginning in the morning of a "day in August, 1912" and concluding "around midnight" on the same day. This "journey" from day into night occurs in the realm of psychological, and perhaps metaphysical, as well as physical action. *Long Day's Journey into Night* interprets the lives of the Tyrones during an extended moment of crisis.

In the progression of consciousness experienced by each of the tormented Tyrones, the problem of existence is encountered in the "climate of the absurd." What is absurd is the comparison between ideal images of life and reality. As Mary says: "None of us can help the things life has done to us. . . . Everything comes between you and what you'd like to be, and you've lost your true self forever" (p. 61). Each of the Tyrones experiences the heightened awareness that results from such comparison, and each attempts to resolve the accompanying suffering differently.

The troubled family holds itself together by maintaining an illusion of stability in a situation characterized by the absence of an ordering principle. Initially they survive by retreating from this terrible reality, as James Tyrone phrases it, "Forget everything and face nothing!" (p. 21). Still, the sense that life is incomplete finally cannot be avoided. The feeling of "longing and loss," first expressed by Robert Mayo in *Beyond the Horizon*, permeates *Long Day's Journey into Night*.

Mary Tyrone suffers a theological loss. As her husband

observes, "she hasn't denied her faith, but she's forgotten it, until now there's no strength of spirit left in her to fight against her curse" (p. 78). She longs for a return to the stability of her youth, and for a state of grace she believes she once had attained. But her life has been marked by instability, suffering and impermanence. The final humiliation in her confused existence is her accidentally acquired addiction to morphine. Mary discovers that she is no longer able to face life. "One day long ago I found I could no longer call my soul my own" (p. 93).

Mary Tyrone arrives at the first stage of the absurd progression of consciousness—awareness. But she is unable to live with the isolation she discovers. Overcome by the pain of being, she withdraws into a drug-induced vision of her past. The drug, she testifies, "kills the pain. You go back until at last you are beyond its reach. Only the past when you were happy is real" (pp. 103–104). Complete escape, however, seems impossible. The nothingness of the present continues to intrude, and she is unable to shake the feeling of religious loss in her life. "What is it I'm looking for? I know it's something I lost. . . . Something I need terribly. I remember when I had it I was never afraid. I can't have lost it forever, I would die if I thought that. Because then there would be no hope" (pp. 172–173).

If Mary Tyrone's loss is theological, James Tyrone's is aesthetic. In his life, the absurd appears in the comparison between the actor he might have been and the material success he is: "That God-damned play I bought for a song and made such a great success in—a great money success—it ruined me with its promise of an easy fortune. . . . What the hell was it I wanted to buy, I wonder, that was worth—Well, no matter. It's a late day for regrets" (pp. 149–50). Tyrone passes beyond his wife's awareness in the absurd progression of consciousness. He sees the absurd in his life, yet he accepts responsibility for himself. If he is unable to transcend the emptiness which he feels in his old age, he does not capitulate to it. Despite the pain of being, he continues to assert that there is meaning in the act of living. Neither the absurd individual in revolt, nor the victim of despair, Tyrone has learned to settle for life as it is; in his own words, "I'm not complaining" (p. 114).

Jamie Tyrone, on the other hand, despairs; his loss is psychological. His suffering is more personal than that of either his father or his mother. Intensely aware of the absurdity in his own directionless life, Jamie assumes the "mask" of the cynic. But underneath this mask, Jamie is a spiritual suicide. Confronted with meaninglessness in his relations with others and with himself, he has given up on life. He is, as he describes himself, "a God-damned shell" (p. 158). He is also the Tyrone who suffers the most severe inner fragmentation; he believes the worst of life because he wants to believe the best. Jamie lives the absurd comparison; his being is defined by the "divorce" of an existence envisioned and existence as it actually is. Quoting sardonically from Rosetti, Jamie provides a precise definition of himself, "Look into my face. My name is Might-Have-Been;/ I am also called No More, Too Late, Farewell" (p. 168).

In Edmund Tyrone, the absurd progression of consciousness reaches its most complex interpretation. He suffers on a metaphysical plane what Camus calls "that divorce between the mind that disappoints."[4] It is Edmund who experiences the crisis of the absurd most intensely in *Long Day's Journey into Night*. He is confronted with the possibility of his own death. He recognizes that life is "damned crazy" (p. 151), and at an earlier time "stopped to think too long" (p. 147), then tried to kill himself. But now, a victim of circumstances beyond his control, he revolts against death and the absurd. He determines to live. Ultimately, Edmund seeks in existence not unity or integration but moments of insight and understanding. He explains such moments to his father: "Then the moment of ecstatic freedom came. . . . Like the veil of things as they seem drawn back by an unseen hand. For a second you see—and seeing the secret, are the secret. For a second there is meaning! Then the hand lets the veil fall and you are alone, lost in the fog again, and you stumble on toward nowhere, for no good reason!" (p. 153).

Of the four tormented Tyrones, Edmund alone is a

survivor. He discovers that he has learned the lesson of Dion-Brown, that "man lives by mending."[5] He is the only one who learns to face life without illusion. In the desolate conclusion of *Long Day's Journey into Night,* as Mary evokes images of the past, Edmund's discovery provides an optimistic note. In answering the fundamental absurd question, judging whether or not life is worth living, Edmund responds in the affirmative.

In *Long Day's Journey into Night,* O'Neill explores the possibility of existing in the climate of the absurd by examining his own life experience in a family setting. The drama is intensely personal, a barely disguised autobiography. In *The Iceman Cometh,* the same problem is investigated in less personal terms.

III

The Iceman Cometh was the last of O'Neill's plays to receive a New York production in his lifetime. Set in Harry Hope's saloon, the "Palace of Pipe Dreams," in the year 1912, the play studies life in terms of the lives led by the derelicts who occupy "The End of the Line Café" (III, 587). Looking out from this "last harbor" (III, 587) of humanity and concurrently looking to the present from the perspective of the past, O'Neill explores the dilemma of modern man "judging whether life is or is not worth living."[6] "To be or not to be" is enacted in modern terms."[7] No thesis is offered; no philosophical position is advocated as the solution to the problem of existence. "O'Neill is reflecting not ethically, on Right Action or Right Thought, but metaphysically, on the very quality of existence."[8]

By presenting an extended moment in the lives of the down-and-outers at Harry Hope's, O'Neill depicts the difficulty of simple survival in the face of ever-present uncertainty. Cut off from the vitality of life, the derelicts who decay at Harry Hope's are unable to create within themselves sufficient energy to overcome the inertia of doubt, and so they retreat from the flow of the present and seek to escape time

by withdrawing into "pipe dreams of the past" or by anticipating "pipe dreams of the future." It is in this disconnected
state that O'Neill presents the question of how to exist in a
situation in which nothing is assured. In the variety of characters who inhabit the world of Harry Hope's, the playwright
portrays the problem of living with the terror of existence.
These individuals survive by eluding the emptiness of reality.

There are three characters who vary from this pattern—
who are at a high level of self-consciousness. Theodore
Hickman, Hickey, is the advocate of negation. He believes he
has found inner peace in the discovery that nothing matters.
Ultimately, Hickey discovers that his belief in valuelessness
is an illusion. A second variation appears in Larry Slade.
Though he begins as an observer-thinker who eschews action,
a self-deluder who sustains himself with the pipe dreams of
philosophical detachment, he becomes the absurd individual
in an absurd world who acknowledges nothingness and defines himself. A third variation is symbolized in the boy, Don
Parritt. His heightened self-consciousness takes ethical-moral
form within a social context.

The "lie of the pipe dream" is, in *The Iceman Cometh*,
"what gives life" (III, 578). The men and women who inhabit Harry Hope's saloon survive by maintaining "a few
harmless pipe dreams about their yesterdays and tomorrows"
(III, 587). They have withdrawn into stayed time. Their mode
of being illustrates what Camus calls "eluding." He writes,
"eluding is the invariable game. The typical act of eluding
. . . is hope."[9] Unable to adapt to the ambiguities of existence
in the present, these characters grasp at fixed illusion, con-
structing themselves in terms of what they were or hope to
be. Each dreamer supports the illusions of others in return
for a supportive reflection of self. They fear to test their
constructed selves in real life, but in the "lie of the pipe
dream" there is a kind of communion of souls. For the
pathetic evaders, it is all that separates them from utter
desolation. They are already stripped of the attachments
which men employ to make life significant. None is married;
they have no families; in fact, they have no identity save the
"lie of the pipe dream." Their lives are affirmed because

each of the dreamers agrees to acknowledge the lies of his comrades as fact. "The truth has no bearing on anything" (III, 578) in this dream world where "worst is best" and "tomorrow is yesterday" (III, 600).

O'Neill depicts illusion as a device necessary to survive the malaise and dissociation which hound man confronted with the unpleasant truths of life. Pipe dreams are an alternative to death. O'Neill explained: "You ask, what is the significance, what do these people mean to us today? Well, all I can say is that it is a play about pipe dreams. And the philosophy that there is always one dream left, one final dream, no matter how low you have fallen, down there at the bottom of the bottle."[10] With his dreamers, O'Neill demonstrates the importance of illusion to survival. Camus writes, "A man defines himself by his make-believe as well as by his sincere impulses."[11] The escapists who retreat into "a world so dark and silent that only conjured illusion gives it substance,"[12] proves Camus' words true.

Into this world comes Theodore Hickman, a man determined to confront the hard truth of life. "Hickey" is a part of the saloon's tradition. Annually, this successful salesman has appeared on Harry's birthday, participating in the proprietor's birthday party by dispensing free drinks and off-color humor. Throughout the first act, Hickey's impending arrival is eagerly anticipated, for he is "a great one to make a joke of everything and cheer you up" (III, 580). He provides relief from the monotony of existence. "Would that Hickey or Death would come!" (III, 596) remarks Willie Oban. When he finally arrives, Willie's words prove prophetic. Hickey is changed. He brings with him "the Iceman of Death" (III, 680).

The amiable Hickey, familiar to Hope's regulars, is transformed. Reputed for his famous drunken "periodicals," the man is now sober, and he asserts, "off the stuff. For keeps" (III, 620). Loved for his kidding good humor and for his ability to make people believe "what they wanted to believe about themselves" (III, 711), he is now deadly serious and determined to sell salvation from illusion to his friends. He tells them that he "finally had the guts to face myself and throw overboard the damned lying pipe dream that'd been making me miserable" (III, 621), and he informs them that they too must confront and reject their illusions. He preaches the destructiveness of the pipe dream. "I know now, from my experience, they're the things that really poison and ruin a guy's life and keep him from finding any peace" (III, 622). Hickey, in his new role as salesman-theologian, attempts to sell personal salvation in secular terms.

Hickey's identity as a messianic figure becomes more apparent during Harry Hope's birthday party. The celebration is described by Larry Slade as "a second feast of Belshazzar, with Hickey to do the writing on the wall" (III, 644). One by one, the derelicts are judged by Hickey and found wanting; and one by one, they set out to implement their pipe dreams. Mosher, McGloin, Willie Oban, Wetjoen, Lewis, and Jimmy Tomorrow venture into the world outside the saloon in search of their dreams. Chuck and Cora leave with the intention of marrying. The Negro, Joe Mott, goes out in search of a stake with which to begin a new gambling house. Rocky admits he is a pimp; Margie and Pearl face their truth, that they are whores. Without leaving the saloon, Hugo Kalmar and Larry Slade face themselves. Hugo discovers that despite his devotion to the ideas of the "Movement," he is an aristocrat at heart. Larry learns that his posture of watching the world while waiting for death in "the grandstand of philosophical detachment" (III, 579) is a pipe dream. Hickey forces Larry to admit his "coward's lie." "I'm afraid to live, am I—and even more afraid to die! So I sit here, with my pride drowned on the bottom of a bottle, keeping drunk so I won't see myself shaking in my britches with fright, or hear myself whining and praying: Beloved Christ, let me live a little while longer at any price!" (III, 689).

Perhaps the most pathetic figure in these efforts to implement a pipe dream is Harry Hope. After twenty years of living in the isolation of his saloon, he sets out for a walk around the ward. As he departs, the motive behind Hickey's desire to make the dreamers face the truth is revealed. He expects, indeed wants, them to fail—"Of course, he's coming back. So are all the others. By tonight they'll all be here again. . . . That's the whole point" (III, 688). Hickey is convinced that his philosophy of denial will bring freedom and peace with self. In a tragic paradox, what he brings is emptiness, meaninglessness, and death. Larry correctly describes Hickey's brand of salvation as "the peace of death" (III, 692). When Hickey compels the derelicts to test their illusions in the hard light of day, they lose these last symbols of "reality." With this loss, they lose their will to live. They are defeated by the images of themselves stripped of the protection of the pipe dream.

Hickey's hard religion of denial does not bring peace to Harry Hope or to any of those who inhabit the saloon. It merely deprives them of all hope. The defeated men have learned what O'Neill's Lazarus revealed—"Life is for each man a solitary cell whose walls are mirrors" (I, 309). They have discovered that they are unable to live in isolation with the reflections of themselves. Hickey acknowledges that the peace he espouses has no joy in it. He begins to question the calm which he claims lies within his own soul. As Larry observes, "He's lost his confidence that the peace he's sold us is the real McCoy, and it's made him uneasy about his own" (III, 703).

The major revelation of the play does not relate to the other men but to Hickey. He finds that he must demonstrate the validity of his new-found salvation for himself and for others. It would appear, however, that his search for truth takes him into a plane of meaning beyond his conscious control. In a trance-like state, he reveals that he has murdered his wife, Evelyn, to free her from the suffering his drunkeness and lechery have caused her, and at the same time to free himself from the guilt and remorse he suffered when, after his debaucheries, Evelyn had forgiven him. Throughout his lengthy confession, Hickey refers over and over to his love for Evelyn, and to her stubborn pipe dream that he would someday reform. He claims he murdered his wife to end the misery and suffering her love caused her, but as he concludes his confession, the truth comes out. "I remember I stood by the bed and suddenly I heard myself speaking to her, as if it was something I'd always wanted to say: 'Well, you know what you can do with your pipe dream now, you damned bitch!' " (III, 716). Hickey appears to discover that he has killed his wife because he could not forgive her forgiveness.

Now the cause of Hickey's transformation and the significance of his gospel become clear. He has told his derelict friends, "Don't you know you're free now to be yourselves, without having to feel remorse tomorrow?" (III, 705). He has, however, failed to realize that when reality fails, men must live by their dreams. Hickey has not understood the simple fact that when people find reality uncomfortable, they adjust it to fit their needs. His gospel of negation, he discovers too late, is the greatest illusion of all.

In the end, Hickey proves unable to accept his own doctrine. Confronted with the fact of his hatred for his wife, he crumbles. In a third development, he evades the truth he has unearthed in his soul, embraces illusion, and claims insanity: "You know I must have been insane, don't you" (III, 716). Ironically, in order for Hickey to save himself from his true feelings, he is forced to bargain with the derelicts whose illusions he has shattered. To achieve the "insanity" he needs to preserve his love for Evelyn, Hickey is forced to recant his gospel of "honesty is the best policy." He admits, "I've been out of my mind. . . . All the time I've been here! You saw I was insane, didn't you" (III, 717). The unmasking of Hickey frees his friends from despair. They are able to conclude that illusions are necessary, and that they never really lost them—"we kidded him along and humored him" (III, 718).

Hickey's progression through the absurd universe is, in some sense, tragic. His tragedy is neither that he has killed his wife, nor that he loses his struggle to save his pals from illusion. Rather it is that fully conscious of the human dilemma in an unreasonable universe, he is overwhelmed by the absurd condition. Ultimately, his only possibility is to embrace death.

IV

Hickey's progression is paralleled, in many ways, by the progression of another character, Don Parritt. Both Parritt and Hickey conceal within themselves the secret of a betrayal. Both love and hate the woman betrayed. Both confront their hatred. And both go to their destruction. It is Hickey who first notices that he and Parritt are "members of the same lodge—in some way" (III, 624). And it is Hickey who recognizes that there is a woman behind Parritt's anguish (III, 643). Toward the end of the play, as Hickey confesses his murder of Evelyn, Parritt confesses his betrayal of his mother in similar language. Further, both Hickey and Parritt are antagonists of the pipe dream. Despite these similarities, the two characters are, in the end, very different.

Parritt's situation is potentially more tragic than Hickey's. His betrayal of his anarchist mother seems to spring from more complex motives than Hickey's betrayal of his wife. Unlike Hickey, Parritt has no illusions of salvation or peace. He is aware of the meaning of his actions and knows that ultimately he must accept guilt and suffer for them. Hickey attempts to live his gospel of negation and fails tragically. Parritt, confronted by a similar crisis of meaning, seeks to evade responsibility for himself and to blame others for his present condition. He gives three accounts of why he has betrayed the "Movement" and his mother with it, excusing himself on patriotic grounds and for monetary reasons before admitting he was motivated by hatred. The ambivalent boy cannot resolve his guilt and self-hatred in death without the reassurance of another. Not until he forces "de old Foolosopher" to take a stand, can Parritt end his life. Larry "snaps and turns on him" telling him "Go! Get the hell out of life, God Damn you, before I choke it out of you!" (III, 720). Then Parritt realizes that death is the only possible way he can free himself from his mother and from his guilt.

Hickey and Parritt demonstrate the failure of disillusion as a mode of survival. Like Hickey, Parritt is unable to discern the contour of reality. Like Hickey's, his life demonstrates the impossibility of certainty. Both Hickey and Parritt illustrate the difficulty of knowledge in an ambiguous universe. As John Henry Raleigh observes, "the classic adage 'Know Thyself' is clearly impossible in this world although there are several different ways of realizing its impossibilities."[13] Hickey's path of impossibility is tragic; Parritt's is pathetic.

A third variation is represented in the character of Larry Slade. Larry's progression from dreamer to absurd hero encompasses both the pipe dreams of Harry Hope's derelicts and the negations of Hickey. Larry confronts the absurd unwillingly but he is, nevertheless, one of the few O'Neill characters to stare into the abyss of emptiness and survive. In the action of *The Iceman Cometh*, he is both a commentator and a participant. Seated in "the grandstand of philosophical detachment," Larry is able to see with special insight into the dreams and illusions of others. But in order to avoid involvement in life, and to escape himself, he practices "the wrong kind of pity" (III, 690), the kind "that lets itself off easy by encouraging some poor guy to go on kidding himself with a lie" (III, 641). Larry pretends a "cynic philosophy" (III, 600), but at the core of his being he is a sensitive individual. Larry sees life too clearly. He knows the degree to which men are involved in the lives of others, and he does not want such responsibility. Rather than being withdrawn from the world, Larry is alienated in it. His cynicism is an attempt to conceal an awareness of the pain of existence. If he seems fascinated with death, it is because among the uncertainties and ambiguities of life, in the midst of a world in which there are no absolutes, death appears as a solid fact. Yet Larry does not "take a hop" off his fire escape. Larry is not, as Hickey claims "just an old man who is scared of life but even more scared of dying" (III, 641). Though he is unwilling to risk commitment in the face of uncertainty, Larry continues "judging whether life is or is not worth living." Larry seeks the absurd mediation—living without consolation.

Unlike the other derelicts who inhabit Harry Hope's

saloon, Larry lives in the present. If he does not appear to be engaged in the life process, it is because his heightened awareness of uncertainty produces doubt. In a life situation without guiding values, one course of action seems as appropriate as another. For Larry, such ambiguity inhibits action. He describes himself as "born condemned to be one of those who has to see all sides of a question. When you're damned like that, all questions multiply until in the end it's all question and no answer" (III, 590).

Because he is painfully aware of the ambiguity of existence, Larry does not find it easy to focus on specific actions. His reflective consciousness, not his pretended objectivity and cynicism, lies behind his assertion that "I have no answer to give anyone, not even myself" (III, 591). He suffers from the existential neurosis, a condition which reduces the ability to engage in the life process.[14] Confronted with nothingness, Larry retreats into himself, but he is unable to remain detached.

In the interaction with Hickey and Parritt, Larry is compelled to reengage with life; that is, to assume responsibility for himself and others and to overcome the inertia of uncertainty and doubt. He ceases to see "faith and treachery" as nothing but "opposites of the same stupidity which is ruler and king of life" (III, 649). Despite the futility of existence, which he clearly sees, he finds he must exercise his judgment. He must act.

Larry's progression from escapism to action occurs in stages. He moves from detachment to life to heightened consciousness and from heightened consciousness to involvement. In the first part of *The Iceman Cometh*, Larry is portrayed as the "old anarchist wise guy dat knows all de answers!" (III, 579). In this attitude, Larry makes acute observations, but his commentary has no effect on anyone. Though he sees reality as clearly, perhaps more clearly, than Hickey, he makes no demands on the bums at Harry Hope's. In the second stage of the progression toward action, Larry's awareness of the true nature of his own being is aroused. In part, his awakening is caused by Hickey, who provokes Larry into admitting a fear of death. In this humiliation,

Larry also learns that he has not given up on life. In the final stage of his journey toward involvement, Larry's ability to judge and to act are revived. This moral regeneration is provoked by Parritt.

Parritt's confessions of guilt to Larry reveal not only the moral vacuity of the betrayer, they also show that Larry's detachment from life is a pretense and a defense mechanism. Gradually, Larry's sense of justice is awakened, and he commands Parritt to kill himself. But he is not the dispassionate "executioner" he feared he would become (III, 701); rather, he is acting out of compassion and from the recognition that death is Parritt's only answer. He understands that "it's the only way out for him!" (III, 726). And Parritt receives Larry's death sentence gratefully, "Jesus, Larry, thanks. That's kind. I knew you were the only one who could understand my side of it" (III, 721). Thus, Larry becomes aware of the meaning of action, and having attained such awareness, he is unable to return to his illusion of detachment.

In the end, only Larry is able to confront the absurd condition and survive. Though in his final awareness he longs for death, he has acknowledged the difficulty of life without retreating into falsehood. Larry arrives at a state of consciousness which no other character in *The Iceman Cometh* achieves. He comes to understand both the world and himself. In his final declaration, "Be God, there's no hope!" (III, 726), he expresses both the tragedy and the redemption of modern man. For without hope, fate becomes a matter which man must settle. And, when the life situation is defined by its absurdity, by an ambiguous universe and the impenetrability of the self, the only certainties by which men may determine themselves are irreconcilable oppositions and death. For Larry Slade, the tragedy of life is seeing reality without blinders; his redemption is in the acceptance of emptiness and death. There is no joy in Larry's final vision. But his recognition is both honest and compassionate. If "life is too much" (III, 726) for him, illusion is not enough. He shows that action is possible only when man faces the terrors of nothingness. In the end he lives without consolation, the absurd individual with a tragic sense of life.

O'Neill's *The Iceman Cometh* abandons the effort to transcend the paradoxes and oppositions of existence. The playwright no longer "exultantly" affirms life as he does in his earlier works. But he does not cease to believe in living. Rather, he explores man's possibilities within the context of the absurd. He anticipated Camus, who was to write, "In this unintelligible and limited universe, man's fate henceforth assumes its meaning."[15] O'Neill, like Camus, "wants to find out if it is possible to live *without appeal*."[16]

O'Neill's sense of the absurd condition led him, as he wrote *The Iceman Cometh*, to express the difficulty of existing in a situation marked by the absence of guiding absolutes. In the lives of the characters in his play, he studied different responses to confusing and uncertain existence. Harry Hope and his regulars cope with ambiguous reality by evasion; Hickey and Parritt face it with denial and despair; and Larry, after great struggle, comes to terms with it. In the end, only denial appears untenable. As the various attempts at survival are enacted on the stage, the characters are seen sympathetically, and yet tragically. Each of the characters is exposed fully, but this is done with understanding and compassion. O'Neill wrote that as the lives of his characters unfold, there are moments "that suddenly strip the secret soul of a man stark naked, not in cruelty or moral superiority, but with an understanding compassion which sees him as a victim of the ironies of life and of himself."[17] To the problem of living, O'Neill offers no answers. The drama reveals, as Brustein observes, "the impossibility of salvation in a world without God."[18]

V

The Iceman Cometh is a tragic study of existence in the absurd situation; *Hughie* is a comic coda in which illusion is affirmed. In *The Iceman Cometh*, illusion separates men from death, but it also separates them from life. Those who survive by the pipe dream exist in stasis, detached from vitality. In *Hughie*, the constructed image of self not only sustains life, it makes dynamic living possible.

The play is an extended conversation between Erie Smith, "a teller of tales," and a Night Clerk, named Charles Hughes. This Hughes is not the "Hughie" of the title, who was the previous night clerk and a friend of Erie. Hughie has died, prior to the beginning of the play, and his funeral started Erie "off on a bat."[19] As the action commences, Erie is "tapering off," but he finds himself confronted with the gloom of death. "And I'm still carrying the torch for Hughie. His checking out was a real K.O. for me. Damn if I know why" (p. 273).

Early in the play then, Erie faces the fundamental question of the absurd—judging whether or not life is worth living. As Ruby Cohn suggests, the play "dramatizes the prototypical Absurdist situation—man's confrontation with mortality. . . . Erie Smith has been shocked by death into an awareness of metaphysical absurdity."[20] But Erie does not meditate upon the absurdity he has discovered. He is "a teller of tales," and his mode of coping with nothingness has been to create a fabric of illusion with which to protect himself. Like all such story tellers, he needs an appreciative listener who will believe him, or at least willingly suspend disbelief. With the loss of Hughie, Erie finds himself without an audience, isolated, alone, and aware of his own mortality.

The play progresses in a manner opposite to that of *The Iceman Cometh*. Most of *Hughie* is devoted to Erie's effort to convert the new Night Clerk into a believer. The former drama moves from sustaining illusion to the naked and destructive truth; the latter begins with truth and proceeds to illusion. The characters in *Hughie* begin in isolation and eventually come together in a kind of communion of souls, a giving of the self to another and a receiving of a positive image of self. But for the majority of the play, the characters remain separate and incommunicative; Erie talks while Charlie listens to his own thoughts and to the sounds of the night. Confronted by the emptiness of existence, Charlie is resigned; Erie, despite his gloom and heightened consciousness of meaninglessness and death, rebels. He is an advocate of and a believer in life. With the death of his friend Hughie, he determines to sell his enthusiasm for living to the new clerk, Charlie.

Erie embarks on this mission for selfish reasons. Hughie, it is revealed, was Erie's luck—"He used to give me confidence" (p. 290). Without Hughie, Erie has been unable to win a bet, a fatal liability for a small-time gambler. If he is to survive, Erie must win from Charlie the acknowledgement to which he had become accustomed while Hughie was alive. Though Erie, like Hickey in *The Iceman Cometh*, is an astute judge of people, able to "size them up" in a glance, he does not win Charlie over easily. The Night Clerk, like his predecessor, has trained himself to ignore others. He is virtually immune to conversation. In addition, the Night Clerk is resigned to boredom: "nothing exciting has ever happened in any night I've ever lived through!" (p. 279). And he is convinced that nothing ever will happen. Erie wheedles and cajoles, insinuates and insults, tells tales and tells the truth, all to little avail. He seems unable to penetrate the shell with which Charlie has surrounded himself. Finally exhausted, and unable to continue the effort to make Charlie participate in life, Erie gives up. He concludes that death is desirable: "But Hughie's better off, at that, being dead. He's got all the luck. He needn't do no worryin' now. He's out of the racket. I mean, the whole goddamned racket. I mean life" (p. 288). Erie is prepared at this point to withdraw from life, to retreat to his empty hotel room. But the word "racket" strikes a chord in the gambling fantasy in which Charlie is indulging, and the Night Clerk responds to Erie. When it is least expected, human contact is made between the two characters.

Though Erie does most of the talking in *Hughie*, it is the Night Clerk who actually tears down the barriers separating him from Erie. This is perhaps ironic. For Charlie, like Erie, acts out of selfish reasons. For most of the play, the Night Clerk tunes out "The Guest's Story of His Life" and focuses instead on the sounds of the night. His thoughts are revealed through a series of stage directions, often accompanied by specific sounds which interrupt or punctuate Erie's lengthy monologue. Charlie's interior monologue, though unvoiced, represents a "stream-of-consciousness" wandering of the mind. The listening to the sounds of the night insulates him from guests' tales of suffering. But Charlie's thoughts only reveal the emptiness of his own life. He vacillates between fear of death and longing for it. Raleigh calls the Night Clerk's inner monologue a "stream of nothingness, beyond and below despair."[21] Yet something in this man clings to life. His fantasies reveal a desire for recognition as strong as Erie's, but his actions suggest that Charlie has long ago abandoned any hope of achieving it.

When the night fails to provide distracting sounds, Charlie Hughes finds that the silence of the city "vaguely reminds him of death" (p. 285). He escapes the "threat of Night and Silence" (p. 287) by becoming involved in the sounds made by Erie. The two men make contact; they recognize one another's humanity and help each other to survive. The loneliness, alienation, emptiness, and despair which accompany recognition of the absurd condition are mediated as Erie and Charlie begin to live through each other. Life may be a "racket," but in the end man survives by resisting. As the play closes, two lives are affirmed, even if each of the characters is the sucker to the other's wise guy. *Hughie* is one of O'Neill's most optimistic plays.

VI

In *Long Day's Journey into Night*, *The Iceman Cometh*, and *Hughie*, the problem of existence is depicted both comically and tragically. The characters include survivors, such as Edmund Tyrone, Larry Slade, and Erie Smith, and casualties such as Hickey, Don Parritt, and Jamie Tyrone. In each of the plays, man is alone; he seeks his reason for being without God. In the face of nothingness, O'Neill's final characters exist in isolation and in pain. Courageous or resigned, they attempt to live. Deprived of any organizing principle, cast into an ambiguous world and uncertain of themselves, these men represent O'Neill's final response to the difficulty of existence. Uneasy in the absurd condition, they show us exile without remedy, but not the defeat of man.

NOTES

[1] Albert Camus, *The Myth of Sisyphus and Other Essays,* trans. Justin O'Brien (New York, 1955), pp. 22–23.

[2] Tom Driver, "On the Late Plays of Eugene O'Neill," in *O'Neill: A Collection of Critical Essays,* ed. John Gassner (Englewood Cliffs, 1964), p. 122.

[3] Eugene O'Neill, *Long Day's Journey into Night* (New Haven, 1956), p. 7. All further references to this play are from this edition and appear in parentheses in the text.

[4] Camus, p. 37.

[5] Eugene O'Neill, *The Great God Brown,* in his *The Plays of Eugene O'Neill,* 3 vols. (New York, 1955) vol. III, p. 318. Future references to this collection appear in parentheses in the text with a roman numeral to indicate volume and an arabic numeral to indicate page.

[6] Camus, p. 3.

[7] Sophus Keith Winther, *Eugene O'Neill: A Critical Study,* 2nd ed. enlarged (New York, 1961), pp. 305–06.

[8] Robert Brustein, *The Theatre of Revolt: An Approach to the Modern Drama* (Boston, 1964), p. 340.

[9] Camus, p. 7.

[10] Croswell Bowen with the assistance of Shane O'Neill, *The Curse of the Misbegotten: A Tale of the House of O'Neill* (New York, 1959), pp. 310–11.

[11] Camus, p. 9.

[12] Travis Bogard, *Contour in Time: The Plays of Eugene O'Neill* (New York, 1972), p. 388.

[13] John Henry Raleigh, *The Plays of Eugene O'Neill* (Carbondale, 1972), p. 162.

[14] Camus, p. 5.

[15] Ibid., p. 16.

[16] Ibid., p. 39.

[17] Eugene O'Neill, "Letters from O'Neill to Lawrence Langner," in *Twentieth Century Interpretations of The Iceman Cometh: A Collection of Critical Essays,* ed. John Henry Raleigh (Englewood Cliffs, 1968), p. 20.

[18] Brustein, p. 343.

[19] Eugene O'Neill, *Hughie* in *The Later Plays of Eugene O'Neill*, ed. Travis Bogard, Modern Library College ed. (New York, 1967), p. 266. All future references are to this edition and appear in parentheses in the text.

[20] Ruby Cohn, *Dialogue in American Drama* (New York, 1964), p. 61.

[21] Raleigh, p. 28.

PART 3

Performers on O'Neill

INTRODUCTION

Virginia Floyd

.

Eugene O'Neill's greatest drama, *Long Day's Journey into Night*, had its American première on October 15, 1956 in Boston. The time and place seem particularly appropriate. First, the première was presented on the eve of the sixty-eighth anniversary of the playwright's birth; and second, it was in Boston that O'Neill had his true beginning, as dramatist, and his end, as man. He spent a year, 1914–15, in George Pierce Baker's "47 Workshop" at Harvard University, where he learned the principles of craftsmanship to which he would adhere throughout his writing career. Boston is the hub of the Puritan stronghold, and O'Neill stated in his last interview with the press in 1946 that he felt closest as an artist to the "battle of moral forces in the New England scene." Ironically, some of his plays were banned there either after they opened or before they even reached that city. Most significantly, O'Neill lived his last years in a Boston hotel, died there, and was buried nearby. With the première of *Long Day's Journey into Night*, he was resurrected in America. For over twenty years, from 1934 to 1956, after the failure of *Days Without End* in 1934, there were no major productions except *The Iceman Cometh* in 1946 and the ill-fated pre-Broadway tour of *A Moon for the Misbegotten* in 1947. It was not until 1956, three years after the dramatist's death and the successful world première of *Long Day's*

Journey into Night at the Royal Dramatic Theatre in Stockholm, that there was what could be termed an O'Neill revival in the United States.

Long Day's Journey into Night had its Italian première in Milan on October 16, 1956, and Eligio Possenti, the theatre critic of *Corriere Della Sera*, reviewed the play the next day, saying: "O'Neill's drama is a re-creation of a past punctuated by sobs as if the author had told his own life weeping. The moans of a soul are heard in this work." In Italy, as in Sweden and other European countries, critics immediately recognized it as a masterpiece, making both a personal and a universal statement. While American critics noted the obvious autobiographical aspects of the play when it was first staged here, some failed to comprehend its true significance and greatness. In his *New York Times* review the day after the play opened in New York on November 7, 1956, Brooks Atkinson ranked *Long Day's Journey* with *Mourning Becomes Electra* and *Desire Under the Elms*, which are both inferior dramas. The critics were, however, unanimous in their praise of Fredric March and Florence Eldridge, who played O'Neill's ill-fated parents, James and Mary Tyrone. Atkinson called the actor's performance "stunning, a character portrait of grandeur" and wrote: "Florence Eldridge analyzes the pathetic character of the mother with tenderness and compassion."

Atkinson would have also noted that Florence Eldridge did indeed capture the essence of Ella O'Neill's character had he spoken to Jessica Rippin, whose mother ran a boarding house located across the street from the O'Neill's New London home, where the family frequently took their meals. O'Neill had lived with the Rippins while recuperating from tuberculosis. Jessica Rippin told me in an interview in 1969 that when she and her two sisters, Emily and Dolly, went to see *Long Day's Journey*, they were especially moved by Miss Eldridge's performance. They had known the O'Neills well, particularly Emily, who had been Ella O'Neill's frequent companion in her afternoon drives. Miss Rippin stated that throughout the play "Em kept whispering, 'she's just like Mrs. O'Neill.'" and added, "to this day Em can't get over how much the mother in the play resembled Ella O'Neill."

Miss Eldridge's response when she was informed of the Rippins's appraisal of her performance was: "You, and inadvertently Miss Rippin, have given me great pleasure, feeling that by following small clues leading here and there, and sometimes contradicting each other, I assembled a lady whom a neighbor recognized. Thank you for sharing this with me." In this same letter of February 27, 1979, Miss Eldridge described an incident that occurred in 1925 when she very nearly became involved in the première production of another O'Neill play, *The Great God Brown*. She states:

> I think it might interest you to know that my first contact with a work of O'Neill was in 1925. I was twenty-four at the time and had just played the stepdaughter in Pirandello's *Six Characters in Search of an Author*. Kenneth Macgowan brought me the script of *The Great God Brown* with the thought that I might be interested in tackling Cybel. I was young enough, and brash enough, to see an Emperor without clothes and dared to suggest that I *would* be interested but felt that certain changes were needed! I shudder when I think of it. Quite recently I received a letter asking for my permission to reprint, in a collection of Mr. Macgowan's letters, "a snarling reply" that Mr. O'Neill made to him when he conveyed my message. Needless to say, the subject of *The Great God Brown* never came up again.

What should be remembered as one reads Miss Eldridge's account of the preparations she made to play Mary Tyrone is the fact that all the actress had to guide her was the actual script of *Long Day's Journey*. The play was not released and published until 1956; who, at that time, had any awareness of the complexities not only of the mother's character but also of her drug problem? Not until the 1960s did we have the enormous spate of books and articles on O'Neill, noting in great detail the autobiographic elements of this play and analyzing Mary Tyrone's drug addiction. Little wonder then that Miss Eldridge speaks of looking for clues—at the O'Neill family home in New London and drug addiction centers.

There were people who tried to convince the actress, as she says, that the play was too long, too repetitious. One statement Miss Eldridge makes reveals her great understanding of what the dramatist was trying to accomplish in *Long Day's Journey*: "The more one worked on the play, the more one realized that it was a symphony. Each character had a theme and the 'repetitions' were the variations of the themes." In the early 1940s, when the play was written, O'Neill was striving to achieve this effect in his work. On February 19 and 21, 1940, he records in his Work Diary ideas that use an orchestral technique—"symphony, characters, chorus, and orchestra (notes)." The very next day, on February 22, he writes: "The Long Day's Journey (notes—and get better title, Long Day's Journey into Night)." As early as 1931, O'Neill acknowledges in his notebooks that he used the structure of a symphony in nearly all his plays with "each character representing a theme." The repetitions that critics found annoying and Florence Eldridge recognized for what they are were part of the dramatist's deliberately conceived pattern.

Since the moving 1956 première, there have been a number of other productions, but perhaps none was more innovative than Arvin Brown's in 1971, with Robert Ryan and Geraldine Fitzgerald portraying James and Mary Tyrone. The two actors were so attracted to these roles that they had rehearsed them informally for years prior to this production as if they knew they would one day play them. Geraldine Fitzgerald claims Mary Tyrone is not a victim of her family but of her own neurosis and is a kind of guilt-ridden Electra who had tried to displace her mother in her father's affections. Like Florence Eldridge, to prepare for this role, Miss Fitzgerald consulted doctors to discuss the effects of morphine on addicts. She and Arvin Brown have a totally new concept of the drug-addicted Mary Tyrone. Most actresses play this character in a dazed, low-key fashion. Miss Fitzgerald maintains Mary gets a "cat reaction" to the drugs and becomes more excited, not depressed. Whereas Florence Eldridge went to Bellevue Hospital to observe addicts in 1956, Miss Fitzgerald, as she notes, had only to step outside the Promenade Theatre in New York City, where she was rehearsing the play fifteen years later, to see drug users "shooting up" in Needle Park. It should be remembered that this is precisely what Mary Tyrone did every time she went upstairs—injected herself with a needle, a terrifying thought for the uninitiated. It was something the playwright could never forget.

There are lengthy explanations of the mother's drug addiction in O'Neill's notes for *Long Day's Journey* at Yale and a statement on the weather progression which denotes the character's regression into her world of oblivion. He describes her condition at 6:30 P.M. after her many trips upstairs that long day: "M very hipped up now, her manner strange . . . at the moment a vain happy chattering girlishness—then changing to a hard cynical sneering bitterness with a bitter biting cruelty and with a coarse vulgarity in it—the last as if suddenly poisoned by an alive demon." Geraldine Fitzgerald's interpretation of this character is a close approximation to the dramatist's vision of her. Although O'Neill's comment here on this character has never, until now, been made public, Miss Fitzgerald's statement on her echoes the playwright's: "Mary is not a victim; she's spoiled, sharp-tongued; she has refused to mature." Compare the choice of words in the two descriptions: vain/spoiled; girlishness/refused to mature; coarse vulgarity/sharp-tongued. For good reason, Tom Burke called Miss Fitzgerald's performance "one of the most shattering pieces of histrionics now available anywhere," one that "brought critics to their knees and audiences to their feet, cheering her artistry."

As the actress states, it was Arvin Brown's courage that gave *her* the courage to risk this new interpretation of Mary Tyrone. Mr. Brown has remarked elsewhere that he directs a play to get the material out of the actor rather than lead an actor to the material. The director's remarks here reveal his dedication to the dramatist and describe his psychological and artistic approach to staging his plays. He and the actress collaborated in another O'Neill production, *Ah, Wilderness!*, thus presenting both the light and dark side of the dramatist's vision of family life. Martin Gottfried in his review of this play writes: "Mr. Brown's work here is major on the international level. The company is the very definition of an ensemble." This type of ensemble acting is especially effective in view of the fact that *Long Day's Journey* and *Ah, Wilderness!* are family plays, and a director must strive to capture not only the complexity of individual characters but also how they function and react as a close unit. O'Neill once stated he would like to see his plays done by a permanent repertory theatre. We have moved one step further toward achieving O'Neill's goal because of Arvin Brown's sensitive interpretation of the plays, his ability to create a sense of oneness and singleness of purpose in an acting company. Together Arvin Brown and Geraldine Fitzgerald created a Mary Tyrone and *Long Day's Journey into Night* that enriched the American theatre and our lives.

Theatre professionals commemorated the twenty-fifth anniversary of the death of America's greatest dramatist with a Special O'Neill Event during the 1978 Modern Language Association Convention. Making one of her rare public appearances in this country, Ingrid Bergman shared reminiscences of her meeting with O'Neill in 1941, when she made her American theatrical debut as Anna Christie, a role also interpreted by two of her countrywomen, Greta Garbo and Liv Ullman.

O'Neill recorded the following statement in his Work Diary for August 9, 1941; "C to S. F. to see Ingrid Bergman in *Anna Christie*—I wouldn't sit through *Anna Christie* for ten grand per minute." In an August 14 entry, the dramatist writes: "Ingrid Bergman to lunch . . . like her, has character, takes work seriously, intelligent, no Hollywood ham stuff."[2] From Miss Bergman's account of their meeting, the actress and playwright seem to be conspirators slipping away from the ever-vigilant wife, Carlotta the caretaker, to discuss his Cycle, "A Tale of Possessors, Self-Dispossessed." It appears Miss Bergman has always regretted "abandoning" the dramatist, as he described her rejection of his plan for her to star in the then nine-play Cycle. Happily for audiences, twenty-six years later in 1967, she appeared in the American première of *More Stately Mansions*, which with *A Touch of the Poet* survived O'Neill's destruction of the Cycle. As Tom Prideaux notes, "For Miss Bergman it was a triumphant return to the stage, and for O'Neill's play, *More Stately Mansions*, which he had ordered burned after his death, it was a resurrection from oblivion." Miss Bergman's sensitive portrayal of Deborah Harford in this production provides one more reason to lament the loss of the other Cycle plays through which the dramatist and actress would have enriched the American theatre.

Reflections on
Long Day's Journey into Night
FIRST CURTAIN CALL
FOR MARY TYRONE

Florence Eldridge

How does one make one's choices, among the various clues offered, and come to certain conclusions about a character one is trying to create and give life to? By now, Mary Tyrone has been played in many different ways so I cannot say, "Mary Tyrone is like this." I can only speak to my own choices for the first American production of *Long Day's Journey into Night* in 1956.

In an attempt to understand the character's drug addiction, I went, through the kindness of a doctor friend, to observe addicts in Bellevue Hospital and noticed their garrulousness and high-pitched voices when they were in need of drugs and the somnolence and peacefulness that followed drug-taking. I tried to fit the knowledge gained from my visit to Bellevue into the pattern of the script in the scenes that preceded Mary Tyrone's going upstairs to find relief and her returns, but there was something that did not fit.

I then went to Dr. Marie Nyswander, an authority on drug addiction, and gave her the play to read. Her conclusion was that if O'Neill had accurately observed his mother's behavior, there was pathology involved as well as addiction, so I made the choice to play what was written. Interestingly, when the curtain came down each night and we "set up our psychiatrists' couches" to receive the traumatized and those whose mothers had been addicts—or alcoholics—or schizophrenics—we discovered *all* had identified.

The next choice to make was how to approach the arthritic hands. Were they that badly crippled? Were they an excuse? I decided not to emphasize Mary Tyrone's crippled hands as I felt that her emotional and spiritual deformity was more important.

Another clue came when we went to New London to see the O'Neill house that is the scene of the play and the cause of Mary Tyrone's lamentation for a decent home. I was surprised to find it full of attractive possibilities and charmingly situated looking out on the sound. I decided then that Mary Tyrone was a victim, not only of her life but also of her own inadequacies, and must be played as an immature person.

José Quintero was particularly anxious for me to meet Carlotta O'Neill as he felt that O'Neill had woven a bit of her into the character of his mother. The director arranged for us to have lunch, and I could find such echoes of Mary Tyrone's speeches in Carlotta's love-hate anecdotes. She would start to reminisce so sweetly and suddenly repressed resentment would burst through into bitter complaints or self pity just as Mary Tyrone does repeatedly when she is reviewing the past with James Tyrone.

Eugene O'Neill and all of us who were fortunate to be part of this rewarding experience owe a great debt to Carlotta O'Neill. When we opened in Boston, prior to the New York opening, and all the smart theatre people came up to see the play, they insisted that it must be cut as it was too repetitious. Fortunately, Carlotta O'Neill stood firm. Not one word could be touched.

The more one worked on the play, the more one realized that it was a symphony. Each character had a theme and the "repetitions" were the variations on the themes. That was the power of the play—the ceaseless pounding of the themes. Had it been cut, it would have unravelled.

STAGING O'NEILL'S
"SIMPLE PLAY"

Arvin Brown

I have been asked why I selected a "simple play" like *Long Day's Journey into Night* when I first started directing in 1965 at the Long Wharf Theatre. The answer would have to be that no one else in the theatre at that time wanted to touch this play. They were terrified of it. I had been promised my first production that season, and I inherited the play—with a very fine American actress, Mildred Dunnock, playing Mary Tyrone. I felt as though I spent that whole first rehearsal period just desperately trying to keep everybody from finding out how totally green I was. I assumed, as I got to know actors better and found out how perceptive they were, that I had not fooled anyone at all. Then, just as a sort of side note, I found myself giving an award to Miss Dunnock several years ago. I told her the story about how silly I was for thinking I could have fooled anyone. She was shocked, and I realized I had done a better job of covering my inexperience than I thought.

Returning to the play in 1971, with Geraldine Fitzgerald in the part of Mary Tyrone, I felt that I had grown tremendously in the six years since I had first done the production. One of the wonderful things about the opportunity to deal with a masterpiece is that one can chart one's own development as a human being in the way one encounters it, the way one perceives it. I felt that I had come to terms with many things about myself and my own family relationships, as well as acquired certain skills just in pursuing my craft for six years. I felt that I had something different to say about the play than I had the first time. Much of what I had to say that was different had to do with the character and treatment of Mary Tyrone. And I was fortunate to have Geraldine Fitzgerald to be able to put it on the stage for me.

I had come to believe in the six years since I had first done the play that most people, but particularly Americans, tend to do a lot of sentimentalizing about neurosis. I think this is especially true in our assessment of O'Neill the man, as well as O'Neill the dramatist, and certainly true of our assessment of the characters he created. Yes, O'Neill was tormented. Yes, O'Neill was tortured. He was also very funny; he was also a tremendous drinker and loved a good time. He was capable of love, and he was capable, in his neurosis, of great cruelty. I looked for all these qualities in the characters in *Long Day's Journey*. They are more immediately apparent in O'Neill's men, particularly the lighter side and certainly the cruel side.

But I believed that there had been a sentimental approach very often in the past to the mother. Yes, she is, in some respects, a victim; she is tormented by the men and feels herself, at times, inadequate to deal with them. But at times she is more than adequate. At times she gives back as good as she gets and, indeed, much of the pain and trauma of the male situation in the play stems from Mary Tyrone's ability (quite unconscious much of the time and resulting from the depth of her despair) to find the sore spots in her loved ones. And she is capable of wounding as only a mother can wound when she really wants to hurt or get back. This is the framework, the launching place, for the work Miss Fitzgerald and I did together in *Long Day's Journey into Night*.

ANOTHER NEUROTIC ELECTRA
A New Look at Mary Tyrone

Geraldine Fitzgerald

There were several things Arvin Brown and I used to talk about when we first started the production of *Long Day's Journey into Night*. First of all, why did the three men in the play, the two sons and husband, put up with Mary Tyrone? Why did they allow her to stay with them? If it is true that at the end of that day when she starts taking drugs again there will be people coming to take her back to the sanatorium, why didn't the sons and the husband send for the doctors immediately? Why do they want her around? If she drifts around in a daze dreaming of the past, complaining—why care about her? They are adults and she is an adult. What is there about her that makes them like her so much—in addition to her being a beautiful symbol as a wife and mother? They seem captivated—but why?

This question led us to ask a second: What are the drugs doing to Mary? Why wasn't she like the people in Needle Park? We rehearsed this play and did it in 1971 at the Promenade Theatre, on that part of Broadway which faces what in those days was called Needle Park because so many there at that time were shooting up! Why wasn't Mary Tyrone like them? The people in the park were all dragging themselves around like wasps at the end of the summer— ready to sting but not reacting if they were left alone. Why was Mary Tyrone different? Why was she still up that night when her family were all falling apart? Why was she still talking? Why was she always so ready to strike back?

Since she was clearly a sick woman, the only way to find an answer to these questions seemed to be consult a doctor. So I went to three doctors. The first was a psychiatrist, the second a surgeon, the third an internist. They each gave the same opinion (as far as an opinion could be given about the health of a character in a play): that Mary Tyrone was a woman who suffered what is called in medical slang a "cat" reaction to morphine (so-called because only women and cats have this atypical response), which would make her overactive and excitable rather than drowsy (the so-called "dog" reaction, the usual one). Although without medical records this hypothesis could not be proved, Arvin Brown and I decided to go with it, because it shed light on so many mysterious moments in the play. For instance, it explained why Jamie, of all the family, is the only one who can tell when his mother has taken drugs—he being the only one whose raffish life might have provided the opportunity to see other women who were also unusual in their response to the same drug.

This choice then led us both to think that the many stage directions describing Mary as responding "from another world" do not necessarily mean another world where the person is half asleep but rather one in which the person is very much awake! And that the actions she was going to take during the play were going to come out of this strange world, in terms of what the other people on the stage or in the audience might think. It was a world that seemed to her to be normal and correct, and the more drugs she took, and the more normal her own strange behavior becomes to her, the more strange it is to the others who were victims of it. If this concept is accepted it becomes clear that she is the victimizer and not the victim. She is really not a victim of her family at all; she is a victim of her own neurosis.

That insight led us to the second terribly important revelation. And it is this: if Mary Tyrone had never had a drug in her life, she would have been more or less the same! She is what she is because of her sense of guilt. She feels deeply guilty about her relationship with her mother, whom she didn't like, and about her father, whom she adored but who died young. Many of O'Neill's characters are based on ancient prototypes, and Mary Tyrone was a kind of Electra. Her behavior is based on the fact that she was a person who felt that she was going to be given the worst of punishment for her own crime of cutting out her mother with her father. When first met, she has already lost her youth prematurely, her talents, her health, and she is about to have the most important thing in life taken from her—Edmund, her younger son, the one who is most like her of the two boys. He is the literary one; and if you pay attention to what they both say, you will find that over and over the mother and the son sound alike. In fact, at times you do not know which one is talking. If you did not have their names written on top of their speeches in the text, you wouldn't know. You would say: "That's Edmund; that's Mary." Their way of expressing themselves would give no clue.

That led us to another discovery: that Mary Tyrone is evidently a very talented person—although perhaps not in music as she believed. She was a literary person and is very eloquent. It may be that her frustrated gift as a writer was passed on to her son and that is another reason why she loved him so.

The thing about this production of *Long Day's Journey* that made it so meaningful for me was the opportunity it provided to work with a director who had the courage to examine the many facets of Mary Tyrone's personality and drug problem. Many people came to me, and to Arvin, and said: "You can't do this to Mary Tyrone. You can't make her be so satirical and witty and needling of everybody on the stage. This cannot be. This is a sacred figure." Yet Arvin had the courage to go forward, and his courage gave me the courage to go along with him.

A MEETING WITH O'NEILL

Ingrid Bergman

I just heard about this [MLA] meeting two days ago. I only came to New York to celebrate Christmas and New Year with my children and grandchildren, but I was pleased to be invited. It may be that you are right. Perhaps it is again Mr. O'Neill coming to tell me that I should be present. It started with *Anna Christie* in San Francisco in 1941. After a performance his wife, Carlotta, came backstage. She said that he was too ill to come but that he would like to meet me. I said that I would like to meet him very much. I was very flattered that he wanted to see me at all, and she said she would come and pick me up two days later for lunch. She pointed out that I must not bring a photographer. I said, "No. I did not bring photographers; they were usually there already." I added: "Be very careful that they do not come without your knowing it. I will not mention to anyone that I am visiting you."

On the way to their beautiful Tao House, Mrs. O'Neill told me that she would give me a sign when I should leave. She stated that he was tired and would not want to stay very long with me. She would nod, and then I should say that I had to go. I promised her that I would do that. So I arrived, and, of course, I was very young and terribly impressed because I knew what a great playwright Mr. O'Neill was. I was also deeply concerned about my part as Anna Christie. The house was very white, and the architectural style was Chinese. There was very little furniture, and the house was airy.

Mr. O'Neill was very tall, but standing there before three staircases—platforms—he looked even taller. He was a very handsome man but quite thin. He came toward me, and there was a silence about him that was so effective. It was the stillness that impressed me. One hardly dared to speak to him. Then, as he came closer, I saw those eyes. They were the most beautiful eyes I have seen in my whole life. They were like wells; you fell into them. You had the feeling that he looked straight through you. Then he sat down, and we talked. He told me that his wife appreciated what I had done with *Anna Christie*. Then we had lunch. I was so awed by the whole thing I cannot remember what we spoke about.

After lunch, Mr. O'Neill made a sign to me that I should come up to his working room. Mrs. O'Neill immediately made a sign that I should not, that I should go home now. I looked from one to the other, and I decided that I would follow him. We went up to his study, which was a remarkable room. He had the nine plays of the Cycle all laid out. He was working on all nine at the same time. He said: "I am writing one hundred and fifty years of American history. It is the same family, and they go from young to middle-age, to old and dying, and then on to the next generation. It is going to be about American history and a family that we follow through the ups and downs of this country." I looked at these plays. They were not finished. He worked on them all at the same time. When an idea came to him, he wrote it into the period where he thought it would be most effective.

Then he said: "I want a company that stays with me. After all, it is the same family that goes through many generations, and I want the same faces. In one play you will have a big part, and in another one you will have a small part. You will play a sister, an aunt, a young daughter." I stood there. I had just started my career in Hollywood, and I had an idea of all the wonderful movies I was going to make. I said to Mr. O'Neill: "But nine plays! You want me to be in *nine* plays?" He said: "Yes. I want this company to stay together for four years. In four years we will have produced them all." Of course, being young and very anxious to have a career in the movies (it was 1941), I said, "No, I am not going to do them." I regretted having to refuse. I remember he looked at me and said: "You're abandoning me." I said, "Not really. Perhaps some other time. Maybe later." I felt terrible about turning down *nine* plays!

As we know, Mr. O'Neill became very ill, and he never finished the nine plays. He completed *A Touch of the Poet* and the play that follows it, *More Stately Mansions*, but all the others were destroyed. He wanted to destroy *More Stately Mansions* also. I do not know if Carlotta, whom I got to know later when I was doing *More Stately Mansions* here, hid the play in a drawer or it was left in a drawer by mistake. She told me how she cried, how very difficult it was to sit there and tear up all these plays. But one copy of *More Stately Mansions* survived and was found. The play was not finished. It was about six hours long if you read it. Mr. O'Neill had just put everything into it; he had not ended it. He had put all of his ideas into this play.

José Quintero came to me—I was then in France—and asked me if I would read it and consider playing it. That's when I remembered Eugene O'Neill standing there saying: "Are you abandoning me?" Then I said: "This time I shall play it—never mind what the play is like." We started out on a version that was different from the Swedish version. There was so much material that we had to select what we wanted. And, of course, the play was not really praised by the critics; they did not like it. However, I thought it was important that the play had been found and that we were producing it. After all, O'Neill is one of America's greatest playwrights. Even if *More Stately Mansions* is not his best play, it was written by a playwright who will go down in history as the greatest of America.

NOTE

[1] O'Neill makes similar comments to Lawrence Langner in a letter dated August 16, 1941, urging the Theatre Guild producer

to attend a performance of the play in anticipation of an *Anna Christie*-Bergman road tour and New York presentation: "We had her out to lunch—and like her a lot. No ham stuff about her. She struck me as intelligent, ambitious, loving her work and willing to work her head off for it, either for films or stage."

Carlotta O'Neill also wrote to Langner (August 10, 1941), praising Miss Bergman:

> I went yesterday, to the matinee of "Anna Christie." (God, what torture, to sit through one of Gene's plays and watch *what* they'll do next!)
>
> To put it in a few words—I liked Bergman & O'Flynn. Bergman was excellent when she had to dig in and work, &, at all times, I felt her the *woman*, not an *actress* acting! She is good property for any producer.
>
> Bergman *can act*, is beautiful & a *woman*—None of *these damned* silly affectations!
>
> (Eugene O'Neill Collection, Yale)

CONTRIBUTORS

Editor Virginia Floyd, Professor of English at Bryant College, has had scholarly essays on O'Neill published in this country and in Europe and is currently completing a book, *Eugene O'Neill's Ideas for Plays*, working with Donald Gallup, curator of the O'Neill Collection at Yale University; he has given her access to the dramatist's notebooks which have never before been made available to scholars and contain his recorded ideas, outlines, and plans for completed and contemplated works—dating from 1918 to 1943. She has worked on a number of projects to promote the dramatist and his work: organizing and chairing sessions with American and European O'Neill scholars and theatre professionals as panelists for the 1976, 1977, and 1978 Modern Language Association Conventions; participating in O'Neill Symposiums in this country and abroad; organizing a Eugene O'Neill Society of which she is a member of the executive board; and acting as advisor for the new national Eugene O'Neill Archival Center and Theatre at Provincetown.

Albert Bermel, Professor of Theatre and Drama at Lehman College, has written numerous books, including *Contradictory Characters: An Interpretation of the Modern Theatre* and *The Comic Agony: Masks of Wit and Humor in the Modern Theatre,* essays, and theatre reviews for which he received the George Jean Nathan Award for dramatic criticism, 1973–74. In addition to writing television and film scripts, he has translated plays, including several of Molière, and has written critical studies. His original full-length and one-act plays have been staged and published in this country and abroad.

Peter Egri is Professor of Comparative Literature and Chairman of the English Department (with over 500 English majors) at the University of Budapest. He is the author of many books: *Hemingway, James Joyce and Thomas Mann, Dream and Reality, The Reality of Poetry*. His *History of the European Drama at the Turn of the Century* has been accepted for publication by The Hungarian Academy of Sciences and his critical studies on American and English authors have appeared in Hungarian, American, French, German, and Italian scholarly publications. An IREX Fellowship in 1970–71 and an ACLS Fellowship in 1976–77 enabled him to do research at Harvard, Yale, and the University of California, Berkeley, for a critical monograph on Eugene O'Neill which he is at present preparing for publication.

Horst Frenz, Professor of Comparative Literature at Indiana University, Bloomington, and author of *Eugene O'Neill*, is currently completing two works on the dramatist: *Eugene O'Neill: World Dramatist* and *Foreign Essays on O'Neill*. He has written a large collection of essays, which have appeared in American and foreign scholarly publications, on O'Neill productions in countries throughout the world and has lectured extensively in the United States and abroad.

Esther M. Jackson, Professor of Dramatic Literature and Criticism at the University of Wisconsin-Madison, is the author of *The Broken World of Tennessee Williams* and essays on Eugene O'Neill and other American dramatists. She was Literary Advisor for the 1974 public television presentation of *The Dreamer*, a ballet choreographed by Birgit Cullberg, based on *A Touch of the Poet*, and for the University of Wisconsin's 1978 production of *Thirst*, one of O'Neill's early one-act plays. She has initiated a number of O'Neill projects, including one to start an O'Neill Theatre and Institute in this country.

Josef Jařab is a graduate of Palacky University, Olomouc, Czechoslovakia, where he currently teaches English and American Literature and culture. He holds Ph.D. and CSc. degrees from Charles University, Prague and was awarded an ACLS American Studies Fellowship in 1969–70 to do research at New York University and Brandeis University. His critical essays on American minority writers and modern fiction and its theoretical problems have appeared in various publications in Czechoslovakia. He also edited a textbook anthology, *American Poetry and Poets of Four Centuries*, and is at present preparing another anthology, *Twentieth-Century American Black Literature*.

Maya Koreneva is affiliated with the Gorky Institute of World Literature of the Academy of Sciences of the U.S.S.R., a research institute. She received her doctorate from Moscow University and is editing her dissertation on American drama since World War II for publication. Her many essays include: "American Drama in the 1960's," "Society's Spiritual Crises and the Individual's Moral Position," and "Literature and War—the American Novel of Two World Wars." She has written the modern American Literature section for the Gorky Institute's ten-volume *History of World Literature* and the chapter on New England literature for *Formation of American Literature—17th to 20th Centuries*. She has translated Edward Albee's *A Delicate Balance*, William Faulkner's *The Unvanquished*, and other works by American and English writers.

Clifford Leech, author of *Eugene O'Neill*, had a life-long interest in the American dramatist. As a student at the University of London, he directed two of O'Neill's early one-act plays, *The Rope* and *The First Man*, and was involved in later O'Neill London productions. Shortly after the publication of his study on O'Neill in 1962, he became Professor of English at the University of Toronto. He retired in 1974 and accepted a teaching position as Visiting Professor at the University of Connecticut. At the time of his sudden death in July 1977, he was planning to participate in an O'Neill session at the 1977 MLA Convention and an international O'Neill conference in 1978. Professor Leech was primarily an English Renaissance scholar and his many publications in this field include: *Shakespeare's Tragedies and Other Studies in Seventeenth Century Drama, Twelfth Night and Shakespearian Comedy, Comedy in the Grand Style*, and critical studies of John Webster, John Fletcher, John Ford, and Christopher Marlowe. He was often a guest lecturer in this country, Canada, and abroad, and in one of his last public appearances, he introduced Marlowe's *Edward II* for the Classic Theatre television series.

Tom Olsson, curator of the archives at the Royal Dramatic Theatre in Stockholm, is the author of *O'Neill and the Royal Dramatic*, a comprehensive study of productions from 1923 to the present. His many articles on the playwright have appeared in *Dramaten*, and he has translated a number of plays by American dramatists. The Zorn scholarship from the Sweden-America Foundation in 1974 and 1975 enabled him to do research on O'Neill in this country. He has presented papers on the dramatist at O'Neill Seminars in the United States and to the Society of Humanities and the Humanistic Society IDUN in Stockholm. He studied theatre in Paris at Louis Jouvet's Théâtre Athénée, was a professional stage and film actor in the 1950s and 1960s, an assistant director to Erwin Piscator, and director of his own experimental theatre in Sweden.

John Henry Raleigh, Professor of English at the University of California, Berkeley, has made a number of significant contributions to O'Neill scholarship—particularly his *The Plays of Eugene O'Neill*, which provides insights into the dramatist's creative consciousness and the psychological, philosophical, and thematic apsects of the plays. He has also edited and introduced *Twentieth Century Interpretations of The Iceman Cometh*, contributed a biographical survey of O'Neill to *Sixteen Modern American Authors*, written a number of scholarly essays on the dramatist, and participated in many O'Neill seminars in this country.

J. Dennis Rich, Professor of Communication and Theatre at the University of Illinois, is administrative director of the university's Circle Theatre Company. He recently completed his doctoral studies. The essay included in this book is from his dissertation on the playwright: "Eugene O'Neill and the Theatre of the Absurd."

Marta Sienicka, Professor of English at the Institute of English, Adam Mickiewicz University in Poznań, Poland, holds a Ph.D. degree in American Literature from the University of Łódź. The topic of her dissertation is "The Structure of the Poetry of William Carlos Williams." Her major publications include a two-volume critical study, *History of American Literature, Dimen-*

sions of Man as Seen by T.S. Eliot in His Early Poetry, and *The Making of a New American Poem: Some Tendencies in the Post-World War II American Poetry.* She is organizing an International Symposium of American Literature, "Tradition in Twentieth-Century American Literature," for December 1979 which will be sponsored by Adam Mickiewicz University.

Timo Tiusanen, Professor of Theatre Research at the University of Helsinki, is the author of *O'Neill's Scenic Images,* which John Gassner called a "truly impressive piece of work, sound and enlightening"; *Durrenmatt, A Study in Plays, Prose, Theory;* and *Lines of Development,* a collection of short studies. From 1970–74 he was manager of the Helsinki City Theatre. His work as a stage director includes *Long Day's Journey into Night, The Visit, The Wild Duck,* and the first Scandinavian performance of Arthur Miller's adaptation of *An Enemy of the People.* He received an ACLS grant for 1978–79 to research a book on Miller at the University of Michigan.

Egil Törnqvist, Professor in Scandinavian Studies at the University of Amsterdam, is the author of *A Drama of Souls: Studies in O'Neill's Super-Naturalistic Technique; Swedish Drama Structures; Bergman and Strindberg: The Ghost Sonata.* He has edited and introduced *Drama and Theatre* and *Plays by Ibsen.* His many essays on O'Neill have appeared in American and European scholarly publications. He was a lecturer in Swedish at Harvard University in 1957–58 and a recipient of an ACLS grant in 1965–66 to research his book on O'Neill at Yale University. At present he is editing a series, *Scandinavian Literature,* in Dutch translation.

Frederick Wilkins is Professor of English and Chairman of the Department of English at Suffolk University. In 1976 he founded, and has since edited, *The Eugene O'Neill Newsletter,* the first and, until now, the only publication in the United States dedicated to fostering O'Neill scholarship and providing information on the dramatist and productions of his plays. He has organized and participated in a number of MLA O'Neill seminars.

Abortion, 16, 65, 132
Absurd, theme of, 206, 257, 258, 259, 260, 261, 266, 268, 270, 271, 272, 274, 275
Acting style, 57, 92, 284
Adaptations, 65, 93, 103
Ah, Wilderness! 39–40, 95, 98, 142, 245, 247, 253, 256, 283–84
Alcohol, use of by characters, 11, 192–93, 202, 231, 247, 248
All God's Chillun Got Wings, 23, 25, 40, 56, 57, 72, 86, 98, 101, 103, 150–52, 154, 155, 156, 161, 162, 164, 218, 255
American character and society as theme, 4–6, 7, 8, 10, 11, 24–27, 31, 147, 169, 170, 190, 193–94, 197, 207
Anna Christie, 20, 37, 43, 54–55, 98, 99, 102, 143, 284, 293, 294
  in Czechoslovakia, 88
  in England, 71
  in Poland, 101, 103, 108
  in Sweden, 36, 42
Aristophanes, 16, 75, 77–78, 79, 81

Aristotle, 88, 117, 118
Aside, use of, 87
Autobiographical elements, use of, 7, 16, 73, 93, 94, 189, 196, 229
  in *Long Day's Journey into Night,* 8, 198, 222, 261, 281

Babbitt, Irving, 253, 254
Barlach, Ernst, 28
Barthel, Sven, 56
Before Breakfast, 132
Bentley, Eric, 96
Bergman, Ingmar, 42
Beyond the Horizon, 5, 112, 150, 162, 254, 258
Blacks, 24–25, 150–52
Boccaccio's *Decameron,* 117–22
Bor, Jan, 91
Boulton, Agnes, 73, 132
Bound East for Cardiff, 132, 148, 254
Bread and Butter, 16
Broadway, break with, 47–48
Brunius, Pauline, 40, 41
Brustein, Robert 253, 271

303

Calvinism, 21, 190–91, 199
Camus, Albert, 257, 260, 262, 263, 271
Čapek, Karel, 19, 23, 85, 93
Capitalism, 25–27, 29, 71
Carlin, Terry, 222
Catharsis, 6–7, 88, 97
Catholicism, 6, 10, 12, 21, 70, 108–9, 190–91, 193–96, 199, 203, 208
    confession in, 212, 213, 217–18, 219, 220, 224–25
Censorship, 15, 17
Cerný, Jindrich, 94, 95
Characterization, 5, 10, 11, 14, 15, 23, 27, 89, 107, 148, 149, 158, 159–61, 162, 163, 164–65, 165–66, 169, 177–78, 181, 182, 189, 191–92, 192–93, 198, 199, 201, 202, 204–5, 206, 218–19, 245, 262, 271, 274, 282, 287, 289, 292
    of Edmund Tyrone, 201, 202, 205, 206, 222, 247, 260–61, 292
    of James Tyrone, 10, 11, 193–94, 196, 197, 232–33, 247–48, 259–60
    of Jamie Tyrone, 222, 224–26, 235, 248, 260
    of Josie Hogan, 232–36
    of Mary Tyrone, 194–96, 222–24, 235, 246–48, 258–59, 280–81, 282–83, 286–87, 288–89, 290–92
    in A Moon for the Misbegotten, 9, 96, 229
Chaucer, Geoffrey, 132, 214
Chekhov, Anton, 22–23, 46, 112, 117, 122–25, 133, 137–38, 208
Comic elements, 39, 42, 66, 95, 96, 97, 231, 233, 274
Communication, theme of, 135, 136–37
Comrades, 74
Confession, theme of, 10, 196, 197, 212–26, 265, 267

Conrad, Joseph, 22, 29, 107, 122, 125–28, 132, 179, 208
Constructivism, 89
Craig, Gordon, 37, 179
Czechoslovakia, 17–21, 24, 84–89

Dahlbeck, Eva, 42, 51
Days Without End, 4, 39, 40, 56, 74, 79, 94, 98, 142, 245, 253, 279
Dear Doctor, The, 132
Death, theme of, 202, 204, 205, 206, 266–70, 272, 273
Desire Under the Elms, 15, 21, 23, 24, 25, 26, 27, 39, 44, 70, 72, 87–89, 98, 101–3, 107–10, 143, 154–55, 157–58, 162, 163, 165–66, 168, 192–93, 239, 242, 244, 280
Determinism, 110, 112, 201
Dialogue, 65, 66, 159, 163
Diff'rent, 239, 240–41
Diotima, 16–17, 75–76, 79–81
Doppelgänger, 160
Dostal, Karel, 86, 88, 89, 90
Dostalová, Leopolda, 89, 93
Dreamy Kid, The, 132
Drug addiction theme, 281–83, 286, 291, 292
Dualism theme, 4, 6, 10, 11, 18, 31, 66, 90, 97, 117, 135, 197, 200
Dukes, Ashley, 29, 178, 179
Dynamo, 25, 30, 74, 163, 181, 182–83, 200, 239, 241–42, 253, 254, 255

Ekerot, Bengt, 49, 50, 51, 54, 59
Ekström, Marta, 39, 40, 57
Eliot, T. S., 116, 146, 236
Emperor Jones, The, 25, 36, 54, 55, 98, 133, 160–61, 163, 164, 182, 204
    in Czechoslovakia, 18, 19, 85–86

expressionist aspects in, 28–30,
172–80
in Poland, 101, 103
racial aspects of, 150–52, 158–59
in Sweden, 18, 40, 52
England, 15, 55, 68–72, 120–21,
214–15
Environment, as antagonist, 164
Epic elements, 23, 117, 135, 136,
151
Euripides, 88
Europe, 3, 4, 12, 13, 14, 15, 17,
30–31
Experimentalism, 4, 19, 20, 28, 40,
52, 55, 66, 71, 85, 90, 92, 97,
103, 112, 255
Expressionism, 18, 19, 28–30, 52,
70, 85–87, 93, 115, 172, 179,
182

Family, theme of, 63, 195–96,
200–1, 206, 233, 248, 259, 283
Fantasy element, 90
Fatalism, 110, 112, 201
Faulkner, William, 116, 146, 168
Faust play, 4
Feminism, 88
Films, 71
First Man, The, 70, 245
Fog, 132
Ford, John, 71
Foreshadowing, 176
Fountain, The, 91, 98, 245, 253
Free will, 112
Freud, Sigmund, 77, 109, 208, 254

Gallup, Donald, 54, 57
Gate Studio Theatre, 71–72
Gierow, Karl Ragnar, 12–14, 18,
20, 40, 42, 44–49, 52–56, 59–
60, 102
Glencairn cycle, 22, 36, 55, 71,
94, 98, 148
Gold, 132
Gorki, Maxim, 23, 96, 115, 117

Gottfried, Martin, 283–84
Götz, František, 18, 21, 83
Great God Brown, 25, 27, 40, 65,
87, 88, 89–90, 98, 103, 163,
164, 204, 281
Greed of the Meek, 8, 9
Greek drama, 88, 112, 163, 208
Gregory, Lady, 234, 235
Grossman, Jan, 94–95
Grotowski, Jerzy, 106, 112
Guilt theme, 196, 197, 199, 218–
19, 224, 225, 235, 267, 270,
291–92

Hairy Ape, The, 10–11, 19, 25–27,
55, 65, 98, 102, 132, 142, 154,
163, 172, 179, 182, 204, 245,
246, 253, 254
anti-capitalism in, 152–53, 160–
61
in Czechoslovakia, 85, 86
and Kaiser's *Coral,* 28–29, 180–
81
in Soviet Union, 154, 156–57
Hammarskjöld, Dag, 13–14, 44–45,
47
Hanson, Lars, 37, 38, 39, 42, 48,
49, 51, 54, 57, 59
Hasso, Signe, 40
Hauptmann, Gerhart, 112, 115,
121–22, 208
Hawthorne, Nathaniel, 215–16,
237
Heller, Agnes, 120
Hellström, Gustaf, 18, 21, 35–37,
56
Hilar, Karel Hugo, 18–20, 24, 84–
88, 91–93
Hitler, Adolf, 17, 18, 20
Hofman, Vlastislav, 86, 91
Hofmannsthal, Hugo von, 115, 122
Hughie, 4, 13, 23, 43, 48, 49, 51–
52, 54, 87, 133–37, 143, 205–6,
271–75
Huizinga, Jan, 220
Human nature, 27, 46, 91, 105

Humanism, 27, 107, 137, 148, 149, 151, 182, 190, 203–4, 252–56
Hungary, 142–143

Ibsen, Henrik, 12, 29, 46–47, 49, 70, 84, 86, 107, 112, 115, 117, 179, 208, 247
Iceman Cometh, The, 4, 5, 7, 13, 23, 27, 41, 46, 48, 56, 58, 59, 68, 72, 96, 98, 103, 110, 133, 143, 149, 168–69, 203, 205, 206, 217, 248, 256, 264–71, 274, 279
confession in, 196–98, 219–21
New York premiere of, 42
pipe dreams in, 261–63
Ile, 40, 132, 239
Illusion and reality theme, 133–34, 138, 201, 202, 206, 261–72
Imagery, 79, 159, 193, 200, 204, 238, 243–44, 249
Imagism, 91
Impressionism, 115, 121, 122
Individual and masses theme, 177
In the Zone, 85, 94, 98, 132
Irish motif, 8, 9, 43, 97, 112, 189–95, 197, 199, 202, 208, 229–36
and Catholicism, 12, 21, 190–91
Isolation theme, 10, 30, 190–91, 206, 274

James, William, 203, 252
Jansenism, 21, 190–91
Jones, Robert Edmond, 36
Josephson, Lennart, 57
Joyce, James, 213, 216, 220, 221

Kaiser, Georg, 28–30, 70, 117, 172–83, 208
Kamerny Theater, 23–24, 154–57
Koonen, Alice, 23
Krutch, Joseph Wood, 256

Lamm, Martin, 56
Land, theme of, 8–9, 21, 88, 107

Langner, Lawrence, 47–48
Language, use of, 14, 66, 110, 111, 176, 254
Last Conquest, The, 18, 207
Lazarus Laughed, 87, 103, 219, 245, 253, 255–56
Life of Bessie Bowen, 8
Lindberg, Per, 18, 36, 37, 40
Linde, Ebbe, 53
Long Day's Joruney into Night, 3, 4, 6, 8, 9, 10, 12–14, 18, 27, 52, 55, 58, 72, 87, 94, 98, 99, 143, 149, 168, 169–70, 192–96, 201–2, 205, 206, 217, 229, 232–33, 235, 246–50, 256, 257–61, 274, 279, 284, 286–87, 288–89, 290–92
American premiere of, 54, 280–82
as autobiography, 197–98
confessional aspects in, 222–23
in Czechoslovakia, 95–97
in Poland, 21, 102–3, 105–7, 110–11
In Sweden, 43, 45–51, 59–60
Long Voyage Home, The, 132
Love, theme of, 16, 73–82
Löwenadler, Holger, 40, 42
Lukács, Georg, 122
Lukeš, Milan, 94
Lungquist, Artur, 57

MacGowan, Kenneth, 36, 180, 205, 240, 281
McLaughlin, Russell, 229, 233
Maher, Beatrice Ashe, 190
Male-Female theme, 16, 40
Marco Millions, 4–5, 25, 90, 91, 98, 143, 253, 255
Marriage, theme of, 16, 73, 75
Marshall, Arnina, 47
Masks, use of, 4, 87, 90, 163, 164, 166, 176, 179, 250
Massachusetts Bay Colony, 237–39, 244
Materialism, theme, 5, 6, 7, 9, 10,

25, 30, 31, 88, 146, 177, 193,
197, 207, 208, 239, 240
Mather, Increase, 239
Meaning, search for, 10–11, 94, 202,
203, 206
Melodrama, 13, 45, 88, 111
Melville, Herman, 64, 95, 97, 116
Metaphysical elements, use of, 28,
29, 258, 260, 261, 272
Meyerhold, 250
Miller, Arthur, 55–56, 104, 116
Milton, John, 215
Molander, Olof, 18, 20, 24, 37–39,
40, 41, 42, 43, 48–49, 51, 56, 57–
59, 85
Monologue, use of, 29, 92, 134,
136, 176
interior, 87, 158, 160, 162, 169,
274
Moon of the Caribbees, 103, 132,
133, 149, 245
Moon for the Misbegotten, 4, 9,
13, 21, 42–44, 46, 47, 48, 49,
59, 96, 98, 99, 102, 103, 106,
109, 110, 143, 190, 193, 197,
229–36, 254, 279
confessional aspects of 217, 224–
26
Irish-Yankee conflict in, 198
Moral content, 5, 11, 21, 33, 199,
203–4, 218, 254, 255
More Stately Mansions, 4, 8, 9–10,
13, 43, 44, 52, 53, 54, 103, 143,
193, 239, 240, 284, 285, 295
Mourning Becomes Electra, 18,
20, 25, 27, 72, 87, 91, 98,
142, 143, 163, 166–68, 200–1,
218, 238, 239, 240, 250, 254,
280
in Czechoslovakia, 91–93
in England, 71
in Poland, 21, 102–3, 109–10
Puritanism in, 241–43
in Sweden, 39, 48, 57, 58–59
Mystic elements, use of, 30, 68, 69,
70, 77, 79, 81, 182, 190, 201,

202, 203, 229, 230, 231, 234,
236, 245–50

Natanson, Wojciech, 105, 106, 107,
108
Nathan, George Jean, 16, 23, 73,
74, 82
National Theatre, Prague, 18–19,
20–21, 23, 84, 87–89, 90, 91
Naturalism, 20, 21, 29, 70, 86, 87,
93, 104, 111, 112, 115, 121, 183
New England, as setting, 6, 8, 12,
21, 88, 109, 189–90, 191–92,
194, 195, 199–200, 201, 208,
230, 237–44
Newcomb, Ruth, 189–90
Nietzsche, Friedrich, 75, 90, 208,
217
Nobel Prize, 15–16, 37, 39, 43, 44
Notebooks, 6
Novellas, 116, 122

One-act plays, 22–23, 117–38
O'Neill, Carlotta, 12–13, 43–49, 52,
53–54, 55, 59, 102, 222, 284,
293–94, 295
O'Neill, Ella, 190, 224, 280
O'Neill, Eugene
biographical information about,
12, 16, 44, 46, 61, 63, 279
Catholicism of, 217, 223
character of, 208, 289, 293–95
quoted, 5, 7, 8, 9, 15–16, 17–18,
19, 20, 23–24, 38, 41, 61–63,
64, 74, 147, 198, 282, 284
reputation of, 3–4, 15, 30, 31–32,
64–65, 66–67, 84, 97, 104, 116–
17, 207–8
"silence" of, 17, 40
O'Neill, James, 231, 232–33
O'Neill, Jamie, 224, 233, 235
O'Neill Theatre Center, 62
Optimism, 256, 261, 274

Pausanias, 16, 75, 76, 81
Pessimism, 97, 137, 147, 170, 256

Plato, and Platonism, 16–17, 74–
   75, 80, 81, 82
Plot structure, 89, 117, 118
Poetic elements, use of 21, 97, 104,
   109, 136, 149, 245–50
Poland, 20–22, 101–12
Possenti, Eligio, 280
Posthumous plays, 13–14, 43, 44,
   53–54, 55
Provincetown Playhouse, 36, 148
Psychological elements, use of, 19,
   28, 55, 57, 104, 105, 106, 109,
   159, 160, 163, 213–14
Puritanism, 5, 6, 9, 11, 12, 14, 15,
   21, 30, 31, 63, 68, 69, 70, 88,
   108, 109, 189, 190–91, 192,
   194, 199–200, 201, 237–44

Quintero, José, 59, 287, 295

Racism theme, 24–25, 40, 146, 150–
   52, 155, 158–59, 176
Radio productions, 40, 103
Realism, 19, 28, 36, 52, 54–55, 57,
   74, 82, 86, 87, 89, 90, 92, 93,
   105, 109, 115, 148, 150, 154–
   55, 159, 160
Recklessness, 16, 132
Reinhardt, Max, 178, 179
Religious themes, 5, 6–7, 10, 16,
   18, 26, 27, 28, 30, 58–59, 74,
   75, 76, 79, 192, 193, 195, 200,
   202, 203, 205, 206, 207, 252–
   53, 254, 255–56
Renaissance, 120–21
Repertory theater, 35, 52
Rippin, Jessica, 280–81
Robson, Flora, 72
Romanticism, 74, 160
Rope, The, 70, 133
Royal Dramatic Academy, Sweden,
   12–14, 17, 18, 19, 20, 23, 34–
   60, 280
Rubin, Jane, 44
Russia, 23–25, 71, 145–70
Rutte, Miroslav, 86, 92–93

Scott, Elizabeth, 42
Sea, motif of, 22, 36, 88, 97, 107,
   149, 157, 161, 201, 202
"Sea-Mother's Son, The," 7
Self, search for, 6, 11, 12, 31
Settings, 23, 245, 248–50
Shakespeare, William, 119, 121,
   214–15, 222, 249
Shaw, George Bernard, 55, 84, 115,
   249
Sheaffer, Louis, 47, 50, 179
Shell Shock, 65, 133
Short stories, 22–23, 117–38
Simpson, Alan, 239
Sin, motif of, 196, 197, 199, 200,
   212, 217, 218, 219, 220, 236,
   244
Sinko, Grzegorz, 104, 107
Sito, Jerzy S., 109–10, 111
Sjöberg, Alf, 39, 40, 50
Smoček, Ladislav, 96
Sniper, The, 132
Socialism, 115
Social themes, 24–27, 28, 30, 86, 89,
   91, 94, 109, 121, 146, 150, 155,
   168, 200
Socrates, 16, 75, 77, 79–80
Soliloquy, use of, 29, 176
"S.O.S.," 22, 128–32
Stace, Walter T., 245–46
Stage directions, 135, 273–74,
Stationendramen, 173
Stoughton, William, 238
Strakosch (Danish publishers), 41,
   45
Strange Interlude, 19, 37–38, 56,
   65, 71, 72, 87, 92, 98, 142, 163,
   219, 253, 255
Straw, The, 7, 65
Stream of consciousness, 92, 136,
   137, 163, 166, 274
Strindberg, August, 13, 14, 17, 23,
   28–29, 34–35, 36, 39, 40–41,
   43, 46–47, 48, 49, 52, 56, 58–
   59, 63, 70, 84, 107, 112, 115,
   117, 183, 197, 208

American productions of, 50
influence of *Dance of Death*, 15, 73–74, 82
O'Neill's debt to, 15–16
Subconscious, projections of, 29
Sweden, 12–14, 17, 18, 20, 21, 24, 34–60, 66
Symbols, use of, 8, 9, 16, 21, 29, 79, 85, 90, 104, 105, 109, 115, 121, 122, 136, 161, 163, 174, 180, 197, 201, 204, 233, 254, 255, 262, 265, 290

Taïrov, Alexander, 23–25, 55, 154–57
Tale of Possessors, Self-Dispossessed, A, 7–8, 52, 147, 284, 294–95
Taylor, Henry Osborne, 214
Technique
of characterization, 163
innovations, 87, 112
orchestral, 282, 287
Teje, Tora, 36, 37, 38, 39, 57
Television productions, 65–66, 103
Tetauer, Frank, 85, 91
Theatre Guild, 47
Thirst, 132, 254
Tidblad, Inge, 40, 48, 54, 57
Toller, Ernst, 28, 70, 208
Torsslow, Stig, 54, 56–57
Touch of the Poet, A, 4, 8, 9, 13, 43, 44, 48, 51, 52–53, 54, 59, 96, 98, 99, 102, 143, 195, 229, 284, 295
Tragedy, 6, 11, 25–26, 27, 29, 30, 43, 45, 46, 66, 88, 89, 90, 92, 94, 95, 97, 105, 127, 149, 256, 266, 267, 268, 270, 271, 274

individual, 157–58, 162, 163, 165, 168
O'Neill's concept of, 147, 164, 202
Greek, 163, 208
universal, 27, 149, 150, 157–58, 162–66
Translations, 18, 21, 23, 31, 36, 39, 44, 56, 65, 85, 86, 89, 91, 94, 96, 102, 103, 104, 110, 111

United States, 14, 30, 116, 145–46
Universality, 105, 107, 149, 190, 208
Utilitarianism, 25

Walter, Rudolf, 86
Warnings, 22, 126–28, 130–32
Web, The, 132
Welch, Mary, 229
Welded, 14, 16–17, 72, 73–82, 245
Wettergren, Erik, 37, 38
Where the Cross Is Made, 132
Whitman, Walt, 64, 101, 153, 255
Wife for a Life, 16, 132
Wigglesworth, Michael, 238–39, 244
Williams, Tennessee, 55, 104, 116, 119
Winthrop, John, 237–38, 239, 243, 244
Witkins, Frederick, 237–44
Women, 19, 88, 197
Work Diary, 8, 16, 17–18, 19, 20, 23, 24, 57, 198, 282, 284
World War I, 28, 115–16
World War II, 17–18, 20, 93–94